BRUCE NORMAN
FOOTSTEPS

For My Family

BBC BOOKS

BRUCE NORMAN

FOOTSTEPS

NINE ARCHAEOLOGICAL JOURNEYS OF ROMANCE AND DISCOVERY

Thanks to Mrs Audrey Fanshawe for permission to quote from the work of her father, Reginald Le May; Alfred M. Bingham for permission to quote from the works of his father, Hiram Bingham; Messrs C. Struik, Cape Town, for permission to quote from *Carl Mauch, African Explorer* and the National Archives, Harare, Zimbabwe, for permission to quote from *The Journals of Carl Mauch*. Especial thanks to editors Nina Shandloff and Talia Rodgers, designer Ann Thompson and picture researcher Frances Abraham. And thanks to my friends and colleagues who have made the films for the *Footsteps* television series: Bryan Adams, Alexandra Branson, Roy Davies, Robert Marshall, Anne Miller, Derek Towers, David Turnbull, David Wallace and presenter David Drew, who kindly wrote the introduction.

Published by BBC Books
A division of BBC Enterprises Ltd
Woodlands, 80 Wood Lane, London W12 0TT

First published 1987
© Bruce Norman 1987
ISBN 0 563 20552 0

Typeset in 11/13pt Century Schoolbook
Printed in Great Britain by Butler & Tanner Ltd, Frome, Somerset
Colour printed by W. S. Cowell Ltd, Ipswich, Suffolk
Jacket printed by Belmont Press, Northampton

CONTENTS

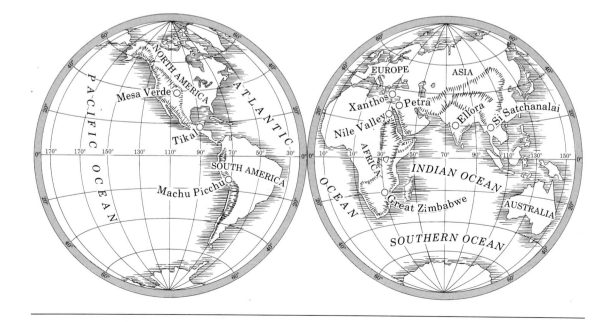

INTRODUCTION

Archaeology today has not lost its capacity for wonder, delight or surprise – far from it, when vast buried armies of terracotta soldiers can still be found in China and whole forgotten cities continue to emerge from the jungles of Central and South America. However, as modern archaeology grows more scientific and sophisticated, it is no surprise if many enthusiasts and even professional archaeologists look back with nostalgia and a certain envy to the great discoveries of the nineteenth century.

In many respects, of course, they were the bad old days of looting and ignorant destruction by people who knew no better. But they were also the heroic, romantic days of archaeological adventure, when the past was a wonderful novelty and, for those extra-ordinary individuals brave and inquisitive enough to search, the opportunities now seem to have been limitless.

As European empires grew and frontiers were pushed back on every continent, completely new and unknown archaeological worlds lay in wait for the explorer. Ancient monuments hidden for thousands of years were revealed: temples, tombs, palaces and great 'lost cities' belonging to glorious civilisations such as the ancient Egyptians, the Maya or the Incas, or mysterious little-understood cultures such as the Shona-speaking tribes of Africa or the Anasazi cliff-dwellers of the American south-west.

The exploits of the original discoverers are now part of the drama of the sites. Their own written accounts describe thrilling moments of revelation: Giovanni Belzoni finding himself spell-bound in the magnificent tomb of Seti I in the Valley of the

Kings; John Seely speechless at first setting eyes on the Kailasa Temple at Ellora; and, a century later, Hiram Bingham hauling himself up the jungle slopes of the Peruvian Andes to stumble upon the greatest lost city of them all, Machu Picchu. Bingham spoke for all of them: 'It seemed like an unbelievable dream ... It fairly took my breath away. What could this place be?'

But such stunning experiences, such great moments in the history of archaeology, were hard-earned, and the romantic appeal of some of their adventures can obscure the sheer drudgery, squalid conditions, and the pain and fear many of them faced. Travel then meant months of journeying, on foot, by mule and on horseback, through deserts, bush and jungle – wild lawless country where an explorer's survival could depend upon the whims of the local people. A strange foreigner looking for ruins, for piles of stones, would seem at best laughably ridiculous and at worst deeply suspicious and threatening to a Bedouin, an African tribesman or a Quechua Indian. Even more perilous were unpredictable natural hazards: extremes of heat and cold, snakes, insects, wild animals and a host of then incurable diseases.

Following the careers of these men is a way of tracing the slow development of archaeology over the century. But it is much more than that. However much the globe may have shrunk in recent years, the country through which they travelled is still often remote and the villages they passed much as they were then. It takes only a small leap of the imagination to project oneself back in time and to share something of their impressions. In Zimbabwe, for example, armed with a good map, you can follow Mauch's exact route through vast expanses of bush. Descendants of the chiefs he met can still tell tales of the wandering white man and point to the old hill-top villages described in his journals, and they will show you the remains of the very hut, close to Great Zimbabwe, in which he stayed.

Finally, in the ruins themselves, there are moments of extraordinary timelessness. In the jungles of Si Satchanalai, in some of the more remote Anasazi cliff-dwellings of Colorado and Utah, in the cave-temples of Ellora, you are in the presence not just of Reginald Le May, Richard Wetherill or John Seely but of the ancient people themselves. It is then that you confront the enduring mysteries all nine of these men faced which even now have few adequate answers – mysteries such as the nature and inspiration of those long-dead people who created the great glories of the past, and the universal inevitability of decay and decline.

David Drew, July 1987

Chapter One

STRONGMAN IN EGYPT
Giovanni Belzoni in the Valley of the Nile

I could not pass without putting my face in contact with that of some decayed Egyptian ... I could not avoid being covered with bones, legs, arms and heads rolling from above. Thus I proceeded from one cave to another, all full of mummies piled up in various ways, some standing, some lying and some on their heads.*

Giovanni Belzoni entered the sacred valley of Beban el Malook, the Valley of the Kings, in February 1817. What he was to discover there and what he discovered at the other great sites of ancient Egypt – Thebes, Abu Simbel and the Pyramids of Giza – was to amaze the British public and provide the British Museum with some of its greatest antiquities. It also began a century of archaeological discovery that was to last well into the twentieth century. Archaeology as a science, however, did not yet exist.

In the eighteenth century, English gentlemen, mostly clerics, began to take an antiquarian interest in the curious sights of their own country such as Stonehenge, and some of them made haphazard collections of old and unusual objects – their Cabinets of Curiosities. The richer English gentlemen travelled around Europe on the Grand Tour, visiting those Greek and Roman sites familiar from their reading of the classics and coming home with collections of antique statues to adorn their houses and

*G. Belzoni, *Narrative of the Operations and Recent Discoveries within the Pyramids, Temples, Tombs, and Excavations, in Egypt and Nubia* (London: John Murray, 1820).

Above: *Giovanni Belzoni (1778–1823) in an engraving published in 1822.*

parklands. Giovanni Belzoni was the least likely person to broaden their interest in the antique to include Egypt.

Belzoni was the son of an Italian barber. He was born in Padua on 5 November 1778, but:

> The greater part of my younger days I passed in Rome, the former abode of my ancestors where I was preparing myself to become a monk; but the sudden entry of the French into that city altered the course of my education and being destined to travel, I have been a wanderer ever since.

In 1803, he arrived in England, the one west European country not in the hands of Napoleon, and, for the next ten years, toured its theatres and fairgrounds as 'The Patagonian Sampson', 'The Italian Hercules', 'Jack the Giant Killer' or 'The Great Belzoni'. For Belzoni was of prodigious size. He was almost 6 foot 7 inches tall and remarkably strong, and it was only by using his strength that he was able to earn a living. Appearing at Sadlers Wells Theatre on Easter Monday 1803 on the same bill as the famous clown Grimaldi, he amazed the audience by hoisting on his shoulders eleven fully grown men. Sir Walter Scott called Belzoni the 'handsomest man (for a giant) I ever saw'. Cruikshank drew a cartoon of him and Dickens made him into a rags-to-riches personification of Victorian virtues: 'The once starving mountebank (who) became one of the most illustrious men in Europe.' In his own account of his life, Belzoni merely says he lived:

> ... on my own industry and the little knowledge I had acquired in various branches. I turned my chief attention to hydraulics, a science that I had learned in Rome, which I found much to my advantage, and which was ultimately the very cause of my going to Egypt.

Whether Belzoni had actually studied hydraulics in Rome is doubtful, but he certainly had some practical experience from the time he introduced fountains and waterfalls into his stage act, and that experience was to pay off. In 1814 he was in Malta, thirty-six years old and still in search of fortune and legitimate fame. There he met an agent of the new pasha (or governor) of Egypt – an Albanian soldier who called himself Mohammed Ali. Ali was attempting to update and Europeanise his 'backward' country and Belzoni saw his opportunity.

> The principal cause of my going to Egypt was the project of constructing hydraulic machines, to irrigate the fields, by a system much easier and more economical than what is in use in that country.

Left: *George Cruikshank's cartoon of Belzoni as the Italian Hercules.*

The visit was to change his life – though not in the way he imagined. Egypt was still an unknown country, the most northerly part of the unknown continent of Africa, and the average Englishman's knowledge of the place was derived from the Bible and Shakespeare; from stories of Moses and Cleopatra. The more educated would know of the references in the classical authors such as Strabo, Herodotus, Pliny and Plutarch, but the first drawings of the country were not printed until 1757. Then, at the turn of the century, Egypt was thrust onto the centre of the political stage when France, having lost the colonial initiative to the British in the East, determined to regain it. To do that, France needed to cut Britain's lifeline to India. Egypt, still ruled by the Mameluke Beys as part of the Turkish Empire (and a vital staging post for India), was the key. On 24 July 1798, Napoleon had invaded and entered Cairo, victorious. Despite the destruction by Nelson of the French fleet at the battle of the Nile a week later, France remained firmly in possession. As well as an army of military men there was an army of cartographers, engineers, scientists and academics: the Commission of Arts and Sciences, whose job was to investigate and record, collect and classify information about Egypt that would be essential for the permanent establishment of colonial rule. The operation lasted three years before the French were finally forced to withdraw, taking with them volumes of notes and not a few antiquities. The British tried to relieve them of their booty but were only successful with a piece of black basalt covered with Greek and other writings which the French had discovered at Rosetta in 1799. The Rosetta Stone, famous as the means whereby the Frenchman Champollion was eventually able to decipher ancient Egyptian hieroglyphics, was placed on display in the British Museum in London. It whetted the public's appetite, as well as the museum's, for more antiquities of the same kind. That appetite was soon to be satisfied.

Belzoni, with his English wife Sarah, arrived at Alexandria on 9 June 1815 to be greeted by sickness and plague. It was a week before they could continue their journey to Cairo. As soon as he arrived, Belzoni couldn't restrain himself from going at once to see 'the wonder of the world, the pyramids':

We went there to sleep, that we might ascend the first pyramid early enough in the morning to see the rising of the sun; and accordingly we were on the top of it long before the dawn of day. The scene here is majestic and grand, far beyond description: a mist over the plains of Egypt formed a veil which ascended and vanished gradually as the sun rose and unveiled to the view that beautiful land, once the site of Memphis. The distant view of the smaller pyramids on the south marked the extension of that vast capital; while the solemn, endless spectacle of the desert on the west inspired us with reverence for the all-powerful Creator.

In Cairo, the Belzonis lodged in a house 'so old and out of repair I expected every moment it would fall on our heads'. There were other dangers too. Cairo, like the whole of Egypt, was a volatile place. Turks were suspicious of the Arabs, the Arabs hated the Turks and both disliked the Europeans (the 'Franks' as they called them) who were bringing in new and unwelcome ideas. Within a few days of arrival, Belzoni was stabbed in the leg by a Turkish soldier and was in bed for a month.

The antagonism towards all things European boiled over into full-scale riot and, although revolution was averted, it had its effect on the construction of the waterwheel that Belzoni had promised the pasha.

There were 'many provoking difficulties to encounter'. Wood for the project was not forthcoming, nor iron, nor, at the outset, labour. Belzoni had to do everything himself. The success of the machine, a large upright wooden treadmill propelled by a single ox, was to be measured against six traditional waterwheels (saqiyas) still in use on the Nile today, driven by as many as four oxen each:

> The machine was set to work and, although constructed with bad wood and bad iron and erected by Arabian carpenters and bricklayers, it was a question whether it did not draw six or seven times as much water as the common machines ... Still, Mahommed Ali perceived plainly the prejudice among the Arabs, and some of the Turks ... for instead of four hundred people and four hundred oxen, they would have only to command one hundred of each, which would make a considerable difference in their profits.

The pasha, for a joke, suggested the wheel should be driven by men. The Arabs obediently got inside, along with Belzoni's Irish manservant. The wheel was brought up to speed and the Arabs leapt off, leaving the Irish boy who was thrown to the ground with his legs broken. The accident was dubbed an ill omen and the pasha had an excuse to abandon the project. Oriental Luddites had destroyed Belzoni's hopes.

Whilst resident in Cairo, however, Belzoni had met the Swiss traveller Jean Louis Burckhardt. Burckhardt had suggested to

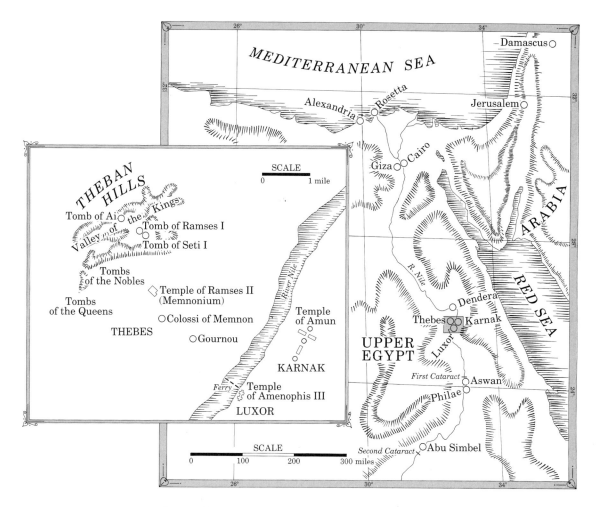

the pasha that, in return for the solicited gift from England of a previous waterwheel, also recently abandoned, the pasha might like to send to the Prince Regent:

> ... the colossal head, or rather bust, known by the name of Young Memnon ... but as it must have appeared to a Turk too trifling an article to send to so great a personage, no steps were taken for this purpose.

The head lay at Thebes on the west bank of the Nile, over 300 miles from Cairo. Its existence was already well-known in England. Sir William Hamilton, husband of Lady Emma, had described it as 'certainly the most beautiful and perfect piece of Egyptian sculpture that can be seen throughout the whole country'. The French had tried to take it away but found it, at almost eight tons, too heavy. The idea of trying to take the head to England was revived by Burckhardt when Henry Salt arrived in Cairo in March 1816, as His Britannic Majesty's Consul. Salt, who had already travelled in India and Abyssinia, had been asked by Sir Joseph Banks, founder member of the African Association and Trustee of the British Museum, to keep his eye open for antiquities that might enrich the national collection. The combination of Salt's commission, Burckhardt's wishes and Belzoni's need for a job conspired to send Belzoni with the pasha's approval on his first journey up the Nile. He received his written instructions from Salt; was told how to recognise the sculpture and not mistake it for any other, and:

> ... he is requested not to attempt removing it, on any account, if he should judge there would be any serious risk of either injuring the head, of burying the face in the sand, or of losing it in the Nile ... Mr Belzoni will have the goodness to keep a separate account of the expenses incurred in this undertaking, which, as well as his other expenses, will gladly be reimbursed.

The tools for the job consisted of a few poles and ropes made out of palm leaves. With Mrs Belzoni, he set off in a Nile sail-boat on 30 June 1816.

At Manfalut, after a week's sailing and half-way to his destination, Belzoni presented his credentials to Ibrahim, pasha of Upper Egypt and heir to Mahommed Ali. He was a man given to punishing his subjects by tying them across the mouth of a cannon and firing cannon-balls through them, or, for variety, roasting them, slowly and alive, like rabbits on a spit. 'What sort of a country must that be', comments Belzoni, 'which allows itself to be ruled by a man of so elevated a mind!' With Ibrahim was Bernardino Drovetti, the Italian-born former French Consul, still a man with influence in the country and a great collector of antiquities. The rivalry that was to grow between Drovetti and Belzoni in their scramble for Egyptian artefacts was to provide an archaeological rerun of the recent war between France and Britain. Drovetti, hearing of Belzoni's plan to remove the Young Memnon, advised him that the Arabs at Thebes wouldn't work for him and then, mockingly, made him a gift of the lid of a granite sarcophagus he'd discovered in one of the tombs:

> ... He said that he had employed several (men) for many days to take it out for himself, but they could not succeed; so that if I could take it out, I was welcome to it. I thanked him for his present and proceeded on my voyage.

Others gave more specific warnings: that there would be difficulty in obtaining labour as well as difficulty in obtaining permissions; difficulty in getting a boat; that the statue wasn't worth

the effort; and finally that Belzoni 'should not meddle in this business'. He continued up the Nile, past the Temple of Dendera which 'left me for a while in a state of suspense and astonishment'. He arrived at Luxor, Thebes, on 22 July and went to the temple:

> It appeared to me like entering a city of giants, who, after a long conflict, were all destroyed, leaving the ruins of their various temples as the only proofs of their former existence ... Who will not fail to wonder how a nation, which was once so great as to erect these stupendous edifices, could so far fall into oblivion that even their language and writing are so totally unknown to us.

Belzoni's knowledge of ancient Egypt had probably increased since his arrival in the country through his discussions with Burckhardt and his reading in Consul Salt's library. He had read Sir William Hamilton's *Ægyptiaca*; he knew Friderik Norden's *Drawings of some Ruins and Colossal Statues at Thebes in Egypt, with an Account of the Same in a Letter to the Royal Society*, published in 1741; he was familiar with those parts of the great French Commission of Arts and Sciences which were already published; and he'd read Herodotus (in translation) and seen d'Anville's map of Egypt published in 1766. There was little more to know. Most of the major monuments visible today were visible then – just – but were inadequately described. The rest of the monuments, which is most of them, were buried under the desert sand. Inscriptions, where visible, could not be read, so it was impossible to tell the date of any of the monuments, to know the incredible length of ancient Egyptian civilisation, or to know anything of the political or social set-up. As Hamilton wrote, all one could deduce was that they were 'the records of a great and learned and wise people'. It was the practical experience of the under-educated Belzoni that was to show, over the next four years, how observation and digging, or in modern archaeological parlance 'field work', could help provide the information that written records could not.

> After having taken a cursory view of Luxor ... I crossed the Nile to the west ... proceeding straight to the Memnonium ... On my approaching these ruins, I was surprised at the sight of the great colossus of Memnon, or Sesostris, or Osymandias, or Phamenoph, or perhaps some other king of Egypt; for such are the various opinions of its origin, and so many names have been given to it, that at last it has no name at all. I can but say that it must have been one of the most venerated statues of the Egyptians.

Opposite (main picture): *Entrance to the Temple of Luxor, published in London in 1804.*
Inset: *Hypostyle Hall, the Temple of Amun, Karnak.*

The Memnonium was a mortuary temple named by the ancient Greeks, misleadingly, after the Homeric hero Memnon. The colossal statue of Memnon, now fallen and broken, was more accurately identified as that of Ozymandias, the king of Shelley's famous poem:

> 'My name is Ozymandias, king of kings;
> Look on my works, ye Mighty, and despair!'
> Nothing beside remains. Round the decay
> Of that colossal wreck, boundless and bare
> The lone and level sands stretch far away.

The name 'Ozymandias' is a corruption of User-maat-Re, one of the names of the XIX Dynasty king, Ramses II, who ruled from 1304 to 1237 BC. The Memnonium is known to all tourists today as the Ramasseum and the Colossus of Ramses was probably venerated most by Ramses himself, inveterate builder and self-publicist who carved over the entrances of his many temples the triumphs of his numerous wars. The Young Memnon was one of two smaller but still enormous statues of Ramses that stood in the second court.

> As I entered these ruins, my first thought was to examine the colossal bust I had to take away. I found it near the remains of its body and chair, with its face upwards, and apparently smiling on me at the thought of being taken to England.

Belzoni set up house with his wife in the Ramasseum and prepared to remove the head. Nine square wooden beams made of tree trunks were laid cross-wise, five underneath and four on top, to form a trolley and underneath were placed four circular tree trunks to act as rollers. The trolley was to be pulled by ropes across rocks and sand. If the exercise wasn't completed before the annual inundation of the Nile the project would have to be abandoned for a year, and the river was already rising. Belzoni couldn't carry out the project alone. He applied for help and permission to the local ruler, the Defterdar Bey:

> He received me with that invariable politeness which is peculiar to the Turks, even when they do not mean in the slightest degree to comply with your wishes.

The Bey promised help, but no men arrived. Only the threat of being reported to the pasha produced any men at all. They were to be paid fourpence halfpenny a day, more than half as much again as they got for working in the fields.

The mode I adopted to place (the bust) on the car was very simple, for work of no other description could be executed by these people, as their utmost sagacity reaches only to pulling a rope, or sitting on the extremity of a lever as a counterpoise. By means of four levers I raised the bust, so as to leave a vacancy under it, to introduce the car; and, after it was slowly lodged on this, I had the car raised in the front, with the bust on it, so as to get one of the rollers underneath. I then had the same operation performed at the back, and the colossus was ready to be pulled up.

The effort of working all day in the burning midday sun produced sunstroke. On 28 July work restarted but Belzoni was 'very poorly' and, the following day, 'found it impossible to stand on my legs'. He retired to bed.

On the 30th we continued the work, and the colossus advanced a hundred and fifty yards towards the Nile. I was a little better in the morning, but worse again in the evening.

On the 31st I was again a little better, but could not proceed, as the road became so sandy that the colossus sunk into the ground. I was therefore under the necessity of taking a long turn of above three hundred yards, to a new road. In the evening of this day I was much better.

The head continued to edge forward at the rate of about 300 yards a day. Then, on 5 August, no one turned up for work. The local overseer, the Caimakan, pleaded that he was acting on orders and that the man that Belzoni had to deal with was

Below: *Belzoni's own drawing of the removal of the head of the 'Young Memnon'.*

the Cacheff and he, with his entourage, was a day's ride away.

> There is certainly something in the ceremonial manners of the
> Turks that is often peculiarly provoking. At the very moment
> they order your throat to be cut, they will not fail to salute
> you, apparently with the utmost cordiality.

To get the Cacheff to give written permission for the project to
continue cost Belzoni a lot of pleasant but plain talk and, of
paramount importance, two fine English pistols as a gift. Immediately, the Cacheff announced, 'We shall be friends.' The following
day, the bust was again on the move:

> On the 9th, I was seized with such giddiness in my head that I
> could not stand. The blood ran so copiously from my nose and
> mouth, that I was unable to continue the operation: I therefore
> postponed it to the next day. On the 10th and 11th, we
> approached towards the river; and on the 12th, thank God, the
> Young Memnon arrived on the bank of the Nile.

Mr Salt the Consul had to be informed; a boat had to be hired;
there would be a delay. Belzoni went to find the lid of the sarcophagus that M. Drovetti had given him as a present and which
lay somewhere in the honeycomb of passages and tombs in the
hills behind Gournou, the Arab village close to the Memnonium.
The people of Gournou were, Belzoni discovered, superior to
all other Arabs in Egypt 'in cunning and deceit'. He was, for
considerable *baksheesh*, conducted into the passages where the
coffin lid reputedly lay. He had to strip, squeeze through narrow
openings between rocks (not easy for one of Belzoni's bulk),
crawl on the ground 'like a crocodile' and then be plunged into
dark and dismay as the lighted tapers went out and his guide
disappeared. 'My situation', he said, with massive under-
statement, 'was not a pleasant one'. He was incarcerated, it
seemed, a quarter of a mile inside the womb of the mountain. It
was only the combination of a cool head, systematic searching
of the passages and chance that brought him out a short distance
from where he'd gone in.

> I was not long in detecting their scheme. The Arabs had
> intended to show me the sarcophagus, without letting me see
> the way by which it might be taken out, and then to stipulate
> a price for the secret. It was with this view they took me such
> a way round about. I found that the sarcophagus was not in
> reality a hundred yards from the large entrance.

The friendly Cacheff who'd been given the present of two pistols
had subsequently been given other presents by the French. He

refused Belzoni permission to remove the lid, saying it had been sold to M. Drovetti. Belzoni said he would write to Cairo. Whilst he waited for an answer and a boat, 'I could not employ my time better than in going up the Nile.' He built an earth wall around the Young Memnon to keep out the rising waters, placed on it a day-and-night guard, and set sail with his unsung heroine, the plucky and patient Sarah Belzoni.

From Luxor to Aswan is a distance of about 150 miles. The Nile winds its way through the desert, lined with palm trees and waterwheels and the green strip of fertile fields which masks the extent of the river's annual flood. It was this flood that brought life to the desert: an annual cycle of birth, death and re-birth that enabled the civilisation of ancient Egypt to grow and flourish. It determined the ancient Egyptian attitude to life, death and life-after-death – the nub of their religion, and was reflected, as Belzoni was one of the earliest to observe, in their way of burial.

At Aswan, the usual routine of lying, deceit, wheeler-dealing and present giving had to be done with the local ruler before permission and a boat was able to take the Belzonis above the first cataract into Nubia and 'the beautiful island of Philae', where:

> I observed several blocks of stones, with hieroglyphics on them in great perfection, that might be taken away, and an obelisk of granite about twenty-two feet in length, and two in breadth … which, if brought to England, might serve as a monument in some particular place or as an embellishment to the metropolis.

The stones were to provide further aggravation with the French and the obelisk, from the moment Belzoni saw it, became a time bomb, ticking quietly over the next two years but which was finally to explode and blow him away.

As he approached the second cataract, Belzoni was entering uncharted territory. During the day the 'barbarian boatmen' were up to their armpits in water, manhandling the boat against the current through the rocks and eddies; at night they were up to their elbows in food:

> When we killed a sheep, I had sometimes the pleasure of seeing the entrails opened, pieces of which, dipped once into the water, were eaten by them raw. The head and feet, with the skin, wool, hoofs, and all, were put into a pot, which is never washed, to be half-boiled, when they drank the broth and devoured the rest.

The nights were cold, the days were hot, there were rats and flies. The Belzonis were in an alien culture, amidst a hostile people, with dirt, disease, danger and the ever-present possibility of death – gentle and slow or violent and short. The difference between their life in Egypt and a decade of comparative ease and civilisation in the theatres of Europe could not have been greater. That both the Belzonis survived, even flourished, without any previous experience of this kind of travel is a measure of their physical stamina and, even more, their indomitable spirit.

They arrived at the temple of Ybsambul – Abu Simbel – its six colossal figures and even larger heads almost buried in the sand. Belzoni calculated that the door was thirty-five feet below the sand's surface. As the sand ran down in a slope from one side of the temple façade to the other, any attempt to make an aperture straight through it to the door would have been like trying to make a hole in water.

To his surprise Belzoni found that he was again following in the footsteps of Drovetti. Drovetti, however, had failed to dig here because, as an inducement to labour, he had offered money, and money, in this remote region, was something the people didn't understand. Belzoni was smarter, he made progress by present. A deal was struck with the local Cacheff:

> He made me promise that, if I found the temple full of gold, I should give him half. To this I agreed, on condition that if I found only stones, they should be all my own property; and he immediately assented, for he said he wanted no stones.

The Cacheff ordered his people to work for money. The people eventually arrived and very slowly the dig began:

> Altogether we had made a considerable advance in the sand, towards the centre of the front of the temple. Next morning, the people took it into their heads to come in such numbers, that I could not employ them all, as the work was directed only to one point.

At paytime that evening, the brother of the Cacheff ordered that all the money be piled in a heap on the floor before being divided out amongst the men. The pile was made, the Cacheff's brother threw himself on top of it, scooped it all up and made off. None of the workers dared to say a word. Whereas, only a week before, money had been a despised article, now it was highly prized. More was needed but Belzoni had no more. Work had to be abandoned an estimated fifteen feet from the temple door.

> Having obtained a promise from the Cacheff that he would not let anyone touch the place ... I contented myself with putting

a mark where the sand was before I commenced the operation; and after taking a drawing of the exterior of the temple, quitted it, with a firm resolution of returning to accomplish its opening.

At Philae, on his way back downriver, he ordered that the stones with hieroglyphs should be cut to transportable size. He then left them – and the obelisk – guarded by the local sheikh. At Luxor, he searched for a boat that could take the Young Memnon to Cairo. Ironically, the boat he found was already carrying two agents of M. Drovetti upriver. They were disparaging about the head, saying the only reason that the French army hadn't removed it was because it was not worth the removal, and their Arab guide:

> On hearing of my fortunate success in collecting several valuable pieces ... observed to me, that, if I persevered in my researches, I should have my throat cut.

Belzoni settled down to wait for the boat's return from Aswan, when the head would be his for the enormous fee of £75. He passed the time, despite the spine-chilling threats, digging at Karnak for more antiquities. He discovered eighteen statues of 'sphinxes', six of them perfect, and a white life-sized statue supposedly of Jupiter Ammon. He then crossed from the east bank of the river, from the land which had been the home of the living ancient Egyptians, to the west, to the vast necropolis of the ancient Egyptian dead. At Gournou Belzoni took a closer look at the tombs and passageways in which he'd been lost a few months before and, despite the acute ophthalmia which for a time made him almost blind, began to research in the valley adjacent to the Valley of the Kings. Almost at once he discovered a tomb with painted walls and a broken sarcophagus. From its size he deduced 'that it was the burial-place of some person of distinction', and he was right. We now know that it was the tomb of the devious high priest Ai, the man who usurped the throne after the death of the boy-king Tutankhamun in 1352 BC.

Money had arrived from Mr Salt in Cairo and the boat had returned from Aswan, but the stones with hieroglyphs that should have come from Philae were not on board. The French had persuaded the Captain that they were too heavy and would sink the boat. They were later found by Belzoni smashed to pieces, presumably by Drovetti's agents as scrawled across them in French were the words 'job spoilt'. Now, with the Nile falling and the opportunity for transporting the Young Memnon falling with it, the Captain refused to honour his agreement. Help came from an unexpected source. The Cacheff, hostile again to the British and expecting big presents from the French, actually received from M. Drovetti a present of just two bottles of anchovies and two bottles of olives:

> Strange as it may appear, it will be seen that the effects of a few salted little fish contributed the greatest share towards the removal of the colossus, which I had so much at heart, and which, in all probability, but for them, would not have been in the British Museum to this day.

The Cacheff was furious at Drovetti's unintended slight and Belzoni struck while the Cacheff's mind was hot. As far as the Cacheff was concerned, Belzoni could take away anything he liked and he could take it in the boat he'd been promised. The Captain was ordered to unload his cargo of dates, labourers were ordered to work free and, on 17 November, the head of Young Memnon was pulled and levered along a specially constructed earthen bank towards the boat.

> The Arabs, who were unanimously of the opinion that it would go to the bottom of the river, or crush the boat, were all attention ... and when the owner of the boat, who considered it as consigned to perdition, witnessed my success and saw the huge piece of stone, as he called it, safely on board, he came and squeezed me heartily by the hand. 'Thank heaven!' I exclaimed, and I had reason to be thankful.

Below: *Belzoni in Arab dress.*

With the statues from Karnak also on board, the boat set sail on 21 November 1816 for Cairo and Alexandria to await shipment to England. The first journey was over.

For any normal person, such an adventure with such an outcome would have been enough, but not for Belzoni. Indeed, his appetite for antiquities and for ancient Egypt had just been whetted.

> I proposed to the consul, to make another trip into Upper Egypt and Nubia, to open the temple at Ybsambul. Nothing could be more pleasing to me, than to find that my proposal was accepted.

He set off on 20 February 1817, on a collision course with the agents of Drovetti. As Belzoni, now in Turkish dress, sailed up the Nile, Drovetti's agents were marching overland to arrive in Thebes before him. Just as the European powers scrambled for colonies so, in their wake, archaeologists scrambled for sites.

I was not long therefore in considering the matter, and resolved to set off immediately, and by travelling day and night was in hopes to reach the place before them.

The race was to take five and a half days by ass, horse and camel, and by sleeping just eleven hours during the entire journey, he beat the agents. But to little effect: on his arrival in Thebes, the French were already in possession of the Temple of Karnak. The Defterdar Bey, already softened up by French gifts, was himself digging in an area claimed by Belzoni and collecting statues on the French behalf.

Belzoni was forced to dig in another area before he crossed the river to Gournou, where the French were not yet in possession and where the search for papyrus and other small objects was more likely to be profitable. He went back into the Gournou caves, the mummy pits, the tombs of the ancient Egyptians:

Of some of these tombs many persons could not withstand the suffocating air, which often causes fainting. A vast quantity of dust rises, so fine that it enters into the throat and nostrils,

Below: *Drovetti with his agents in Upper Egypt.*

and chokes the nose and mouth to such a degree that it requires great power of lungs to resist it and the strong effluvia of mummies. This is not all; the entry or passage where the bodies are is roughly cut in the rocks, and the falling of the sand from the upper part or ceiling of the passage causes it to be nearly filled up. In some places there is not more than a vacancy of a foot left, which you must contrive to pass through in a creeping posture like a snail, on pointed and keen stones, that cut like glass. After getting through these passages, some of them two or three hundred yards long, you generally find a more commodious place perhaps high enough to sit ... But when my weight bore on the body of an Egyptian, it crushed it like a band-box. I naturally had recourse to my hands to sustain my weight, but they found no better support; so that I sunk altogether among the broken mummies, with a crash of bones, rags and wooden cases, which raised such a dust as kept me motionless for a quarter of an hour, waiting till it subsided again. I could not remove from the place, however, without increasing it, and every step I took I crushed a mummy in some part or other.

Despite the initial havoc he caused, Belzoni found, under arms, between knees and folded in linen, the papyri that he was looking for. He was a plunderer, as the British Museum had asked him to plunder and as others were plundering, but he also took careful note of the objects around him – the wall-paintings, the pottery, the linen, the gilding, the sculpture, the architecture and the embalmed animals – as well as the embalmed people. He began to acquire sufficient firsthand information to contradict 'my old guide Herodotus'. He found that the Greek historian was not well-informed about the Egyptians; that mummies in their cases were not buried erect ('I never saw a single mummy standing') and the lower classes were not buried in cases at all but dried in the sun. Belzoni was, from practical experience, becoming what would today be called an archaeologist.

He discovered enough material for a second boatload to be dispatched to Cairo, and the boat got away just before the Bey announced that no article should be sold to the English, only to the French. Belzoni withdrew to the Nile and continued his way to Abu Simbel in a temperature of 124°F. His party was bolstered by the addition of two British army officers and Consul Salt's secretary. At Abu Simbel they decided they should continue the digging themselves. They found that they were more efficient by five times than 'the barbarians' even though, with the occasional addition of members of the boat crew, they were only eleven people. As the dig went deeper, palisades had to be erected to stop sand falling into the hole. At twenty-five feet, the cornice of the door surround came into view; the next day the decorative frieze, and the next day:

> ... to my utmost satisfaction saw the upper part of the door as the evening approached. We dug away enough sand to be able to enter that night, but supposing there might be some foul air in the cavity, we deferred this till the next morning ... (when) we went to the temple in high spirits at the idea of entering a newly discovered place.

It was, for Belzoni, 'one of the most magnificent of temples', both in terms of size and decoration. He recognised, too, the 'same hero' that he'd seen in Thebes – Ramses II – but he could only guess at the date of the temple's construction and, whilst the discovery itself was satisfying, there was very little that could be taken away. The party embarked for Luxor virtually empty-handed on 4 August.

At Luxor, Belzoni abandoned Karnak to Drovetti and moved back to Gournou and the valley of Beban el Malook, the Valley of the Kings, with permission from the Cacheff to dig. The ancient Egyptians had originally buried their dead in chambers inside pyramids, but the tombs were broken into, the grave goods stolen and the bodies desecrated. For greater security, the later royal tombs were constructed in the Theban hills in chambers hollowed out of the rock, but these too, despite constant vigil by the high priests, were broken into either in ancient times or by curious Greeks and Romans. The Greek historian Herodotus had written that there were about forty royal tombs. Strabo, writing at the time of Christ, reckoned there were forty-seven but that only eighteen of these could be seen. Two thousand years later, the French expedition had confirmed that there were still eighteen visible, but Belzoni doubted whether more than ten of them had been royal. He had already found, however, that authors such as Herodotus could be wrong:

> ... particularly when they speak from hearsay, I put them out of the account, and proceeded entirely on my own judgment to search for the tombs of the monarchs of Thebes. I began in the valley to the westward of Beban el Malook, near the same place where I discovered the tomb the year before.

Belzoni, when it came to tomb hunting, seemed to possess the magic touch. He was a tomb diviner. The Arabs thought that he was concocting magic spells as he wrote in his notebook, but what he was actually doing was writing down his observations: that the piles of stones and rubbish on the valley floor might have been washed down from tombs on the mountainside; that the piles of rubbish themselves might conceal tomb entrances. In the entire valley he found only one likely spot. The rubbish was removed and a passage revealed, blocked after a few yards by a wall of stones:

> The following day I caused a large pole to be brought, and by means of another small piece of palm-tree laid across the entrance, I made a machine not unlike a battering-ram.

Inside the tomb were four mummies in their cases. Belzoni examined them minutely:

> Among the others I found one that had new linen, apparently, put over the old rags; which proves that the Egyptians took great care of their dead, even for many years after their decease.

His success caused him to move into the Valley of the Kings itself. He began excavating on 6 October and made his first discovery three days later:

> The painted figures on the walls are so perfect, that they are the best adapted of any I ever saw to give a correct and clear idea of the Egyptian taste.

On the same day he entered another tomb:

> At one corner of this chamber we found two mummies on the ground quite naked, without cloth or case. They were females, and their hair pretty long, and well preserved, though it was easily separated from the head by pulling it a little.

Two days later a third tomb, now known to be that of Ramses I:

> We found a sarcophagus of granite, with two mummies in it, and in a corner a statue standing erect, six feet six inches high, and beautifully cut out of sycamore-wood: it is nearly perfect except the nose.

He took a rest for four days, during which time he discovered two mummy pits at Gournou before returning to his excavations in the valley of Beban el Malook on 16 October.

> Not fifteen yards from the last tomb I described, I caused the earth to be opened at the foot of a steep hill, and under a torrent, which, when it rains, pours a great quantity of water over the very spot I have caused to be dug. No one could imagine that the ancient Egyptians would make the entrance

into such an immense and superb excavation just under a torrent of water; but I had strong reasons to suppose that there was a tomb in that place, from indications I had observed in my pursuit. The Fellahs who were accustomed to dig were all of opinion that there was nothing in that spot, as the situation of this tomb differed from that of any other. I continued to work however, and the next day, the 17th, in the evening, we perceived the part of the rock that was cut, and formed the entrance. On the 18th, early in the morning, the task was resumed, and about noon the workmen reached the entrance, which was eighteen feet below the surface of the ground. The appearance indicated that the tomb was of the first rate: but still I did not expect to find such a one as it really proved to be. The Fellahs advanced till they saw that it was probably a large tomb, when they protested they could go no farther, the tomb was so much choked up with large stones, which they could not get out of the passage. I descended, examined the place, pointed out to them where they might dig, and in an hour there was room enough for me to enter through a passage that the earth had left under the ceiling of the first corridor ... I perceived immediately by the painting on the ceiling, and by the hieroglyphics in basso-relievo, which were to be seen where the earth did not reach, that this was the entrance into a large and magnificent tomb.

Belzoni had found what was, and still is, the most magnificent tomb in the entire Valley of the Kings, the tomb of King Seti I who died *c.* 1300 BC, father of Ramses II, the Young Memnon. But the name of Seti I was a name that Belzoni, who died before the hieroglyphics were deciphered, would never know.

Belzoni and his colleagues penetrated along the corridor that led down a flight of steps into the bowels of the mountain. At the end of a second long corridor their progress was checked by a pit, 30 feet deep, on the opposite side of which was a small gap some 2 feet wide and high. A rope, still hanging there after more than 3000 years, was the means across – but when touched it crumbled to dust.

The pit was bridged on the following day by two wooden planks. Belzoni climbed through the small gap into a beautiful hall held up by four pillars and then through into yet another hall, 28 feet square and covered with figures:

> ... so fine and perfect, that you would think they had been drawn only the day before ... We perceived that the paintings became more perfect as we advanced farther into the interior.

Right: *Sketch by Belzoni of the wall painting 'Sacrifice of the Bull', from the tomb of Seti I.*

> ... From this we entered a small chamber, twenty feet four inches by thirteen feet eight inches, to which I gave the name the Room of Beauties.

They then entered another large hall, covered with paintings and supported by two rows of square pillars, three on each side and then, one step further, into a vast saloon with an arched roof. In the flickering light from the torches they could see the roof painted blue like the sky and decorated with figures of the zodiac. On the floor was the embalmed carcass of a bull. Belzoni called it the Bull's or Apis' room:

> But ... what we found in the centre of the saloon ... merits the most particular attention, not having its equal in the world, and being such as we had no idea could exist. It is a sarcophagus of the finest oriental alabaster, nine feet five inches long and three feet seven inches wide. Its thickness is only two inches; and it is transparent when a light is placed inside it. It is minutely sculptured within and without with several hundred figures, which do not exceed two inches in height, and represent, as I suppose, the whole of the funeral procession and ceremonies relating to the deceased, united with several emblems, etc. I cannot give an adequate idea of this beautiful and invaluable piece of antiquity, and can only say that nothing has been brought into Europe from Egypt that can be compared with it. The cover was not there: it had been taken out and broken into several pieces, which we found in digging before the first entrance.

News of Belzoni's discovery spread rapidly. It even reached the Aga of Kenneh, two days ride east of Thebes, who appeared within thirty-six hours, demanding the treasure. He and his soldiers were like hounds, searching in every hole and corner, but they found nothing. The Aga insisted that Belzoni had discovered a large golden cock filled with diamonds and pearls and demanded to know where it was. Belzoni denied this and asked the Aga what he thought of the 'beautifully painted figures'.

> He just gave a glance at them, quite unconcerned, and said, 'This would be a good place for a harem, as the women would have something to look at.' At length, though only half persuaded there was no treasure, he set off with an appearance of much vexation.

In one remarkable week, Belzoni had increased the number of royal tombs known in the Valley of the Kings by half. He left Thebes with another boatload of antiquities, the fruit of ten months' exploration, and arrived back in Cairo on 21 December where he was to experience 'much vexation' in his turn. Belzoni found that, as well as being able to command only a small price for the sale of those antiquities that were his (to the Count de Forbin, Director of the French Museum), even worse, his discoveries were being credited in the French Press to other people: to Consul Salt, to M. Drovetti, even to the Count de Forbin himself. The academics in France even disbelieved that the sarcophagus in the Apis tomb was actually made of alabaster. The English *Quarterly Review* hit back, sensing national honour to be at stake, accusing the French of sour grapes. As the tension increased, Sarah decided that she'd had a long felt want to visit Jerusalem – alone. Giovanni revisited the pyramids and, in particular, the second great pyramid, the Pyramid of Chephren:

> I seated myself in the shade of one of those stones on the east side, which form part of the temple that stood before the pyramid in that direction ... The sight of the wonderful work before me astonished me as much as the total obscurity in which we are of its origin, its interior and its construction. In an intelligent age like the present, one of the greatest wonders of the world stood before us, without our knowing even whether it had any cavity in the interior or if it were only one solid mass.

A chamber existed inside the great Pyramid of Cheops but not, according to Herodotus, inside the Pyramid of Chephren. Herodotus, however, had been wrong before:

With all these thoughts in my mind I arose, and by a natural impulse took my walk towards the south side of the pyramid. I examined every part, and almost every stone. I continued to do so on the west, and at last came round to the north. Here the appearance of things became to my eye somewhat different from that at any of the other sides.

The practical experience gained from observation and excavation at Abu Simbel and, especially, in the Valley of the Kings, was about to pay off. As Belzoni himself said, making a revolutionary observation for his time, 'in many cases practice goes further than theory' – a reproof to all the know-all academics and classically educated gentlemen who had never turned a spade in their lives.

I observed on the north side of the pyramid three marks, which encouraged me to attempt searching there for the entrance into it ... I observed that just under the centre of the face of the pyramid the accumulation of materials, which had fallen from the coating of it, was higher than the entrance could be expected to be, if compared with the height of the entrance into the first pyramid ... I resolved to make a closer examination.

Work began on the east and the north sides, forty Arabs on each side working with just thin hatchet-like spades in an attempt to find the pavement on which Belzoni believed the pyramid was built. The work was painfully slow, the hatchets broke on the stones and rubble and, whilst the pavement was eventually reached on the east side and most of the accumulated rubbish had been removed on the north side, there was no sign of an entrance, until:

... after sixteen days of fruitless labour, one of the Arabian workmen perceived a small chink between two stones of the pyramid.

The workers, whose work-rate had declined with their enthusiasm, were galvanised, stones removed and a cavity revealed:

To introduce many men to work in this place was dangerous, for several of the stones above our heads were on the point of falling; some were suspended only by their corners ... and with the least touch would have fallen ... one of the men narrowly escaped being crushed to pieces ... that I thought it prudent to retreat out of the pyramid ... for the danger was not only from what might fall upon us, but also from what might fall in our way, close up the passage, and thus bury us alive.

Belzoni deduced that this passage was not the true entrance to the pyramid but a forced passage partly driven into the pyramid in an attempt, in antiquity, to discover the pyramid's central chamber, if it had one. Despite his disappointment, Belzoni was obdurate. He looked again at the first pyramid to see if it would help him with the second. He looked at the first pyramid's entrance. It was not positioned as he had at first thought, exactly in the centre. He returned to the second pyramid and decided that he had been digging in the wrong place, that an entrance, if the first pyramid was to be any guide, would be thirty feet to the east of centre.

> This gave me no little delight, and hope returned to cherish my pyramidical brains.

He began to dig again with the Arabs muttering to themselves 'magnoon' – madman. Three days and many huge blocks of stone later:

> I perceived in the excavation a large block of granite, inclining downward at the same angle as the passage into the first pyramid, and pointing towards the centre ... The discovery of the first granite stone occurred on the 28th of February, and on the 1st of March we uncovered three large blocks of granite, two on each side and one on the top, all in an inclined direction towards the centre. My expectation and hope increased, as to all appearance, this must prove to be the object of my search.

It took the rest of the day to extract the stones blocking the passage before it could be entered and then, apparently jointed into the stonework, was:

> ... a fixed block of stone, which stared me in the face and said *ne plus ultra*, putting an end to all my projects as I thought.

The stone proved to be a portcullis that had to be raised slowly by levers, with a stone propped under the portcullis as it was raised inch by inch, until it was high enough for a man to squeeze through:

> I continued to raise the portcullis, and at last made the entrance large enough to squeeze myself in; and after thirty days exertion I had the pleasure of finding myself in the way to the central chamber of one of the two great pyramids of Egypt.

Along a steeply descending and then a steeply rising dark and airless passage, Belzoni reached the door at the centre of a large

chamber. His torch threw long shadows on the walls. In the gloom he could just make out a painted roof and, buried in the floor, a huge sarcophagus of the finest granite, unadorned and empty. In one corner of the room, words were scrawled in a strange Arabic script. Translated they revealed that the pyramid had actually been entered in about the year AD 1200. The romantics, Belzoni thought, would be disappointed at this revelation, but he was not. It was 'a very interesting circumstance'. He had come a long way from being merely a hired looter of antiquities to an archaeologist in embryo, interested in information for its own sake.

Belzoni was delighted at his discovery: he had solved an age-old mystery and he had financed it himself. Consul Salt offered to pay his expenses but he declined. There was bad feeling between Salt and himself, a smouldering antagonism that had recently burst into flame. Salt believed that the agreement between them was for Belzoni to work on Salt's behalf. Belzoni believed he was working for the British Museum and not as a Salt employee. A new agreement was drawn up between them. Salt handed over to Belzoni two statues of the goddess Sekhmet, a coffin lid, a half share of whatever price the Apis sarcophagus might fetch, and agreed to pay him £500 over the next year. In return Belzoni was to 'help' Salt, not as an employee but working under Salt's auspices. The master-servant relationship had gone. On the wall of the chamber in the Chephren pyramid he wrote the name G. B. Belzoni in letters three feet high. This find was *his*.

He prepared for his third and final journey up the Nile. He wanted to draw and make wax impressions of the reliefs in the Seti tomb – there were to be 182 of them life-size, 800 small ones and 500 hieroglyphs – and he wanted to dig and make a collection of antiquities of his own. Also, an English aristocrat, William Bankes M.P., had seen the giant obelisk at Philae and wanted Belzoni to get it for him. The attempt was to lead to the final, cataclysmic fight with the French.

Belzoni was met by Drovetti at Luxor and given some curious information. Someone masquerading as himself had been hiding in the Karnak temple deliberately to discredit him and even drawing fire:

> I informed Mr Drovetti that I hoped he would tell his European people to inquire before they should fire at the supposed person representing me, whether it was the real or the sham Belzoni, as it would not be quite so pleasant or satisfactory to me if the mistake had been found out after.

Was this just another attempt to frighten him or was his life really in danger? He mentioned the obelisk at Philae: Drovetti, surprised, claimed that it was his. Drovetti's agent hurried to Aswan in an attempt to persuade the Aga not to allow the obelisk to be removed. The Aga, anticipating presents from the English, refused and the removal began, using the same techniques that had been successful with the Young Memnon. At the water's edge an earth ramp had been built in order to load the obelisk onto the boat:

> The pier appeared quite strong enough to bear at least forty times the weight it had to support; but, alas! when the obelisk came gradually on from the sloping bank, and all the weight rested on it, the pier, with the obelisk, and some of the men, took a slow movement, and majestically descended into the river.

Concerned at the opprobium of the antiquarian world, and even more concerned that the French would have the last laugh, Belzoni spent two days levering the obelisk out of the water, onto the boat and down the cataract:

> In the boat there were only five men; and on the rocks, on each side of the cascade, a number of others in various places, with ropes attached to the boat, so as to put it either on one side or the other, as it required, to prevent its running against the

stones; for if it should be touched in the smallest degree, with such a weight on board, and in such a rapid stream, the boat could not escape being dashed to pieces.

The successful navigation of such an enormous and unwieldy load, in a fragile boat going down a waterfall at twelve miles an hour through large rocks, was a considerable feat of engineering, 'and I was not a little pleased to see it out of danger'.

The boat reached Aswan safely and Belzoni hurried back to Thebes where he spent Christmas camping in the tomb of Seti I with Sarah, now returned from Jerusalem. The boat, following him down the river, arrived at Luxor and was parked almost literally under the noses of the French, '... and it irritated them to such a degree, that they premeditated the mode of revenge.'

Belzoni, riding over from the west bank to the east to examine some ground at Karnak, was leaving the temple when one of his Arab workers came running towards him, crying from having been beaten by the French. Belzoni refused to be drawn until a crowd of some thirty Arabs also came running towards him, headed by two European agents of Drovetti, demanding:

> ... what business I had to take away an obelisk that did not belong to me; and that I had done so many things of this kind to him, that I should not do any more.

Belzoni's bridle was seized, a double-barrelled gun pointed at his chest, and the Arabs waved threateningly with sticks shouting 'that I should pay for all I had done to them'. He tried to push his way through the mob but was prevented by yet another group of Arabs, this time led by Drovetti himself. A pistol was fired. Fortunately, blood was not shed. Drovetti calmed the situation and a discussion ensued, characterised by mutual suspicion and misunderstanding. Despite Belzoni's righteous indignation at the charges levelled at him:

> I returned to Beban el Malook, and immediately commenced my preparations to depart for Europe, as I could not live any longer in a country where I had become the object of revenge.

He loaded the alabaster sarcophagus, the wax impression of the reliefs and some small artefacts onto the boat carrying the obelisk. He mourned the damage he felt water and inconsiderate visitors would do to the Apis tomb he was leaving behind him and he mourned leaving Thebes. At Alexandria he was delayed several months so that an action could be brought against his attackers. The newly appointed French Consul, on finally hearing the case, ruled that as the men concerned were actually Italians, he had no jurisdiction over them and Belzoni should go to court in Turin.

> In the middle of September, 1819, we embarked, thank God! for Europe: not that I disliked the country I was in, for, on the contrary, I have reason to be grateful; nor do I complain of the Turks or Arabs in general, but of some Europeans who are in that country, whose conduct and mode of thinking are a disgrace to human nature.

Belzoni was back in London in March 1820. He'd been away for four years and he returned a celebrity. *The Times*, announcing his arrival, called him 'the celebrated traveller' and catalogued his discoveries. His book describing his experiences was published by John Murray (who corrected the appalling spelling) and preparations were made for an exhibition of Belzoni's own antiquities to be displayed inside a full-scale replica of the Apis (Seti I) tomb. It opened in Piccadilly on 1 May 1821: the showman had reasserted himself. The book promoted the exhibition, the exhibition promoted the book and the imminent arrival of the obelisk and the sarcophagus kept interest in both at a maximum. One of the mummies was publicly unwrapped, more, one has to believe, as a publicity stunt than a scientific experiment and Egyptomania was let loose. Belzoni was lionised by society. *The Times*, commenting on the exhibition, praised him for ingenuity and diligence, and an artistic sagacity combined with an ability to discover his subject matter that 'has distinguished him above all European travellers in modern times'.

The British Museum, however, did not altogether share *The Times*' enthusiasm. The collection of antiquities that Salt offered the British Museum was initially rejected as too expensive. The newly arrived alabaster sarcophagus was impounded by them and, whilst they wouldn't buy it, they wouldn't release it to Belzoni either, who had a legitimate share in it and wanted to display it. Disillusioned, he auctioned the contents of his exhibition and funded a new expedition.

During his third journey up the Nile, Belzoni had gone beyond the second cataract into the Nubian desert in search of the lost city of Berenice. This experience had stirred his enthusiasm for greater travel and even greater fame. Neither England nor Sarah could hold him. As he wrote to a friend, Burckhardt's ambition to find the source of the Niger was now Belzoni's:

> Should I succeed in my attempt I shall add another 'votive tablet' to the Temple of Fortune; and if on the contrary, my

Below: *The sarcophagus of Seti I in Sir John Soane's Museum, Lincoln's Inn Fields, London.*

Above: *Belzoni's name chiselled on a monument still in Egypt.*

project should fail, one more name will be added to the many others which have fallen into the River of Oblivion.

Before he left England he presented to the Fitzwilliam Museum at Cambridge the prize of his own collection: the red granite coffin lid of the sarcophagus of Ramses III. Academic and scientific recognition was, to the end, more important than money. He arrived on the Benin coast of Africa in October 1823. Within two months he was dead of dysentery.

Consul Salt called Belzoni 'the prince of ungrateful adventurers'. The *Quarterly Review* wrote more accurately, 'Though no scholar himself he may justly be considered as a pioneer of antiquarian researches'. Until recently, Belzoni has been more often dismissed as 'plunderer' than praised as 'pioneer', but his attitudes and methods, although reprehensible with hindsight, were no more than usual for his day and more caring than most. Unwittingly, Belzoni was the first of a new generation of Egyptologists who, instead of making a detailed study of classical authors, emphasised firsthand, on-site observations and excavation. The subject was soon to be revolutionised by Champollion and his reading of the hieroglyphs, but Belzoni was the catalyst.

The obelisk from Philae is now in the grounds of William Bankes' old home at Kingston Lacy in Dorset; the alabaster sarcophagus of Seti I is in Sir John Soane's Museum in Lincoln's Inn Fields; an unsold head of Sekmet is over the entrance to Sotheby's in Bond Street; but the vast majority of Belzoni's pieces are in the British Museum, including the Young Memnon, the centrepiece of a vast display. But the name of Belzoni is not much in evidence in the museum. It is necessary to search for it where he carved it himself, obsessively, on the base of his statues – Belzoni, Belzoni, Belzoni ...

'But pray,' added he, smiling, 'have you a scarcity of stones also in Europe, that you come here to fetch them away?' I answered that we had plenty of stones, but we thought those of Egypt were of a better sort.

Chapter Two

THE ROSE-RED CITY
Jean Louis Burckhardt
in Petra

I was without protection in the midst of a desert where no traveller had ever before been seen; and a close examination of these works of the infidels, as they are called, would have excited suspicions that I was a magician. *

In Cairo in 1815, Giovanni Belzoni met the man who was to start him on his career: Jean Louis Burckhardt, the young Swiss waiting in the city for the caravan that would take him forward on his journey of exploration into Central Africa. He had been waiting for almost three years. During that time he had visited many of the ancient sites of Upper Egypt including Abu Simbel and the temples at Thebes, where he had seen the colossal head of the Young Memnon. It was Burckhardt who was determined that the head should go to Britain and who introduced Belzoni to Consul Salt.

Belzoni, who was not easily impressed by his fellow men, thought Burckhardt 'the most candid, disinterested and sincere being I ever met with'. At the time of their meeting, Burckhardt's career was almost over. His fame would rest on a goal already achieved, a discovery made by stealth and almost by accident. On 22 August 1812, on his journey to Cairo, Jean Louis Burckhardt had become the first westerner to see perhaps the most romantic of all 'lost' cities: Petra, 'the rose-red city, half as old as time'.

Men's lives are predestined; we all obey our fate. For myself,

*J. L. Burckhardt, *Travels in Syria and the Holy Land* (London: John Murray, 1822).

Above: *Jean Louis Burckhardt (1784– 1817).*

I enjoy great pleasure in exploring new and unknown countries and becoming acquainted with different races of people. I am induced to undertake journeys by the private satisfaction that travelling affords and I care little about personal fatigue.

Burckhardt was born on 25 November 1784, in Lausanne, Switzerland. He was christened Johann Ludwig and his first language was German, but he was known in the family by the French version of his name – Louis.

His father was a wealthy businessman in Basle; a cultivated Anglophile and friend of the English writer Edward Gibbon. The Burckhardts' affluence and family harmony were shattered by the French Revolution: business suffered and the family's name was placed on a list of 'enemies of France'. In 1796 the Basle City Council, fearing their neutrality was being compromised, accused Burckhardt's father of high treason and imprisoned him. In 1798, the French invaded Berne; they ransacked the town and used the loot to finance their military expedition against Egypt. The Swiss cantons became subject to the French and, at the age of fourteen, Burckhardt's wanderings began. First, to school in Neuchâtel and then, from 1800 to 1805, to university in Leipzig and Göttingen. Here, reacting against family disgrace and financial hardship, he lived so wildly and ran up such enormous debts that it was to take him the rest of his life to atone for what he saw as his 'crime' against his family.

In 1806, Burckhardt sailed for England in search of a job. It was not immediately forthcoming, but he made useful contacts: Joseph Planta, Chief Librarian at the British Museum; Henry Salt, who was to be the future British Consul in Cairo; and, above all, Sir Joseph Banks, long-standing member of the African Association. Burckhardt wrote home to his parents:

(I) mingle with the great in the daytime and buy for the evening, secretly in a back street, provisions for a few days. I shall never forget it – and I hope it will do me good.

It did, although for a period of two months he almost starved.

The African Association had been formed in 1788 by a group of wealthy and learned men. According to its acting Secretary William Henry Leake, Editor of Burckhardt's journals, it was 'a Society whose sole professed object is the promotion of discoveries in the African continent.' In an age of colonial expansion, the nation with the most knowledge of Africa would be the best placed to gain the most from its colonisation. Many young men were already dead or posted missing in the Association's service, all searching for the source of the River Niger: the

American Ledyard, the German Hornemann, the Scot Mungo Park (the most famous of them all) and now the Englishman Henry Nichols, who was reported dead of fever at Calabar on the Atlantic coast of what is now Nigeria. The Association was looking for a replacement explorer just as Burckhardt was becoming desperate for a job. As minutes of the Association committee meeting on 21 March 1808 record:

> A letter from Mr Burckhardt a Native of Basle in Switzerland was read together with several notes from him to Sir Joseph Banks ... offering his Services to the Association for the discovery of the Interior Parts of Africa which being considered & in general approved: Mr Burckhardt was desired to attend the Committee when he very fully explained to the Committee his views and intentions and also the Route by which under the direction of the Committee he proposed to direct his enquiries.

The plan was simple: to travel to Malta and there become conversant with African ways before travelling to Tripoli; then across the Sahara by caravan to Timbuktu and on to the River Niger itself, where 'he proposed to hide in the character of a Moorish merchant provided with the usual Species of Merchandize'. After the risks and dangers were pointed out to him and Burckhardt expressed himself 'undismayed', the proposal was considered:

> From Mr Burckhardt's conversation and Habits of Life & the recommendation of him by Mr Professor Blumenbach of Göttingen in a Letter to Sir Joseph Banks, the Committee is of opinion that Mr Burckhardt should be employed in the Service of the Association.

Between May 1808 and the start of 1809 Burckhardt went up to Cambridge to begin his preparations. He learnt the basics of Arabic; he studied medicine; mineralogy; chemistry; anatomy and astronomy; anything that would be of use to him in his enterprise. He began to toughen his physique by walking long distances bareheaded in a rare summer heatwave; living on a sparse diet of vegetables and water; sleeping on the ground. There was a Teutonic diligence about him as well as a Teutonic love of the romantic.

His instructions were issued on 5 January 1809. They differed slightly from the original plan, as notes received from the missing explorers suggested that the best route to the west coast of Africa was not via Tripoli but by pilgrim caravan from Cairo. He was told to proceed to Cairo via Malta and Aleppo.

Above: *Portrait of Burckhardt as an Arab.*

His contract was for eight years, which was the estimated time that it would take him to reach his destination and, hopefully, return. The first two years were to be spent in study in Syria, for which he was to be paid a daily rate of 10s.6d.; after that he was paid a guinea a day. He wrote again to his parents:

During this long period I shall be accustomed to living more moderately. I shall learn to make do with less and to strengthen my moral and physical character through self-denial. I have at last achieved what I have been craving for during eight years – a definite sphere of activity. I have at last found a goal ... This journey, and what I shall observe while I travel, requires not a genius but a straightforward, clear mind and some ability.

The 'crime' of his wild years during university was about to be expiated. He left Cowes, Isle of Wight, in March 1809 as John Lewis Burckhardt and arrived in Malta as Sheikh Ibrahim Ibn Abd Allah. For the rest of his life, apart from with close friends, he was to speak nothing but Arabic.

The French had recently been ousted from the Maltese Islands and the British were in the process of taking them over. For two months, Burckhardt lodged in rooms overlooking Valetta harbour, watching the Arab traders and learning their ways. He had time to consider the enormity of his enterprise:

The fear of death has left me since I have been at ease with my conscience and ... I shall not hastily expose myself to death, but shall not be afraid either when I am faced by it.

His confidence grew as, in full Arab dress, he passed undetected among the people that thronged the harbour. But would he remain undetected in an Arab country? He left Malta in June, bound for Aleppo in Syria, part of the Ottoman Empire. On his journey from the coast to the city, something about his appearance attracted attention. He was accused of being an infidel, a European up to no good:

When the man saw that nothing in my manners betrayed my Frank origin, he made a last trial, and pulling my beard a little with his hand, asked me familiarly 'Why I had let such a thing grow?' I answered him with a blow upon his face, to convince the by-standing Turks how deeply I resented the received insult; the laugh now turned against the poor Dragoman (guide) who did not trouble me any further.

Shortly afterwards, however, a more serious breach of etiquette almost blew his disguise completely. Answering a call of nature,

he completed his ablutions with his right hand: 'It is an offence to use the right hand as it is the social and the eating hand.' He was dubbed unclean and was abused by his fellow travellers. It was a useful lesson. He wrote to the Association from Aleppo:

> This trial has so far been satisfactory to me, that, in the first place I am persuaded that nothing of my pursuits has transpired at Malta, which will always be of material consequence to me; secondly, in being landed at a remote corner of Syria, I have avoided the general intercourse of a mercantile seaport such as Acre, Beirout, Tripoly or Latakia; and finally, it has created within me the confidence that ... I may be able to call in support of a similar disguise, a fluent utterance of Arabic, and a habitude of Oriental manners.

But why the need for disguise and why Aleppo? Outside Europe there were very few European travellers and a European's presence in Arabia or North Africa was immediately noticed and his progress watched with suspicion. He was a target for robbery at least and, at most, for killing as a spy, as all Franks were viewed as infidels bent on exploitation. The only way to prevent any of this happening was to cease to be a European, to integrate, to become like one of them. Only this way could an explorer like Burckhardt protect both himself and the information he'd been hired to discover.

Aleppo was an ideal place to complete his transformation. It teemed with traders from India, Turkey, and Kurdistan as well as Arabia, and many languages were spoken. He could pass unrecognised as he improved his Arabic and learnt how to behave. He also made short journeys into the surrounding regions to prepare himself for the first leg of his journey.

His first foray was in March 1810, when he went into the mountains east of Aleppo searching, ostensibly, for herbs. He returned safely. His second took him into the desert, where he succeeded in reaching the great ruined city of Palmyra, some years before the fabled Lady Hester Stanhope. It also gave him his first experience of being robbed and stripped, an experience that was repeated on his third journey when he travelled to the Euphrates where he lost not only his clothes but his camel as well, though not his notebook (perhaps concealed in his underwear) nor his life. 'Arabs', he found, 'never maltreat the traveller who agrees to be robbed.'

These experiences confirmed the travellers' tales of robbery and sudden violence. It was as if the whole region, a mixture of different races and different religions – Islam, Christian, Druse and Jew – was in a perpetual state of turmoil. The Turkish overlords and the local rulers were against the people; the townspeople were against the desert dwellers; the desert tribes were against the government and the town as well as each other. It was a region where the rule was 'rob or be robbed', where the locals preyed on the travellers and the travellers stole what they couldn't buy from the locals. Even with the pilgrims on the Hadj, the sacred journey to Mecca:

> Thieving and robbery have become general among them, and it is more the want of sleep from fear of being plundered, which causes the death of so many pilgrims, than the fatigues of the journey. The Pasha's troops ... which bring up the rear of the caravan, are frequently known to kill the stragglers during the night, in order to strip them of their property. The Pasha, it is true, often punishes such delinquents, and scarcely a day passes without someone being empaled alive; the caravan moves on, and the malefactor is left to be devoured by the birds of prey.

The people of the desert were as harsh as the land they lived in, but they were also, conversely, as kind as they could be cruel:

> A traveller may alight at any house he pleases; a mat will be immediately spread for him, coffee made, and a breakfast or dinner set before him ... and this hospitality is not confined to the traveller himself, his horse or his camel is also fed ... It is

a point of honour with the host never to accept the smallest return from a guest.

Burckhardt was convinced that his method of travelling incognito was vastly preferable to the methods of the English aristocrats that he met on tour:

I stop at the dirtiest caravanserai, use the floor as my mattress and my coat as a blanket, eat with camel drivers, and brush my horse myself, but I see and hear things which remain unknown to him who travels in comfort.

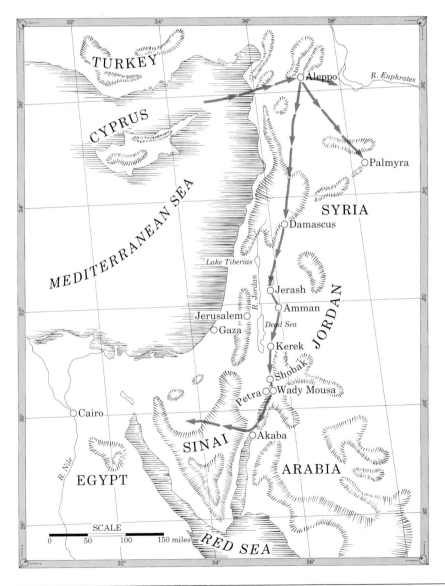

The things he saw and heard were more than sufficient to satisfy his and the Association's natural curiosity. Quite innocent was their desire to have information on what was coyly known as 'sacred geography', the identification of holy sites referred to in the Bible. Less innocent was their need for detailed information on physical geography that could be of vital use to an invading army, and information on deposits of rock salt and sulphur that might be suitable for commercial exploitation.

He also supplied detailed information on the political divisions of the country, the effective rulers, the strongest tribes, the most powerful religious groups and the effect that any of these might have on the traveller. His disguise was proved successful when he travelled for a brief spell with an Englishman he'd known in Aleppo, John Fiott. Fiott was also dressed as an Arab but the Arabs and Turks who passed him on the road called him a 'Frank' and laughed, but Sheikh Ibrahim who rode with him was saluted with decorum.

By the late spring of 1812, Burckhardt had completed what he called his 'preliminary exercises' and was ready to plunge south to Cairo, through some of the least known and most dangerous territory in the Near East:

> Wishing to obtain a further knowledge of the mountains to the east of the Jordan, and being still more desirous of visiting the almost unknown districts to the east of the Dead Sea ... I resolved to pursue that route from Damascus to Cairo, in preference to the direct road through Jerusalem and Ghaza, where I could not expect to collect much information important for its novelty. Knowing that my intended way led through a diversity of Bedouin tribes, I thought it advisable to equip myself in the simplest manner. I assumed the most common Bedouin dress, took no baggage with me, and mounted a mare that was not likely to excite the cupidity of the Arabs.

He left Damascus on the night of 18 June, following the traditional pilgrim route to Mecca. The Hadj, the pilgrimage, had not travelled for six years because of danger from warring tribes:

> Several heaps of stones indicate the graves of travellers murdered in this place by the Druses, who, during their wars with Djezzar Pasha, were in the habit of descending from the neighbouring mountain, Djebel el Sheikh, in order to waylay the caravans.

He joined a small caravan heading towards Lake Galilee:

It was now about midday, and the sun intensely hot, we therefore looked out for a shady spot, and reposed under a very
large fig-tree, at the foot of which a rivulet of sweet water
gushes out from beneath the rocks and falls into the lake at a
few hundred paces distant.

At night he slept in the khans, or public inns, or was given
hospitality in private houses in the villages or the tents of the
Bedouin. Guides were essential but guides were difficult to find:

... no person seemed to be inclined to undertake the journey,
except in the company of an armed caravan.

He reached the valley of the Jordan, the El Ghor, where the
harsh mountains and the sandy desert on all sides contrasted
with pistachio trees and grass:

A stranger who should venture to travel here unaccompanied
by a guide of the country would most certainly be stripped.

The climate and the terrain were constantly changing. The
danger, however, remained constant:

In three hours and three quarters we descended the southern
side of the mountain, near the tomb of Osha, and reached Szalt,
four hours and a half distant from Meysera. Near the tomb of
Osha was an encampment of about sixty tents of the tribe of
Abad; they had lately been robbed of almost all their cattle by
the Beni Szakher, and were reduced to such misery that they
could not afford to give us a little sour milk we begged of them.

It was Burckhardt's first contact with the Beni Szakher, the
bogeymen of the desert, but it was not to be his last. The Beni
Szakher were at war with everyone 'and we heard daily of skir-
mishes taking place between the contending parties'. No one in
Szalt would take Burckhardt to Amman. He eventually managed
to engage four armed men and was on the point of leaving when
'their wives came crying to my lodging, and upbraided their
husbands with madness in exposing their lives for a couple of
piastres'. The men refused to go. Impatient, Burckhardt left
anyway, alone – until he was able to hire a guide friendly with
the Bedouin:

July 7th. We set off before sunrise ... At the end of three hours
and a half we entered a broad valley, which brought us in half
an hour to the ruins of Amman ... one of the most ancient of
the cities recorded in Jewish history.

When Burckhardt visited Amman, now capital of Jordan, it was no more than a collection of tumbled stones beside a little river. There were the identifiable remains of a bridge, a colonnade with eight columns still upright and a Roman theatre, the largest he had seen in Syria. It was while examining the theatre that he was suddenly interrupted:

> My guides had observed some fresh horse-dung near the water's side, which greatly alarmed them, as it was a proof that some Bedouins were hovering about. They insisted upon my returning immediately, and refusing to wait for me a moment, rode off while I was still occupied in writing a few notes upon the theatre. I hastily mounted the castle hill, ran over its ruins, and galloping after my guides, joined them at half an hour from the town. When I reproached them for their cowardice, they replied that I certainly could not suppose that, for the twelve piastres I had agreed to give them, they should expose themselves to the danger of being stripped and of losing their horses, from a mere foolish caprice of mine to write down the stones.

The days were broiling hot and the nights were cool; there was often little food and a desperate need for water; the road was rough, sometimes impassable, there were flies and mosquitoes. But Burckhardt's three long years of preparation were paying off. His disguise held. He reached the rim of the Wady Modjeb, the Grand Canyon of Palestine, on 14 July:

> The view which the Modjeb presents is very striking: from the bottom, where the river runs through a narrow stripe of verdant level about forty yards across, the steep and barren banks arise to a great height, covered with immense blocks of stone which have rolled down from the upper strata, so that when viewed from above, the valley looks like a deep chasm, formed by some tremendous convulsion of the earth, into which there seems no possibility of descending to the bottom; the distance from the edge of one precipice to that of the opposite one is about two miles in a straight line.
>
> We descended the northern bank of the Wady by a footpath which winds among the masses of rock, dismounting on account of the steepness of the road, as we had been obliged to do in the two former valleys which we had passed in this day's march; this is a very dangerous pass, as robbers often waylay travellers here, concealing themselves behind the rocks, until their prey is close to them. Upon many large blocks by the side of the path I saw heaps of small stones, placed there as a sort of weapon for the traveller, in case of need. No Arab

passes without adding a few stones to these heaps ... I had never felt such suffocating heat as I experienced in this valley, from the concentrated rays of the sun and their reflection from the rocks. We were thirty-five minutes in reaching the bottom.

It took nearly four hours to climb out the other side:

We had now reached a high plain ... in half an hour, we met some shepherds with a flock of sheep, who led us to the tents of their people behind a hill near the side of the road. We were much fatigued, but the kindness of our hosts soon made us forget our laborious day's march. We alighted under the tent of the Sheikh, who was dying of a wound he had received a few days before from the thrust of a lance; but such is the hospitality of these people, and their attention to the comforts of the traveller, that we did not learn the Sheikh's misfortune till the following day. He was in the women's apartment, and we did not hear him utter any complaints. They supposed, with reason, that if we were informed of his situation it would prevent us from enjoying our supper. A lamb was killed, and a friend of the family did the honours of the table; we should have enjoyed our repast had there not been an absolute want of water, but there was none nearer than the Modjeb, and the daily supply which, according to the custom of the Arabs, had been brought in before sunrise, was, as often happens, exhausted before night; our own waterskins too, which we had filled at the Modjeb, had been emptied by the shepherds before we reached the encampment. This loss was the more sensible to me, as in desert countries where water seldom occurs, not feeling great thirst during the heat of the day, I was seldom in the habit of drinking much at that time; but in the evening, and the early part of the night, I always drank with great eagerness.

Kerek, with its city walls and strong Saracen castle, provided Burckhardt with a three-week break from the desert. It was a town consisting of four hundred Turkish families and a hundred and fifty Christians. Between them, they mustered over a thousand guns and held sway over the neighbouring country. Everybody over ten knew how to fire a gun.

Burckhardt was greeted with overwhelming enthusiasm and pressed with incredible hospitality; people vied with one another to grab the bridle of his horse and take him off to their house. Hospitality was part of the Kerekian way of life and a measure of social standing. The more a man entertained, the higher his reputation. In Szalt, free hospitality at the khan was provided by public levy; in Kerek, on the arrival of a stranger, one citizen would declare that he intended to furnish the entire day's entertainment – and so on till the stranger left. It had the collective result of no one in the town, except the sheikh, being worth more than £1000.

It was at Kerek that Burckhardt met the sheikh who was to give him, instead of help, unexpected hindrance. Having asked for a guide, Burckhardt was told that he could ride with the sheikh himself and was asked in return for both payment and a present. The present Burckhardt refused to give on the grounds that it breached traditional hospitality and the payment for the guide he kept as small as possible on the grounds that he had hardly any money. The sheikh took a cut of the guide's money and then kept his guest waiting until, after almost three weeks, he was ready to depart with a retinue of forty horsemen. Progress was slow:

> Our Sheikh had no pressing business, but like all Arabs, fond of idleness, and of living well at other people's expense, he by no means hastened his journey, but easily found a pretext for stopping; wherever we alighted a couple of sheep or goats were immediately killed, and the best fruits, together with plenty of tobacco, were presented to us.

Having guided Burckhardt only half the agreed distance he demanded more money or 'he would not take charge of me any farther'. Burckhardt was forced to pay up. The sheikh then demanded an exchange of saddles; a saddle worth forty piastres in exchange for one worth only ten. Burckhardt was blackmailed into submission. The sheikh's son now demanded an exchange of the inferior saddle his father had given Burckhardt for the even more inferior one of his own. Burckhardt complained that the son's stirrups were almost unfit for use and would damage his ankles as he didn't wear boots:

> But it was in vain to resist. The pressing entreaties of all my companions in favour of the Sheikh's son lasted for two whole days; until, tired at length with their importunity, I yielded, and, as I had expected, my feet were soon wounded.

The sheikh eventually left Burckhardt to the services of another guide:

> Looking down into a valley, we saw at a distance a troop of horsemen encamped near a spring; they had espied us, and immediately mounted their horses in pursuit of us. Although

several people had joined our little caravan on the road, there was only one armed man amongst us, except myself. The general opinion was that the horsemen belonged to the Beni Szakher ... There was therefore no time to lose; we drove the cattle hastily back, about a quarter of an hour, and hid them, with the women and baggage, behind some rocks near the road, and we then took to our heels towards the village of Dhana, which we reached in about three quarters of an hour, extremely exhausted, for it was about two o'clock in the afternoon and the heat was excessive. In order to run more nimbly over the rocks, I took off my heavy Arab shoes, and thus I was the first to reach the village; but the sharp flints of the mountain wounded my feet so much, that after reposing a little I could hardly stand upon my legs. This was the first time I had ever felt fear during my travels in the desert; for I knew that if I fell in with the Beni Szakher, without anybody to protect me, they would certainly kill me, as they did all persons whom they supposed to belong to their inveterate enemy, the Pasha of Damascus, and my appearance was very much that of a Damascene.

The horsemen turned out not to be Beni Szakher after all but friendly Howeytat – friendly, that is, to all the company except the two who hadn't fled because they were from Maan and friends of the Beni Szakher. These friends, instead of finding themselves safe, were, in the ways of the desert, stripped by the Howeytat.

Finding a guide continued to be a problem. Burckhardt was cheated twice before he found a man willing to take him the rest of the 400 miles to Cairo for the price of four goats and 20 piastres (about £1) payable on arrival. Had he been recognised as a European, the price would have risen from 20 piastres to at least 1000. On 19 August he visited the Saracen castle of Shobak where, written in Arabic script high up on the walls of one of the towers, was the name Salah al-Din – Saladin the Great. In the ruins of the castle, he bought provisions from an encampment of Bedouin peasants and, as he no longer had any cash in silver and didn't want to reveal the small amount of money he had to get him to Egypt, he had to pay in kind – his spare shirt, his red cap and half his turban.

August 22nd – I was particularly desirous of visiting Wady Mousa, of the antiquities of which I had heard the country people speak in terms of great admiration.

It was this visit to Wady Mousa, the Valley of Moses, that was to provide him with the greatest experience of his life:

Right: *The hall of the Crusader castle in Shobak where Burckhardt exchanged his spare clothes for food from the camping Bedouin.*

The road from Shobak to Akaba, which is tolerably good and might easily be rendered practicable even to artillery, lies to the E. of Wady Mousa; and to have quitted it, out of mere curiosity to see the Wady, would have looked very suspicious in the eyes of the Arabs; I therefore pretended to have made a vow to slaughter a goat in honour of Haroun (Aaron), whose tomb I knew was situated at the extremity of the valley, and by this stratagem I thought that I should have the means of seeing the valley in my way to the tomb. To this my guide had nothing to oppose; the dread of drawing upon himself, by resistance, the wrath of Haroun, completely silenced him.

As Burckhardt and his guide travelled over hilly country in the direction of the Wady, he could see, in the distance, the top of the mountain which contained the prophet's tomb. His guide tried to persuade him to do what most other pilgrims did, to make his sacrifice here, in view of the mountain, but Burckhardt was not to be deflected. He pretended that he had vowed to slaughter the goat at the tomb itself. At the small fortified village of Eldjy, at the mouth of the Wady, he hired a local man to show him the way. For the price of a pair of old horseshoes, the man carried the goat whilst Burckhardt carried a waterskin. They descended into the valley. After about half a mile, the antiquities began:

Of these I regret that I am not able to give a very complete account, but I knew well the character of the people around me; I was without protection in the midst of a desert where no traveller had ever before been seen; and a close examination of these works of the infidels, as they are called, would have excited suspicions that I was a magician in search of treasures; I should at least have been detained and prevented from prosecuting my journey to Egypt, and in all probability should have been stripped of the little money which I possessed, and what was infinitely more valuable to me, of my journal book.

But in the next ten hours Burckhardt witnessed a succession of architectural wonders unseen by Europeans for 1000 years:

At the point where the valley becomes narrow is a large sepulchral vault ... a little further on, I saw some other sepulchres with singular ornaments ... A few paces lower, on the left side ... is a larger mausoleum similarly formed, which appears from its decayed state, and the style of its architecture, to be of more ancient date than the others. Over its entrance are four obelisks, about ten feet in height, cut out of the same piece of rock; below is a projecting ornament, but so much defaced by time that I was unable to discover what it had originally represented; it had, however, nothing of the Egyptian style.

Two hundred yards further on, the valley narrowed to a point where it seemed to be entirely enclosed by high rocks but:

Left: *The obelisk tomb (top centre) with its row of four decorative 'pyramids'. Like the square stone blocks (left), they represent the Nabatean god Dusares. From a drawing by David Roberts, published in the mid-1840s.*

Right: *The Arch, now fallen, spanning the Syk at Petra, by David Roberts, published in 1842.*
Opposite: *The Treasury at Petra drawn by David Roberts in March 1839, showing the fallen pillar and the urn peppered with gunshot.*

... upon a nearer approach, I perceived a chasm about fifteen or twenty feet in breadth, through which the rivulet flows westwards in winter; in summer its waters are lost in the sand and gravel before they reach the opening, which is called El Syk. The precipices on either side ... are about eighty feet in height; in many places the opening between them at the top is less than at bottom, and the sky is not visible from below.

He entered the dark, winding passage between the cliffs. Here and there were remains of a paved road. Cut into the cliff walls on either side were channels that once carried a water supply. At fifty paces there was an arched bridge across the chasm; perhaps the gate of the city.

Nobody had ever been able to climb up the rocks to the bridge, which was therefore unanimously declared to be the work of the Djan, or evil genii.

Below the bridge there were niches in the rock, probably for statues, and all the way down were smaller niches carved in the rock, some just holes, others decorated with small pilasters, others still with bases for statues.

After proceeding for twenty-five minutes between the rocks, we came to a place where the passage opens, and where the bed of another stream coming from the south joins the Syk. On the side of the perpendicular rock, directly opposite to the issue of the main valley, an excavated mausoleum came in view, the situation and beauty of which are calculated to make an extraordinary impression upon the traveller, after having traversed for nearly half an hour such a gloomy and almost subterraneous passage as I have described.

The Khasneh (or Treasury) is carved entirely out of the rock; the great Corinthian columns of its façade, its intricate decoration, preserved from the desert wind and rain by the rocky overhang. It measures approximately 90 feet wide by 140 feet high, about the same as the great west portico of St Paul's Cathedral, and is crowned by a classical urn. It is this feature that gave the Treasury its name. For decades the local Arabs believed that the urn contained treasure; for decades they had been peppering it with bullets in a vain attempt to bring the treasure down.

Under the watchful eye of his guide and remembering the Arabs' obsession with hidden treasure, Burckhardt entered the building. Behind the façade were richly carved doorways which led into three vast chambers, completely bare. Who had built it and what its function was there was no clue but:

It is one of the most elegant remains of antiquity existing in Syria; its state of preservation resembles that of a building recently finished ... The natives ... pretend that it was the residence of a prince. But it was rather the sepulchre of a prince, and great must have been the opulence of a city, which could dedicate such monuments to the memory of its rulers.

From the Treasury the Syk widened out into a spacious passage between cliffs:

Several very large sepulchres are excavated in the rocks on both sides; they consist generally of a single lofty apartment with a flat roof ... Of those which I entered, the walls were quite plain and unornamented; in some of them are small side rooms with excavations and recesses in the rock for the reception of the dead.

The exterior shape of the tombs reminded him of truncated pyramids with elegantly ornamented doorways, similar to those he'd seen at Palmyra but:

I do not think, however, that there are two sepulchres in Wady Mousa perfectly alike; on the contrary, they vary greatly in size, shape and embellishments.

The effect was overwhelming:

In some places, three sepulchres are excavated one over the other, and the side of the mountain is so perpendicular that it seems impossible to approach the uppermost, no path whatever being visible.

As he progressed, the valley widened out. He passed a theatre cut entirely out of rock, its benches, tier upon tier, capable of containing perhaps 3000 spectators but now choked, like the tombs, with sand and gravel.

One hundred and fifty paces further, the rocks open still farther, and I issued upon a plain two hundred and fifty or three hundred yards across, bordered by heights of more gradual ascent than before. Here the ground is covered with heaps of hewn stones, foundations of buildings, fragments of columns, and vestiges of paved streets; all clearly indicating that a large city once existed here.

All around him were the great mountains that formed the rim of the bowl in which the city sat and which provided it with a natural wall of protection. In the distance to the east he glimpsed what seemed the finest sepulchres in the entire Wady:

I counted upwards of fifty close to each other. High up in the cliff I particularly observed one large sepulchre, adorned with Corinthian pilasters.

To the west:

> ... are the remains of a stately edifice, of which part of the wall is still standing; the inhabitants call it Kaszr Bent Faraoun, or the palace of Pharaoh's daughter.

That it could once have been a palace of a daughter of Pharaoh was unlikely, but it reminded Burckhardt that Egypt was scarcely more than 200 miles away. It also very nearly provided him with his undoing:

> In my way I had entered several sepulchres, to the surprise of my guide, but when he saw me turn out of the footpath towards the Kaszr, he exclaimed: 'I see now clearly that you are an infidel, who have some particular business amongst the ruins of the city of your forefathers; but depend upon it that we shall not suffer you to take out a single part of all the treasures hidden therein, for they are in our territory, and belong to us.' I replied that it was mere curiosity, which prompted me to look at the ancient works, and that I had no other view in coming here, than to sacrifice to Haroun; but he was not easily persuaded, and I did not think it prudent to irritate him by too close an inspection of the palace, as it might have led him to declare, on our return, his belief that I had found treasures, which might have led to a search of my person and to the detection of my journal, which would most certainly have been taken from me, as a book of magic.

Burckhardt, irritated by this conviction of the Turks and the Arabs that ruins contained treasure and that strangers were there to magic the treasure away, left the temple ruins and returned to the path that was to lead to the Tomb of Aaron.

> A little farther on, we reached a high plain called Szetouh Haroun, or Aaron's terrace, at the foot of the mountain upon which his tomb is situated ... The sun had already set ... it was too late to reach the tomb, and I was excessively fatigued; I therefore hastened to kill the goat, in sight of the tomb, at a spot where I found a number of heaps of stones, placed there in token of as many sacrifices in honour of the saint. While I was in the act of slaying the animal, my guide exclaimed aloud, 'O Haroun, look upon us! It is for you we slaughter this victim.

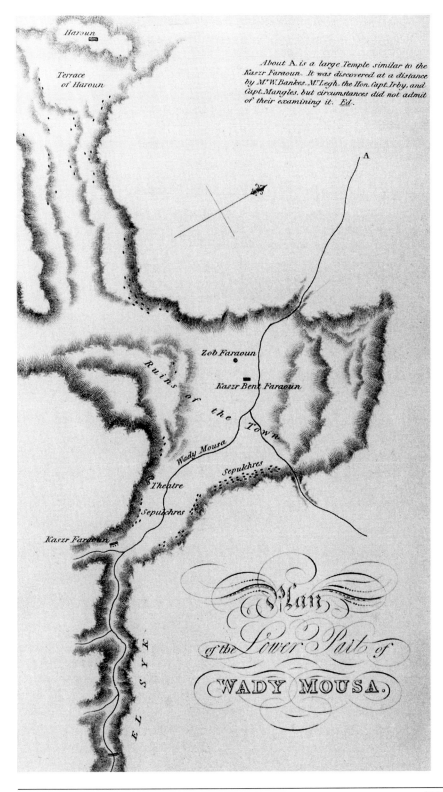

About A. is a large Temple similar to the Kaszr Faraoun. It was discovered at a distance by Mr W. Bankes, Mr Legh, the Hon. Capt. Irby, and Capt. Mangles, but circumstances did not admit of their examining it. Ed.

A

Haroun

Terrace of Haroun

Ruins of the Town

Zob Faraoun

Kaszr Bent Faraoun

Wady Mousa

Sepulchres

Theatre

Sepulchres

Kaszr Faraoun

EL SYK

Plan of the Lower Part of WADY MOUSA.

Left: *Burckhardt's own plan of Petra, of necessity drawn from memory but surprisingly accurate. The entrance of the Syk is at the bottom of the picture.*

O Haroun, protect us and forgive us! O Haroun, be content with our good intentions, for it is but a lean goat! O Haroun, smooth our paths; and praise be to the Lord of all creatures!' This he repeated several times, after which he covered the blood that had fallen on the ground with a heap of stones; we then dressed the best part of the flesh for our supper, as expeditiously as possible, for the guide was afraid of the fire being seen, and of its attracting hither some robbers.

It was the end of Burckhardt's tour of Wady Mousa and he could only speculate on what he had found. The classical authors provided some hints. Eusebius described the location of Aaron's Tomb and Strabo referred to the capital of a people called the Nabateans as a place called 'Petra', describing its situation as: 'On ground in general even and level, but guarded all around by rock, outside precipitous and abrupt but inside having abundant springs for drawing water.' The description fitted. The very name Petra, which is Greek for 'rock', could not have been more apt. On balance, Burckhardt concluded, 'It appears very probable that the ruins in Wady Mousa are those of the ancient *Petra*.'

Since Burckhardt's time the ruins have been explored and recorded in considerable detail and we now know more than he did. Surprisingly, however, not much more.

Excavation has shown that the first inhabitants of the area were Neolithic people of 4000 years ago. Their pottery links them with the Neolithic people of the Jordan Valley at nearby Jericho, but the first people of whom there is any written record are the Edomites. It was here, according to the Bible, around 790 BC that King Amaziah of Judah cast down from a high rock 10,000 of his Edomite captives. Some Biblical scholars believe that the location of 'Sela in the Wilderness' can be identified with the great rock Umm el Biyara, which rises 1000 feet from the valley floor. There is no evidence of the massacre, but on the rock's summit are the excavated remains of an Edomite village of the seventeenth century BC and quantities of Edomite pottery. The Edomites were described by the British archaeologist Crystal-M. Bennett as 'that elusive, enigmatic people who flit intermittently across the pages of the Bible, who refused Moses passage through their territory on the return from Egypt, who invoked the wrath of the later prophets, notably Jeremiah, and who ultimately were dispossessed of their land by the Nabateans.'

The Nabateans first appear in the pages of recorded history as one of the enemies of Assurbanipal, King of Assyria in 647 BC, but they were not yet in Petra. They arrived there sometime in the fourth century BC, taking over the area from the Edomites and descending from the clifftops to settle on the floor of the valley. But why should the Nabateans, a desert people, herders and traders like many of today's Bedouin, settle at all? And why in Petra?

Above: *Nabatean coin, showing the fighting camel and saddle that allowed the rider to keep both hands free.*

Five hundred years before Christ, the Arabian Peninsula was at the heart of a growing international trade, from the Indian Ocean to the Red Sea, which linked Mesopotamia with Egypt and Arabia with Europe. Many of these routes crossed Nabatean territory and the Nabateans discovered that the control of this trade, the levy of taxes, was a lucrative business. It was best controlled from the central fastness provided by the mountain redoubt of Petra; a place that had adequate water in a water-starved area, a place that could be easily defended. Once the decision was made to settle, the town grew quickly and so did the territory the Nabateans controlled, stretching from the Sinai Peninsula to Damascus and from Gaza to the eastern desert region of El Hejrah. Their prosperity was reflected in the buildings they carved from the cliffs of their capital city.

But the Nabateans were not the only tribe in the desert. What made them superior, the Beni Szakher of their day? The most recent and one of the most plausible theories has been advanced by the Director of the German School of Archaeology at Amman, Dr Axel Knauf, who believes the answer lies in the camel saddle. From the few coins and other scraps of evidence remaining, Knauf has shown that before Nabatean supremacy, the camel saddle was inefficient for warfare in the desert. It was their invention of a camel saddle suitable for fast movement that made the Nabateans masters of cavalry tactics and therefore masters of the trade routes for 400 years.

Despite the rising power of Rome in the west, the Nabateans were able to remain independent until, in the year 63 BC, the Roman general Pompey was sent to subdue them. They bought him off, but in AD 106 they finally yielded, quietly, and Petra became a Roman province.

Very little in the way of domestic artefacts, apart from enormous amounts of broken, porcelain-thin pottery, has survived at Petra; only the buildings on the valley floor and the wind-ravaged tombs in the cliffs, 4000 of them over an area of five square miles. They range from quite small caves in the rock – with just a small door with a strip of decorative frieze above it – to the enormous and probably royal tombs such as the Urn Tomb, the Palace Tomb or the Corinthian Tomb, with gigantic façades, enormous columns and pediments, many openings and, inside,

enormous chambers with niches for coffins. The interiors are absolutely plain apart from the extraordinary decorative effect of the natural colours of the rock which swirl across the walls and ceilings in bands of red, pink, orange, grey and white. In the absence of written records historians have tried to date the tombs from their style of architecture, but it is impossible. The style is, in general, 'classical', and similar to that of the Hellenistic buildings found in other great desert cities in the area such as Palmyra and Hatra. There are later Roman influences, however, as well as earlier Assyrian influences and a style that seems to be uniquely Nabatean – the square-stepped half gables which appear at the top of so many of the tombs. It would be simple to believe that the gabled tombs were the earliest Nabatean ones and that the classical ones were later, but at Petra the styles are all mixed together with 'Nabatean' gables on top of classical porches. The Kasr el Bint, once thought to be Roman, is now thought, from archaeological evidence, to be a late Nabatean work dating from the reign of King Obadas II, who died just before Christ was born. The Treasury, the most Hellenistic of all the great monuments and showing no 'Nabatean' influence at all (and therefore probably dating from after the Roman occupation), is now considered to be earlier – even earlier than the Kasr el Bint; dating from the reign of King Aretas III (84–56 BC) and the work of imported craftsmen. The Roman theatre, too, probably dates from before the arrival of the Romans. The only building that can be dated with any real accuracy is the tomb of the Roman governor of Petra, 'Sextus Florentinus'. Over the main door of his tomb is recorded in Latin the dead occupant's honour and attributes. Sextus was Governor of Arabia in about AD 127. His tomb, therefore, must date from between about AD 130–150.

Of the other inscriptions in the city, a small niche in the Syk records the name, in Greek, of a trader called 'Sabinos Alexandros'; in the Urn Tomb another inscription, also in Greek, records that the building was converted into a Christian church in AD 446, long after the city was in decline; and on the Turkamaniya Tomb is the best preserved inscription in Nabatean. Nabatean was a mixture of Aramaic, the language spoken by Christ, and early Arabic. The inscription reads:

> This tomb and the large and small chambers inside ... and the porticos and the dwelling places within it ... and the remainder of the whole property which is in these places, is the consecrated and inviolable property of Dusares, the God of our Lord ...

Dusares was a local deity, probably inherited by the Nabateans from the Edomites. His name means the Lord of Shera and even today the local mountains are called the Shera range. All over Petra he is represented by a simple squared-off block of natural stone twenty or more feet high and sometimes in more decorative forms like the four obelisks on the Obelisk Tomb. In life, the Nabateans worshipped him in the High Place, the altar formed by the artificially flattened tabletop on the summit of the cliff behind the Treasury. Here blood was let, human and animal, an actual death to symbolise the renewal of life. Burckhardt's animal sacrifice to Aaron was a faint echo of it. In death they worshipped him by being buried in the sacred rocks, enclosed by him, for the rocks not only represented the god, they were the god. There are echoes in the imagery of the Bible:

> The Lord is my rock, and my fortress, and my deliverer;
> The God of my rock; in him will I trust.

Because of the survival of the great tombs, Petra appears today to be one vast necropolis, a city of the dead; but it was never that. The tombs are actually all on the periphery of the city, and it is the vast open area between them that contained the city's life. Now, apart from the Kasr el Bint, the colonnaded main street and the remains of a triumphal arch, this area is still as Burckhardt described it, a jumbled mass of fallen stones and collapsed pillars, of vast mounds of debris which conceal the temples, public baths, civic buildings, shops and houses that once stood there. For when the Romans moved their administrative centre further north to Bozra, the city was slowly reclaimed by the tribes of the desert. The Bedouin took over the tombs and sepulchres as homes in winter and storehouses in summer. The roofs of the caves are blackened with the smoke from their fires. They remained there until 1986, selling coins and artefacts to the visitors: their belief that the ruins contained 'treasure' was not altogether unfounded.

The first visitors arrived shortly after Burckhardt's account was published in 1822. They came, as he suggested, with armed guards. Among them was the Victorian graphic artist David Roberts, who painted wild and romantic views of the place. Relying on Roberts' pictures, Dean Burgon penned the immortal but misleading line, 'A rose-red city half as old as time.' When he actually got to Petra he realised that every other shade of red it might be, but rose-red it wasn't.

Burgon was able to see many sights that were denied to Burckhardt. As well as the High Place and the Royal Tombs were smaller but equally attractive tombs like the Lion Tomb and the Tomb of the Roman Soldier and, at the furthest extremity from the Syk, 600 feet up, approached by a rugged narrow Wady that looks out over the entire city, the one building which can rival

The Pyramids at Giza, c. 2500 BC. 'We admired at some distance the astonishing pile that stood before us, composed of such an accumulation of enormous blocks of stones, that I was at a loss to conjecture how they could be brought thither.'

Inset: *The Temple of Abu Simbel, built by Ramses II c. 1250 BC and saved by UNESCO from the rising waters of Lake Nasser in 1969.*

Right: *The Colossi of Memnon, built by Amenhotep III in 1400 BC as a funerary monument and only later misleadingly called the Colossi of Memnon by the Greeks. Belzoni passed them on his way to the Ramasseum. 'I need not say I was struck with wonder. They are mutilated indeed, but their enormous size strikes the mind with admiration.'*

Left: *The giant head of Ramses II at the Ramasseum. Its fellow, 'the Young Memnon', was removed by Belzoni to the British Museum in 1816.*

Opposite: *The Khasneh (Treasury) at Petra, Jordan, 'one of the most elegant remains of antiquity'. The urn which the local Arabs believed contained the treasure is situated at the very top of the central cylindrical temple above the portico.*

Left: *The giant pillars of the Treasury. Each pillar is constructed of three separate blocks of stone. When Burckhardt first saw it, the pillar on the right had fallen and was broken.*

Right: *The Palace Tomb, one of the largest tombs at Petra, is named after its supposed similarity to the façade of a Roman palace.*

Below left: *The Street of Tombs, Petra. 'In some places, three sepulchres are excavated one over the other, and the side of the mountain is so perpendicular that it seems impossible to approach the uppermost, no path whatever being visible.'*

Below right: *El Deir, 'The Monastery', the largest tomb at Petra, which Burkhardt never saw.*

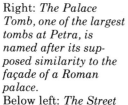

Above and left: *The Kailasantha Temple, Ellora, India. It was cut from the solid rock of the mountainside c. AD 750. The triple peaks of the temple represent the peaks of the sacred Mount Kailasa in the Himalayas, house of the Hindu god Shiva. The elephants crouch under the weight of the mountain.*

Left: *The Buddhist Temple at Karla, built c. 80 BC. Wedding guests are sculpted almost life size on the main façade.*
Below left: *The upper gallery of the Indra Sabha Temple at Ellora. Seely considered this Jain temple, built c. AD 1200, 'for grandeur and size, second only to the Keylas'.*
Below: *Interior of the temple at Karla. Hollowed out of the rock, its roof struts are made to appear like wood. The stupa (stone altar) is placed under its sacred umbrella at the far end. Seely described it as 'an object of wonder; a ponderous arched roof of solid stone supported by two rows of pillars (and) at the further end ... an immense hemispherical altar of stone with a kind of wooden umbrella spreading over the top'.*

the size and beauty of the Treasury itself. It is called El Deir, the
monastery. Carved out of the shoulder of a mountain it is vast,
bigger than the Treasury, its one doorway of 26 feet high,
dwarfing a man. But unlike the Treasury, there is scarcely any
decoration, a simple, sublime architectural statement of windows
and columns. In contrast, carved on the face of a rock nearby is
a figure of a man leading a camel, so weatherworn as to be almost
indistinguishable.

Burckhardt left the city at night, winding his way out of the
darkened Syk, ready to continue his journey the next day. He
spent almost five years in Cairo, waiting for the caravan to Africa
which never came. He died of dysentery on 15 October 1817: he
was thirty-two. Mourned by Giovanni Belzoni, Sheikh Ibrahim
was buried in the Muslim graveyard in Cairo, but Jean Louis
Burckhardt's memorial is the city of Petra itself:

Of this at least I am persuaded, from all the information I

Above: *El Deir, the
Monastery, Petra.
David Roberts'
romantic view shows
the Royal Tombs in the
distance.*

procured, that there is no other ruin between the extremities of the Dead Sea and Red Sea, of sufficient importance to answer to that city. Whether or not I have discovered the remains of the capital of Arabia Petraea, I leave to the decision of Greek scholars.

Chapter Three

THE WONDERS OF ELLORA
John B. Seely in India

*Innumerable works have been published on the antiquities of Greece, Rome, and Egypt; but, with the exception of two or three incidental notices by travellers, scanty and imperfect, the wonderful caverned Temples of Elora are known but to a very few.**

The exploits of men such as Burckhardt in Arabia and Belzoni in Egypt created an enormous interest in the monuments and artefacts of ancient civilisations. The general public could not yet travel, but, increasingly, they could read. There was a growing demand for accounts of the exotic and it was probably the publication of Belzoni's book in 1820 that caused an obscure Captain in the Bombay Native Infantry to write his own narrative of a journey in India, one of the most exotic lands of all. In 1810 John Seely set out on a perilous 300-mile route to see the spectacular cave temples of Ellora. It took him through country overrun by bandits, through jungle infested with tigers and snakes, over mountain passes, across unbridgeable rivers in temperatures well into the hundreds and under constant threat from hostile natives and malarial mosquitoes. He travelled because he was interested, and simply because the caves, like Everest, were there:

> It is my humble opinion that no monuments of antiquity in the known world are comparable to the Caves of Elora ... whether we consider their unknown origin, their stupendous size, the

* J. B. Seely, *The Wonders of Elora* (London: G. & W. B. Whittaker, 1824).

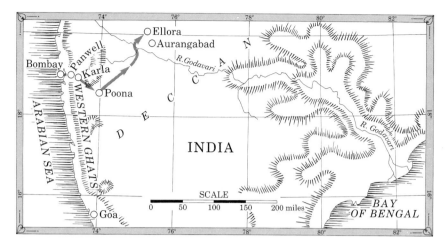

beauty of their architectural ornaments, or the vast number of statues and emblems, all hewn and fashioned out of the solid rock! ... Reader, is not this entire temple wonderful? Or does it yield the palm to many places mentioned by ... Belzoni?

As he travels, Seely gives a fascinating insight into the people and places, the habits and customs of an Indian way of life that existed at the start of the British Raj. He is equivocal about the benefits of the Empire, but he is one of the very first in a long line of Britons to be fascinated by India, a fascination that continues to this day. Of Seely himself we know nothing apart from what he tells us in his book and the few facts which survive in the records of the East India Company in Bombay. He had an association with Wyke Regis, near Weymouth in Dorset, but he was probably born in London, in 1788. In 1804, at the age of sixteen, he was sent to China as a midshipman; in 1807 he was commissioned into the Bombay Native Infantry, the youngest officer in the corps, and was stationed on the island of Versovah, fourteen miles north of Bombay. Seely was to play his part in the defence of an India that was not yet entirely British, and which was still vulnerable to attack by the French.

> We had every amusement and comfort that men could require: an excellent mess, good houses, a number of books and newspapers, a sailing boat, a billiard table, cricket, quoits etc. Our station was also made more agreeable by a constant intercourse with Bombay; the journey to which place, both by land and water, was very agreeable, and rendered cool by the sea breezes.

But Versovah was like the great Hindu god Siva: both creator and destroyer. Few officers and even fewer men reached the age of forty. Within fourteen years, only four out of Seely's fifteen fellow officers were still alive and not one had died in battle. Weakened by the debilitating humidity and exposure to the sun they succumbed to malaria, dysentery, cholera and a multitude of illnesses that could only be described by the general term 'fever'. If they didn't die, they often lost the use of a limb or went blind:

> Had not I a constitution of iron, I must long before this have been with those I am lamenting; and were I to relate the quantity of medicine I have taken, the operations I have undergone, and the torture I have suffered in the space of twenty-four hours, my statement would be disbelieved.

Bombay was an obscure and fairly useless island when it came into British possession in 1662; but it had an enormous natural harbour that the British were quick to exploit. By 1800, ruled on behalf of the British Crown by the British East India Company, it was a metropolis of 170,000 people.

> The prospect is as grand and as beautiful as can be imagined: the mighty range of the G'hāts towering in the clouds and extending as far as the eye can reach; the bold views on the continent; the diversified objects on the island; old ruinous convents and monasteries erected by its former conquerors, the Portuguese; the noble country-houses of the Europeans; Hindoo pagodas, Mahometan mosques; the remains of Mahratta forts and buildings: these, with the rural appearance of Hindoo villages, where every patch of ground is richly cultivated or ornamented, and interspersed with groves of date and cocoa-nut trees, afford a prospect of luxuriance and beauty to be met with nowhere . . .

At the far tip of the island was the town: the native section of small, mud-walled houses with thatched roofs and the European section laid out in squares and terraces as neat and Georgian as the climate would allow. Here, too, were the fort and barracks; the custom house and government buildings; the warehouses and the docks, packed with the tall masted ships of the East India Company from all over the world, teeming with activity.

Seely's journey began in September 1810, after the crippling heat of midsummer and after the monsoon. It began with 'an aquatic excursion'. With three friends, all of them under the age of twenty-three, he rowed and sailed across the bay from Bombay Island to the mainland of Mahratta:

> An excursion of this kind, with agreeable companions, after a month's *grilling* in the interior, makes the mind joyful and the

soul glad. On one side, as you proceed up the harbour, you have the mighty range of mountains stretching away their cloud-capt tops in every fantastic and romantic shape ... The curious-looking hill called the Funnel, from its similarity of shape, rises abruptly in front, while on the right a Mahratta fort, called Shoon Ghur ... raises its romantic turrets in solitary grandeur in the heart of the mountains. Surrounded by jungle, in all the wildness of nature, on the left the view is bounded by the hills of Salsette, which afford an agreeable back-ground to the whole of this magnificent scenery.

The party had lunch in the middle of the bay on Butcher's Island, 'Deva Devi!, Island of the Gods', and on it was His Majesty's Hospital Barracks for Seamen and the graves of the British sailors who had died there:

Reader, reflect: though here I lie,
As you are now, so once was I:
As I am now, so you must be;
Therefore prepare to follow me.

The young officers amused themselves chasing snakes in the cemetery before setting sail again for the neighbouring island of Gharri-pouri, or, as the Europeans named it after a rocky outcrop fashioned in the shape of an elephant, Elephanta Island. It is famous for its Hindu cave temples cut into the mountainside

Below: *Entrance to the Cave Temple on Elephanta Island.*

250 feet above the sea. Stifled by the stench of thousands of bats squeaking and squabbling in the gloom of the cave roof, Seely saw one of the finest sculptures in the whole of India – the Trimurti, or the Three-headed Bust of Siva. Nineteen feet high and with each face over five feet long, the giant sculpture represents Siva in the characters of Brahma the creator; of Rudra the destroyer; and of Vishnu the preserver, holding a lotus flower in his hand. Sacred to the Hindu, the caves, within easy reach of pleasure parties from Bombay, were not sacred to Europeans:

> For Europeans (shall I say gentlemen?) were found not only sufficiently vicious to try to injure the figures and ornaments, but were actually so depraved as to indecently disfigure the deities with a variety of disgusting ornaments and appendages, so that a respectable female could not, without having her feelings outraged, visit these wonderful caverns.

The party spent the night on the mainland at the village of Billapore. Their boat was fastened to a large wooden stake driven into the bank of a small creek and their camp was the ground alongside it, as distant from the jungle as possible. In the creek were alligators but in the jungle were tigers.

> At daylight we cast off; and, what with rowing and occasionally sailing, we arrived at Panwell in time for a good breakfast.

In the two days, they had rowed and sailed a distance of twenty miles. Panwell was the mainland starting point for the road to Poona, the Mahratta capital. The Mahratta confederacy stretched over much of western India and was still ruled by its native Hindu ruler, the Peishwah, 'the foremost', but under a treaty of 1803 the British had several military stations in the country in order to protect the Peishwah from his Indian enemies. These stations were to provide Seely with hospitality and, for as long as they existed on the route, security. Seely had been warned by the authorities of the dangers: apart from the constant threat from wild animals and bandits, the British military stations didn't exist further than 100 miles and the military were not 'on very amicable terms' with the Mahratta chief Holkar who held sway over the territory in which the Ellora caves were. Seely was censured by several and was considered if not actually unpatriotic, certainly unbalanced as no individual had travelled direct from Bombay to Ellora before. Seely was not to be deterred:

> To a young and always ardent mind this objection appeared of very slight import: a little management with the natives is all that is necessary; and, if a man has health and a good stock of

patience, he may surmount more difficult journeys than mine promised to be.

Nor was he actually to travel alone. Although his colleagues were returning by boat to Bombay, Seely, admittedly the lone white man, was to proceed with a veritable cavalcade. Three bullocks, with drivers, carried his tent, which was 12 foot square; three more bullocks carried clothes, food, books and medicines; two porters carried his camp cot and his writing desk; another carried pots, pans for cooking and utensils for eating: there was a pony to carry the head servant and two other ponies for the other four servants he had with him. There was an armed escort of six Siphauees (native militia men) and a corporal:

> Several native travellers accompanied my people for their own security, as the country was sometimes infested with robbers.

After breakfast and an early 'tiffin' (luncheon) with his departing friends, the cavalcade lumbered off with Seely on horseback at its head. The road was no more than a dirt track through the jungle and was often rocky and rugged. Progress was slow and could never be more than twenty miles a day. On the first day, having started late, they made only fourteen miles to the village of Choke, where he found lodgings in a Hindu pagoda:

> The part of the pagoda that the traveller occupies is a large convenient apartment. Towards the night it is rather cool, as the front is entirely open and exposed: the breeze at night is very chilly. Robberies are not very frequent, the Patel of the village having within these few months inflicted a summary punishment upon some Bheels who had begun to infest the neighbourhood. Two of them being detected in plundering, he had them hung up by the heels, perfectly naked, and exposed to the fury of the midday sun, till they were dead.

An advance party of one servant, a porter and a guard would be sent on in the evening with instructions to get as far as they could by nightfall before pitching camp. The next day, Seely would travel the five or six miles to catch up with them and arrive in time for an already prepared breakfast and a rest. The rearguard would follow on after having struck camp and loaded everything onto the bullock carts to meet the resting advance guard at about midday, when they would all move off together again until the same routine was repeated in the evening.

From Choke to Capooly was another fourteen miles over winding roads even more rugged than before and through countryside desolate from the recent local Mahratta wars:

The state of the country and the condition of the inhabitants cannot be imagined; at all times living under the very worst system of government, but in war assailed by the additional calamities of plunder, burnings, and captivity; so that the country and its inhabitants were in a constant state of indescribable and heart-rending distress ... The poor wretched people ... are, among themselves, mild, charitable, and affectionate; while their superiors, for tyranny, avarice, and treachery, are unparalleled by any order of men on the face of the known earth.

At Capooly was an enormous water tank:

> ... after the perspiration produced by walking about the village had subsided, I jumped in ... clothes and all, which, without apprehension of danger, I left to dry upon me.

The shade temperature was 104°F. The village tank served the same purpose as the village pond in England, to provide a water supply in the dry season and a place to wash both clothes and bodies. Some were little more than holes in the ground; others, like the tank at Capooly, were circular, like a small lake, and built of stone with steps leading into the water:

> In this tank several young females, both beautiful and innocent, were bathing and playing, quite unconcerned at my near approach. Had they been spoken to they would have fled like the timid deer, or if only on a *probable* chance of pollution, they would have drowned themselves instantly, or stuck a dagger in their hearts. These are the same women who cheerfully burn themselves alive with the dead bodies of their husbands. Their life is that of pure innocence and chaste love. They are idolators, and can neither read nor write, unsophisticated and untaught, yet possessing the highest moral attributes.
>
> We, forsooth, are a polished nation, and purpose reforming the Hindoos, poor creatures! It is a pity that such a virtuous, docile, affectionate, sober, mild, and good-tempered people should be calumniated by the whining cant of the day.

Seely, a young man of twenty-two in pre-Victorian society, was surprisingly thoughtful, unblinkered, open and free in his attitudes to a country that many of his fellow officers casually dismissed as 'barbarian'. And he appreciated beauty, in all forms:

> These girls were symmetry itself – small, but exquisitely proportioned; their feet and hands slender and delicate; flowing

and thick black tresses, *daily* washed and perfumed; small but remarkably regular features, piercing black eyes, good teeth and a graceful and firm step.

But the beauty didn't last. The girls married at 12 or 13 and, by the age of 25, were old and ravaged by disease and childbearing. By the age of thirty many if not most of them were dead. The practice of suttee (widow burning) which so horrified the British in India and which was eventually outlawed was in fact neither general nor widespread. There were known to the British authorities less than 1000 cases a year at that time for the whole of India, and the numbers were declining. The victims, under the influence of Siva the destroyer, were willingly taking part in a solemn act that would bring them salvation:

> I have witnessed two Suttees, both of which were voluntary on the part of the women; nor were they intoxicated by any drugs, or tied down to the faggots. To one of these females I spoke, and asked her if it was her own choice, and whether she still wished to burn. She replied, with great calmness and dignity: 'It is my fervent desire – nothing shall prevent me – if it did, I would stab myself.' She gave me a bunch of the *Moogree* flowers, and ascended the pile with the same alacrity and cheerfulness as a love-sick bride goes to the altar – the latter seeking for earthly happiness, the former for eternal happiness with her departed lord.

Capooly lay at the foot of the Western Ghats, the chain of mountains which stretches down the western side of India for 1000 miles and, like a vast retaining wall, supports the tableland of central India known as the Deccan. The mountains rise almost sheer from a little above sea level to over 5000 feet:

> Above and beyond these mountains we fancy another world, of whose inhabitants we know nothing; how to visit them, how to penetrate their country, or how to scale their inaccessible looking wall ... Whilst taking a glance at the frowning aspect they present, one imagines there can be no ingress; for unlike Sterne's bird, it is not how to get *out*, but how to get *in*.

It was to be another seventy-five years before the British engineered a railway route through the mountains. It took 40,000 men, of whom a third died from injury or disease. Now there was nothing but a winding jungle track, but it was not unused: convoys of laden bullocks stumbled their way between Poona and the coast; on the day previous, a lady of the Poona court had passed on her way to Bombay with her baggage carried by two elephants and eight camels. She also had a dozen horses and was herself protected by 30 horsemen and ten gunners. This morning, however, Seely was alone apart from his own cavalcade:

> Proceeding onwards on foot, the path at an abrupt angle overhangs a frightful precipice and valley, covered with an eternal jungle, and where probably the foot of man never penetrated.

He climbed on foot as it was too steep for a horse to carry a rider, and as he climbed higher the views became wider. In the jungle were glimpses of water in the valley bottom; around him was the sound of waterfalls and the jungle was so dense in places that the rays of the morning sun couldn't penetrate. The vast tank at Capooly below him now looked like a tiny horse pond. He paused, after two hours, to rest and drink. Monkeys chattered in the trees all round him; peacocks screamed:

> As I stood on the brink, I shuddered at looking into the vast chasm beneath. The three sides are almost perpendicular. Here and there, through an interstice of the rock, a stunted tree has forced its way out. The bottom of this valley is overrun with trees, which appear like small bushes; and it requires some nerve to look even at this natural basin, much less to calmly explore it with the eye.

He continued to climb, almost encircled by mountains and cascades, until he reached the summit at Cundalla at 9.00 a.m. It had taken him six hours, but it was another six yet before the rest of the party arrived at three in the afternoon for a meal and rest, 'sweating and dreadfully fatigued from their labour'. This was one of the very few passes in the Ghats known to the British and, despite Seely's own efforts, the rest were to remain unknown and unmapped for several decades. They were literally uncharted territory. On 24 September:

> I proceeded across the open country ... to the mountain of Ekverah; where, at a considerable height above the plain, stands a large temple, hewn out of the solid rock. The path by which the temple ... is reached is very steep and difficult, winding along the face of the mountain: in fact it is little better than a water-course, broken, rugged and precipitous ... On the left of a terrace at the end of the footpath, excavated from the bowels of the mountain, stands, in solemn magnificence, the great arched temple of Karli with its noble vestibule and entrance, and the sitting figure of Budha. On looking into the temple, an object of wonder presents itself: a ponderous arched roof of solid stone, supported by two rows of pillars; the capitals

Above: *Entrance to the Karla Temple, painted by Henry Salt (Belzoni's consul in Egypt) in 1804.*

of each surmounted by a well-sculptured male and female figure, seated, with their arms encircling each other, on the back of elephants, crouching, as it were, under the weight they sustain. At the further end of the temple is an immense hemispherical altar, of stone, with a kind of wooden umbrella spreading over the top ... At Karli, Budha is the paramount deity.

Buddha remained a paramount deity in India until the eighth century when Hinduism reasserted itself and before the rise of Islam in the twelfth century. The Temple of Karla is Hinayana Buddhist and was constructed about 80 BC. Outside the cave stands a single stone pillar topped by four lions back to back, the emblem of Ashoka, the great king of the Mauryan Empire. It was his grandfather who expelled the Greeks from India after the death of Alexander the Great in 323 BC and who was the first king of India to accept the teachings of Buddha. The temple itself is set slightly back from the cave entrance to form a vestibule covered with sculpture. Above a low carved stone entrance door is a large 'sun window' which filters light into the interior, a roof, ribbed with wooden rafters like an upturned boat and lines of columns as in a Christian church. The elephants and seated human figures on the columns make obeisance to the stupa, the stone altar which signifies the presence of God.

The temple was inhabited by a group of holy men supported by the Peishwah:

> One of them, an aesetic of high renown, had a singularly mild and serene countenance: he was sitting before a flame of fire day and night, with a cloth over his mouth, to prevent his inhaling pollution or destroying any living substance: he was regularly fed with parched grain, and his water for drinking was strained through a cloth. I addressed him with reverence: he turned up his fine placid countenance and looked at me with eyes that spoke of heaven. I almost wished at the moment to be a Brahman. This man appeared the image of self-denial, absorbed in contemplating the wonders of God.

Religion was an abiding presence in India, unlike England. Seely was deeply affected by it, but he could also see its ridiculous side when taken to extremes, and he could understand how European influence was bound to destroy so much that was traditionally Indian. He tells the story of a holy man in the city of Benares who had vowed never to cause the death of a living creature; who swept the floor before him as he walked, and who brushed the air with a fan as he breathed:

> Some mischievous European gave him a microscope, to look at the water he drank. On seeing the animalculae, he threw down and broke the instrument, and vowed he would not drink water again: he kept his promise, and died.

After leaving the Temple of Karla, Seely continued across the plains. At midday the sun was so hot and the glare so intense that the land appeared to be in motion, undulating like waves on a calm sea. He stuck the broad leaf of a plantain under his hat to try and keep cool and to act as a primitive sunshade. He arrived in Poona near sunset:

> ... the setting rays of that glorious orb reflecting its beams on the venerable roof of the Parbutti temple, on turreted walls, large white terraced houses, lofty shining spires, and on handsome looking pagodas, intermingled with Moghul buildings, Hindoo palaces, castles and gardens.

The streets were crowded, 'a diversified moving mass' of Brahmin priests, Arab horsemen, Mahratta foot soldiers, near naked Fakirs – Hindus, Muslims, Portuguese, Christians and Jews:

Above: *Poona, capital of the Mahratta Confederacy, in 1804. The Parbutti Temple is on the hill (left) in the middle distance.*

This living picture has the addition of state elephants, splendid cavalcades of public officers, decked out with parade and show, accompanied by richly-caparisoned horses and camels trotting along at a quick pace, with rows of little tinkling bells suspended round their necks. If to all this we add crowded markets, religious processions, and bands of noisy musicians, some idea may be formed of the tumult and bustle of the capital city of the Mahratta empire towards evening.

The Mahrattas were Hindus and champions of Hinduism against the Muslim Mogul princes of northern India, and it was the Mahratta leader Shivaji (1627–1680) who first carved out a coastal kingdom from the Mogul empire at the same time that Cromwell was defeating Charles I in England. The kingdom was extended in 1707, after the death of Aurangzeb, last of the great Mogul emperors, and Poona became the capital of the Mahratta confederacy which, by 1795, covered almost half of India. It was this 'native' administration that the British East India Company hoped would provide the stability in the west of the country that they themselves had provided in the east at Calcutta. But the first British Ambassador to the Poona court was appointed in 1786, a time when certain factions within the confederacy were challenging the Poona authority. There was civil war. The Peishwah, facing defeat, turned to the British for help. In return for certain trading and other concessions, Sir Arthur Wellesley, later Duke of Wellington, occupied Poona and the Peishwah (Baji Row II) was reinstated. He was not a trustworthy man. He was also not a wise man, turning on his British allies and giving them the opportunity they had been waiting for. The Peishwah was defeated at the battle of Kirkee on 5 November 1817 and the British, under the British East India Company, took over the administration of most of the rest of India. Poona became the summer capital of the British Bombay government and the music-hall home of Colonel Blimp until Independence in 1947. It was during the brief settled period after the civil war, before the anti-British insurrection, and when the city was still capital of the Mahratta confederacy, that Seely passed through and made straight for the British military station on the city outskirts.

Poona was like an island in a devastated rural sea. Seely continued his journey through vast barren wastelands, where villages were marked by crumbled and fallen remains of mud-walled houses and fields by overgrown clumps of prickly pear cactus and milk-bush plants. The people, where there were any, were almost naked. At Corygaum he crossed the Bhema River in a basket boat made of split bamboo wickerwork covered with hides: it was like a coracle but big enough to carry three bullocks and a dozen men at the same time. He arrived at Seroor, a neat British cantonment with neatly laid out streets and spacious houses with gardens bounded by thick hedges of prickly pear.

At Seroor, he changed his guard, hired fresh coolies, bought fresh bullocks and a camel as he intended, for the rest of his journey to Ellora, to force march across bandit country.

> I was cautioned to keep my Siphauees and baggage close at hand, as the G'hāt was infested by Bheels. Some few I saw, but they did not offer to molest me, and I passed by quite unconcerned.

The Bheels were, according to the locals, 'licensed' bandits, not only tolerated by the Mahratta court but often employed by them to bully the peasants into submission. Herdsmen in the fields protected themselves with bows and sharply barbed arrows; the headman at Wamborey even kept a private army of thirty-five Arab soldiers and Seely resorted to the expedient of paying a Bheel to play gamekeeper over his brother poachers – especially at night. Seely was now beyond the range of British protection.

> I had been so accustomed to supplications for medicine, that I always carried a stock with me, chiefly of calomel pills: these often procured me a fowl or an extra cooly when entreaty and money failed; and if to my medical donation, to any person of consequence, was added a black lead pencil, I was overloaded with civilities.

At Toka, on the bank of the Godavari river, he needed, literally, a dose of his own medicine. He was overcome with fever brought on by fatigue and overexposure to the sun. To bring down his temperature he took nine grains of calomel pills and a glass of hot brandy and water spiked with aloes and black pepper. After a good night's sleep he was still tired but the fever had gone and he was able to continue across the Godavari river, sacred like the Ganges, back into jungle country infested with Bheels:

> During the journey, I could not have seen less than 150 of them in different parties. Several accosted me; but having three Siphauees with me, their muskets loaded, and myself armed, they offered no interruption to us: but my servant, who had preceded me, rather than have an altercation, had paid a tribute of 4 rupees (10s), greatly in opposition to the wishes of the Siphauees, who objected to any compromise with the Bheels.

Beyond the jungle was open country again, cultivated land and fields. The road showed signs of having been tended and was lined with trees. In the distance was the spire of a temple and, according to Seely:

> It was not without emotion I entered the pretty little rural village of Elora, embosomed in a grove of trees.

It was excessively hot and, as he couldn't expect his baggage to arrive for three or four hours, Seely sought shelter in the pagoda of the Grishneshwar Temple, but he couldn't settle. Near the pagoda was the village tank:

> ... the masonry of which, for beauty and uniformity, I never saw equalled. It must have been a work of immense labour, and would be deemed a fine ornament to the grounds of the most costly mansion in England.

Despite being dreadfully fatigued from his ride and having had a meagre breakfast of three dry biscuits and some bad milk, Seely surveyed the tank. He always carried with him a measuring tape and, in the heat of the sun, found the tank to be 151 feet square, with five flights of steps going down to a pool of water, separated by terraces. Eight small temples stood in pairs at each corner of the tank, the domes supported by four carved pillars and each containing a lingam, a small sacred phallus of stone. In the pool:

> I observed Brahmans and Brahmanees promiscuously bathing, nearly in a state of nature.

When Seely visited it, the upper part of the tank was shaded with trees:

> Such lovely spots are rarely met with. About 1 p.m. my people arrived, and I hurried them on to Elora, distant about a mile; for, although both tired and hungry, I could not resist proceeding on at once to the glorious scene which awaited me at

Left: *The 18th-century village tank at Grishneshwar, Ellora, with its collection of small shrines containing the lingam.*

the eternal temples and houses in the mountain. No inducement could have prevailed on me to stop another half-hour.

He had been travelling for ten days:

> ... but it is totally impossible to describe the feelings of admiration and awe excited on the mind upon first beholding these stupendous excavations. On a close approach to the temples, the eye and imagination are bewildered with the variety of interesting objects that present themselves on every side. The feelings are interested to a degree of awe, wonder and delight that at first is painful, and it is a long time before they become sufficiently sobered and calm to contemplate with any attention the surrounding wonders. The death-like stillness of the place, the solitude of the adjoining plains, the romantic beauty of the country, and the mountain itself, perforated in every part, all tend to impress the mind of the stranger with feelings quite new, and far different from those felt in viewing magnificent edifices amidst the busy haunts of man. Everything here invites the mind to contemplation, and every surrounding object reminds it of a remote period and a mighty people, who were in a state of high civilisation, whilst the natives of our own land were barbarians, living in woods and wilds.

There are thirty-four temples in the mountain at Ellora: Buddhist, Hindu, and Jain. Most of them are caverns tunnelled out of the mountain, but two of them are free-standing temples. These have been formed by the mountain itself being gradually cut away to leave, in one instance, a temple so large, so complex and so profusely decorated that it must rank as the largest and most sophisticated piece of sculpture in the world: the Kailasantha Temple, known variously as the Kailasa, the Keylas, Paradise, the Holy Mountain, residence of Lord Siva:

> To build the Pantheon, the Parthenon at Athens, St Peter's at Rome, our own St Paul's, or a Fonthill Abbey, is a task of science and labour; but we understand *how* it is done, how it proceeds, and how it is finished: but to conceive for a moment a body of men, however numerous, with a spirit however invincible, and resources however great, attack a solid mountain of rock, in most parts 100 feet high, and excavating, by the slow process of the *chisel* ... appears beyond belief, and the mind is bewildered in amazement. I think the caverned temples of Elora far surpass, in labour, design, etc. any of the ancient buildings that have impressed our minds with admiration; nor do I think they yield the palm of superiority to anything we are told of in Egypt.

The Kailasa, dedicated to Siva, is arguably the noblest and certainly the most extraordinary Hindu temple in India. The local Brahmins believed the temple was built by heavenly influence and supernatural power: Seely could only guess as to its construction. What we now know from stylistic as well as written evidence is that the temple was most likely begun by a Rashtrakuta king, Dantidurga, who lived AD 725–755. An estimated 200,000 tons of black volcanic rock were excavated to produce a pit 100 feet deep with a floor area of 276 by 154 feet on which the free-standing parts of the temple rest. There are three main sections. Facing away from the mountain and out across the plains is the high entrance gate, screening the sacred precincts from the outside world. Beyond, and linked to the gate, is the shrine to Siva's mount, the bull Nandi, on either side of which are two giant elephants and two huge columns which reminded Seely of Cleopatra's Needles. Beyond the Nandi shrine and linked to it by a bridge is the main temple itself. It rises up in imitation of its namesake Mount Kailasa, like the Olympus of the Greeks,

Below: *The Kailasa Temple from the south-west, drawn by James Wales and published in 1803. The elephant on the right has lost its head. Seely's favourite resting place was on the terrace immediately to the left of the obelisk.*

the sacred home of Lord Siva in the Himalayas and still in places covered with white stucco in imitation of Himalayan snows. Round its base are elephants, like caryatids, bearing the weight of the holy mountain on their backs; sculptured scenes from the *Ramayana*, the sacred stories of Hindu mythology; and sculpted reliefs such as the figures of the demon Ravana shaking the mountain to its foundations and disturbing Siva and his lovely goddess Parvati. And over all, on every surface, Siva dancing, Siva angry, Siva benign and the asparas, the angels, celestial consorts of the gods fluttering in the sky. The endless catalogue, says Seely, of Hindu mythology that:

> ... after the deepest research and closest investigation, produces neither amusement nor information, being monstrous lies and fabled imposture from beginning to end.

The upper storey of the temple is reached either by a flight of steps from the courtyard or by the bridge from the Nandi shrine to a porch.

Below: *Seely's drawings of the Hindu deities at Ellora.*

> Here viewing the wonders around you, the piazza below, with its deified inhabitants, the court, and the various apartments, the mind may enjoy for hours a rich feast of delight, while the body reclines on one of these massy stone ottomans. I have at times, in the deep solitude of this place, not a voice or sound disturbing me, found myself, as it were, in another world, the sole tenant and master of these retreats, the former inhabitants of which have for ever fled, leaving behind them these stupendous relics of their ingenuity and perseverance – a glorious memento of a superior race to the present, and of happier periods than the modern age.

Behind the porch is a central hall, dark in contrast to the brilliant sunlight outside, its roof supported by sixteen massive columns and, at the far end, guarded at the door by the goddesses of the rivers Ganges and Jumna, the holy shrine in which:

> ... is placed the *Lingham* of Mhah Deo (Siva), the presiding deity of the temple. This symbol, which is placed in the centre of the *sanctum sanctorum*, is a stone of cylindrical shape, bedaubed with red ochre and sweet-scented oil, and strewed with odoriferous flowers. The worship of this stone, with the ceremonies observed, need not be detailed: they are of an impure kind. It is an emblem of the generative power.

At least Seely mentions the lingam; most Victorian writers who followed him ignored it altogether.

My tent was pitched and my horse picqueted nearly in front of Keylas, in a fine open spot – a necessary precaution in India, on account of reptiles or beasts of prey; but I purposed residing entirely in the great hall.

A plan not approved of by the 'ignorant, bigoted and indolent fakeers' – the holy men who were already in residence – but Seely was able to buy their acquiescence, as he cynically expected, with metaphorical beads in the form of three bags of rice. The rice had to be bought for them by his Brahmin as Seely's own Christian and unhallowed hands would have constituted the bribe impure and therefore unacceptable. However, as fakirs in particular and Indians in general were of a somewhat litigious nature, the bribe was accompanied by a written agreement signed by both parties, an agreement that Seely drew up with the mock solemnity of a state paper. It provided that the fakirs should leave the great hall to Seely's party on condition that none of them cooked meat or smoked tobacco. The fakirs were to be allowed in to worship at the lingam at specific times only; one spring of water was for Seely's sole use, whilst the butchering of any animal (and indeed any cooking) had to take place away from any of the temples. The agreement was signed on 10 October

Left: *Sculpted scenes from the* Ramayana, *the sacred stories of Hindu mythology, at the Kailasa Temple.*

1810 by Somekee Ram Vystnam, Brahmin, and on Seely's behalf by Nulla Rao, Brahmin and pundit. As there was no mention of beef in the agreement, 'as the mere mention of it would bring out a high caste Hindoo in a cold sweat', Seely concealed the fact that he had salt beef in his provisions. He ate his beef, surreptitiously, staring into the eyes of the sacred bull Nandi himself. Nandi, he said, didn't even blink.

That night, having seen the sculpture of a sphinx on one of the porticoes of the temple door, Seely amused himself by thinking of the links that might exist between the mythology of the Hindu and that of Egypt and of Greece. As the shadows spread across the floor of the great hall and darkness fell, the gloom and the silence grew oppressive:

> Nothing can be better adapted to estrange the soul from all mundane ideas than the deep gloom of these temples at the hour of midnight ... the grandeur, gloom and stillness of the place were insupportable. My faithful Siphauee guard told me at last we had better retire ... and we both quietly sneaked out of Paradise to my tent.

His spirits rose with the morning sun on what he called one of the happiest days of his life. He spent it exploring, recording and drawing; marvelling at the sculpture; wondering at the colours which had survived; climbing into the galleries and smaller temples that were hewn out of the rockface on all sides surrounding the courtyard. It was here, up a dark winding staircase, that he discovered the Lankeswar – the Great Lanka – a chapel bigger than the great assembly hall of the Kailasa itself and hewn out of the rock. Its roof was supported by twenty-seven columns of solid rock, massive pillars carved with figures, scrolls, leaf forms and geometric patterns, and pillared aisles burrowing into the heart of the mountain. It was an indication of the richness of the cave temples that he still had to see.

To the south, facing the main entrance to the Kailasa, were the Buddhist cave temples; away to the north were the Jain. He began at the south on 10 October, not without a slight expectancy of anticlimax after the wonders that he had seen. In spite of this, however, and also in spite of the oppressive heat and the sheer effort of concentrated looking, he continued to be amazed by the variety of temple design, the profusion of carving and the incredible amount and quality of sculpture, from sculpted panels to giant, free-standing Buddhas. The Teen Tal, the three-storey temple, stood back from the face of the mountain in its own excavated courtyard, its three plain balconies a foil for the sculpture inside. On the top floor, facing out towards the light at the cave entrance, were perhaps the most remarkable sculptures in the whole of Ellora: a line of seven Buddhas in teaching posture, their heads shaded by the umbrellas that symbolised their strength and power:

> Their faces are painted with oil and red ochre, though not quite so tastefully or delicately laid on as the cosmetics at home.

And on the far wall was the Buddha himself, shown teaching in the Deer Park at Sarnath in northern India, the site of the first historic sermon in 528 BC:

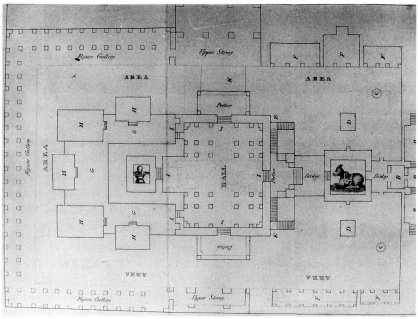

Left: *Ground plan of the Kailasa Temple drawn by Seely. The entrance to the complex is from the right. The Nandi shrine is depicted by a reclining bull. The main temple is the central pillared hall with the lingam on the left. All these parts are free standing. The outer galleries are hollowed out of the surrounding rockface.*

To perpetuate the glories of ancient days, the founders of Elora could not have conveyed to posterity a better idea of their genius than in these colossal figures of gods and stupendous excavations ... (We) cannot fail to be excited as we reflect that man, with his limited powers, has been able to effect such glorious works, surpassing all possible belief.

The Buddhists were sculpting the Teen Tal some time between AD 700 and 750, at the same time as the Visvakarma Temple. Like the Temple of Karla, the Visvakarma was built in imitation of earlier wooden structures, with the window throwing light onto the interior hall with its lines of columns, its stone-ribbed roof in imitation of wooden beams and a huge figure of Buddha carved in front of the stupa:

I was very much inclined to be sacrilegious here, by purloining one of those pretty little sitting figures (but) ... two strong objections existed to my possessing one of these figures: first, the Brahmans would not allow of my taking away one; and, if they had, there would have been *much* difficulty in separating it from the parent rock. Had I succeeded, my prize would have been surely as valuable and as curious as some of the unintelligible fragments brought over from Italy ... that in a few places adorn the lower statuary room of the British Museum.

This was, of course, before Belzoni had been to Egypt. Beyond the Visvakarma was a line of ten more Buddhist temples: small monasteries with cells for the monks and all of them sculpted, all of them quiet and contemplative, like the religion, all of them with individual beauty:

It is unusual as it is novel to be living solitarily in a rocky mansion, feeding on vegetable diet and drinking only of the limpid springs of Elora. First and foremost, I discarded the salt beef ... and the little brandy I had ... went to my servants ... They did not in their conviviality get drunk, but just 'agreeably confused' ... but for the fourteen days I continued on a vegetable and milk diet, I never was more cheerful and healthy. It gave an elasticity and serenity to the spirits that were quite enviable ... At day-light I bathed in one of the cisterns appropriated to my service; after that, I rode hard for a few miles or looked out for a fox or jackal; then came home to my tent, ate voraciously of rice and eggs ... Then came surveying the temples until 2 p.m. ... The afternoon I lounged and whiled away with some book ... The front portico at Keylas, or the upper storey of Teen Tal, were my usual places of retirement.

He went to study the temples to the north. To get there he had to cross almost a mile of rough ground, broken with the deep watercourses of streams, small lakes left by the monsoon and thick vegetation. These temples were built between the eighth and thirteenth centuries by the Jains, a religious sect which developed from Buddhism but which has its own pantheon of gods – the tirthankaras. In the temple of Indra Sabha was a seated figure of the twenty-fourth (and last) tirthankara, Mahavira:

> I really do not think there are five square inches of the walls left undecorated, as minutely as it is perfectly done, with figures, emblems of religion, tasteful ornaments, and wreaths of flowers ... for grandeur and size ... considering the infinite variety of sculptural ornaments, (it) is second only to Keylas.

The Indra Sabha was also the last of the great cave temples of India. From then on, temples were built in the open, in the sun, but inside they were to remain as dark, enclosed and mysterious as the caves from which they had sprung.

Seely, dressed in white linen shirt, jacket and trousers and sitting on a little camp stool with notebook and pencil in hand, contemplated the sculptures and the religion and the India around him:

> The bull alone is not only worshipped, but the cow likewise. A Hindoo will with ecstasy run after a cow, and think himself particularly happy if he can but catch some of her falling urine to drink and wash his face with: and happy is the Hindoo who is thus blessed before his morning ablutions and prayers.

But the effort of prying into every nook and cranny, thick with dust and the home of scorpions and centipedes, began to tire him:

> In endeavouring to penetrate into the cave, partly filled with water ... I was nearly suffocated and drowned by falling into it, in a kind of giddiness that overcame me, probably from the foul air it contained. Many snakes were in the pool at the time.

He decided, after a few more days, to quit. Seely had been able to respond to the wonders of Ellora, their beauty and romance but, despite his wide reading and his personal experience of India, intellectually, archaeologically and historically he was at a loss. Mr Reuben Burrows, writing in the *Edinburgh Review* in July 1804, was not:

> The pyramids of Egypt, as well as those lately discovered in Iceland, and probably, too, the tower of Babel, seem to have been intended for nothing more than images of Siva.

Above: *Visvakarma
Temple, drawn
(inaccurately) by Seely
in September 1810.*

Stonehenge is evidently one of the temples of Budha ... That
the Druids of Britain were Brahmans is beyond the least
shadow of doubt.

India, despite the British presence of almost half a century, was
still essentially as unknown as Africa. What Seely did know,
however, and advocated in advance of his time, was that:

> ... A powerful, scientific, and generous nation, like the
> English, ought not to allow any injury to happen to these
> mighty works, which can, by a very little trouble, and by
> incurring no expense, be prevented.

A series of photographs taken in 1890 show the temples in much
the same state of picturesque decay as Seely described them but,
since then, rubbish has been removed, the ground level lowered
and the structures restored. Whilst some of the romance has
gone, the beauty and the wonder remain.

With the discovery in 1819 of the nearby Ajanta Caves by
another British officer chasing tigers, and work done on other
cave sites in India, it is possible today to put Ellora into artistic,
historical and chronological context. The caves stretch in unend-
ing succession along the mountains south to north, from the
earliest (Buddhist) caves which were begun somewhere between

the second and fourth centuries at the furthest south, through the eighth-century Hindu (Brahmin) caves in the middle of the line to the eighth-to-thirteenth-century Jain caves in the north. The progression and the dates of construction correspond to the dominant religious influence in the area at the time. Ellora had been an important site from the early centuries when Hinduism was establishing itself. It was at a crossroads of India where artistic as well as religious influences came from both the north and south as well as from the west, from Arabia and even Europe. However, much of the Hindu iconography in the Brahmin temples that so baffled Seely was local. It was the record of myths and cults which grew up in the neighbourhood; the outward signs of a religious tradition that was wide enough to include the philosophy of the high-caste Brahmin at one extreme and the simple worship of goddesses of earth and water by the humble peasant at the other.

With the rise of the Mogul Empires in the north, and the spread of Islam to central India, Ellora became a target of Muslim pillage, but Hinduism survived. The Emperor Aurangzeb, the Cromwell of India and the man whom Seely rightly thought responsible for some of the damage to the statues at the Kailasa, was forced to desecrate the linga in order to try and establish

Above: The Temple of Indra Sabha at Ellora, drawn by Seely and used as the frontispiece to his book The Wonders of Elora. *It is only a very approximate representation.*

the supremacy of Islam over a Hindu cult that refused to die; but he failed. The Mahratta rulers revived Hinduism in the eighteenth century; some of the painting that Seely discovered and dubbed 'modern' probably dates from that time. And Ellora was still a sacred Hindu place when Seely was there: a stronghold of Brahminism, of high-caste Hindus where, as Seely records, only Rajput (royal) troops were allowed to be stationed. But the focus of religious devotion was no longer the Kailasa but the temple in the village of Grishneshwar, home of one of only twelve Siva jyotorlingas in the whole of India and restored in the eighteenth century after Muslim destruction. It is still the focus of attention, with pilgrims coming from all over western India to worship the linga and to bathe in the tanks.

Seely travelled extensively in India, recommending road improvements, recording his journeys and publishing a book of recommended routes. He often travelled with his young family and was devastated when his young son Richard died of cholera. Seely was no scholar but he was widely read, tolerant of different traditions and cultures and not blind to the faults of his own. He was upright, even puritanical, yet at the same time attracted by the pagan and the sensual he saw around him.

India finally caught up with him, as it had with his colleagues. He fell ill, he could scarcely see in one eye, and an overdose of 'medicine' partly paralysed his arms. He returned to England where, partly for money, he wrote his book complaining of rapacious relatives and the meanness of the East India Company after fifteen years' service:

> I may be bent, but I am not to be subdued. To repine is a sin; to be dissatisfied with what cannot be helped is folly.

He didn't get better and returned to India to die. A letter from his wife to the authorities about his condition and a brief entry in the army records are the last we hear of him. He was, perhaps, just forty years old when he died in 1824 and was probably buried in the military cemetery on Bombay Island, which was built over in the 1950s. There is no known portrait of him, except the written one that he gives of himself through his book:

> Some say that a soldier's job is fighting, not writing, but ... I have never written much, nor need I tell the reader I do not write well; but still I conceive there is some intrinsic worth in this *solitary* account of the temples of Elora; for such it certainly is, no book having ever been written professedly and distinctly on the subject ... and that is some satisfaction to a soldier, should other merits be denied him.

Chapter Four

THE MARBLE HUNTERS
Charles Fellows in
Asia Minor

The most acceptable presents to the inhabitants are not such as are of the greatest intrinsic value, but articles of use which it is difficult for them to procure ... I have been often asked in a delicate manner ... if I possessed a picture of our queen or reigning sovereign; a common print of this kind would be highly prized.*

Charles Fellows made his first excursion into central Turkey in 1838. The fact that he termed his gruelling and often dangerous journey 'an excursion' is indicative, for Fellows was a 'gentleman', a man of private means. He was an active member of the British Association who travelled for instruction and pleasure, uncommissioned and at his own expense.

Fellows was born in 1799 in Nottingham, the younger son of a banker father. He showed an early interest in drawing and in the antique and, at the age of fourteen, illustrated a trip to Newstead Abbey (home of Lord Byron) in sketches which later appeared on the frontispiece of Moore's famous *Life of Byron*. He also liked adventure. In 1827, he made the thirteenth recorded ascent of Mont Blanc and pioneered a new route that is still used today. In 1832, he travelled widely in Italy and Greece.

In the early nineteenth century, the concept of the Grand Tour was still alive. A tour which focused on the classical civilisations of Greece and Rome, and which included the purchase of 'souvenirs' in the form of classical sculptures or marbles,

* C. Fellows, *A Journal written during an excursion in Asia Minor* (London: John Murray, 1839).

THE MARBLE HUNTERS 101

for edification and display at home in Britain. But the Tour was still limited to the Western and European locations of the Roman Empire: to Rome, Pompeii and Athens. Fellows' excursion into Asia Minor was the natural extension of the Grand Tour – a journey into that part of the Roman Empire which had survived the fall of Rome and lived on as Christian Byzantium until the fall of Constantinople to the Ottomans in 1453.

Although on Europe's very doorstep, apart from the Aegean coast it had been very little explored by Europeans. The Ottoman Empire remained the mysterious East and the Turks the destroyers of the twin prongs of European civilisation – Christianity and the culture of ancient Greece. With the establishment of a Greek state in 1832, however, and the earlier defeat, in 1827, of the Turkish fleet at the battle of Navarino, the Europeans were beginning to fight back.

Fellows was strongly biased in favour of the Greeks, and Turkey was of interest only because of the survival there of ancient Greek cities whose remains were unvisited and, in many instances, unlocated. Fellows' hope was to locate them again. He landed at the port of Smyrna (Izmir to the Turks) on 12 February 1838:

> I can scarcely believe that I am in Asia Minor, for my inn (the Navy Hotel) is just like an English public house (but) on looking out of my window this morning, I found that I was really in the East. I beheld a whole city of Turks, a very gay scene; but the people struck me as being disgustingly fat (and) I have just seen a man with a turban, which I took for a small sack of flour placed upon his head.

Streets were narrow, camels and children a pedestrian hazard:

> The children are still brought up in national prejudices; they hoot after a European and call him Frank, Frank-dog and other such epithets ... They are afraid of the consequences of their impertinence, and generally secure a retreat behind some doorway before they even call after the stranger.

But, unlike Burckhardt thirty-six years before, Fellows, with his Greek servant Demetrius, was safe to travel undisguised. He was referred to by the Turks as 'Milordos', a name:

> ... given to persons of all nations who travel without any visible motive. Who is he, a messenger of government or a merchant? The Turks can conceive no other motives for travelling; and if the stranger disowns both of these, he must be *Milordos*.

Left: *Street in Smyrna (now Izmir) showing typical Turkish dress and wooden houses with overhanging storeys.*

Fellows' plan was to make a circular tour north from Smyrna to Constantinople; then south through the central highlands of Anatolia and west along the Mediterranean coast back to Smyrna. It was to take him through those countries known to the ancients as Lydia, Phrygia, Pamphylia and Lycia; semi-independent states which existed on the periphery of the expanding Greek world in the seventh century BC. The first stage of the journey, via Pergamum and Troy, was already known to European travellers. Small Turkish towns teemed with relics 'of

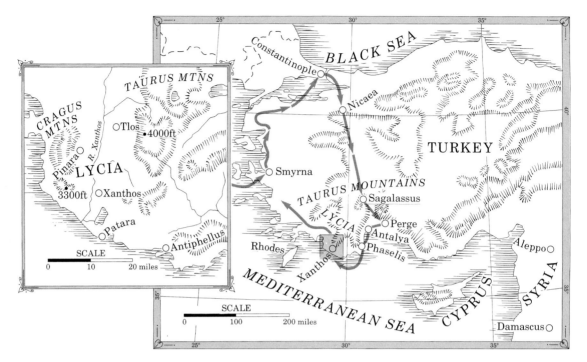

former splendid cities' and, from all these sites, sculptures were being dug up by 'gentlemen' and carted off to the museums of Europe, both legally and illegally. All around him in the fields were reminders of the life of ancient Greece:

> In cultivated districts (the head of the ox) is placed on a stick, or hung on a tree, as a scarecrow. This custom prevails in Greece as well as here: the heads are always beautifully white and retain the horns, which are in this part of the world exceedingly short and thick. The skull, with its horns, has thus been constantly presented to the eye of the Greek artist blanched white as marble, and hence the introduction of precisely this figure in the friezes of their architecture; and perhaps the vine or clematis wreathing about the horns may have suggested the frequent accompaniment of this ornament.

He arrived in Constantinople on 9 March. Classical remains were disappointing; a classical pillar incorporated in a mosque wall here; a Roman sarcophagus there; a fine obelisk brought by the Romans from Egypt. Of much greater interest were the Whirling Dervishes:

Below: *Skull of a bull, sketched by Fellows.*

> ... a most extraordinary sight. There is no doubt that it has high antiquity as a religious ceremony, and the performance is not so laughably ridiculous as I had expected from descriptions and pictures. There were fifteen dancing at the same time, and

during the whole service of prayers and dance I never saw more signs of devotion; the dance indeed appears to be a religious rhapsody. The performers generally continued to turn during three or four minutes, then bowed, and almost immediately recommenced turning; during the whole time the eyes appeared closed, and the peculiar effect was given by the perfect fixedness of the body, head, and arms. They assumed a certain position, and I could with difficulty perceive the movement of their feet, and almost felt at a loss to account for the rotatory motion given to the figure.

Above: *A Whirling Dervish, sketched by Fellows.*

The 'Europeanisation' of Turkey was further advanced in Constantinople than elsewhere. Under orders from the modernising Sultan, the fez was replacing the turban, trousers replacing robes, boots replacing slippers, highly inconvenient, Fellows thought, 'as they must slip them off six times a day for prayers'. The religious power of Islam, like the temporal power, was beginning to weaken. There was religious freedom in the city:

> Curious instances are shown, however, of the difficulty of subduing the prejudices of an ignorant people. One very unpopular reform which the Sultan had to effect, in the formation of his troops, was that of their wearing *braces,* a necessary accompaniment to the trousers: and why? Because these form a cross, the badge of the infidel, upon the back: many indeed will submit to severe punishment, and even death, for disobedience to military orders, rather than bear upon their persons this sign, hostile to their religion.

Fellows was won over by Constantinople, the most picturesque city that he had ever seen; and by the Turks, who, he discovered, were kind, hospitable and clean:

> I know no European country where there is so little annoyance from offensive impurities in the streets. I do not remember ever seeing a Turk spit: what a contrast to the manners of France, Italy and Germany!

However, because of the rapid changes in progress in the city, he felt that the villages and the countryside promised to be more interesting. He left Constantinople on 17 March and headed south, crossing the Bosphorus from the European to the Asian side and taking the new road, the only road in Asia Minor. It went for sixty miles and was under construction by the Austrians, against the opposition of the locals. Although the road still needed to be surfaced by McAdam, charges for using the new road were already fixed. His horses had to be changed three times

Right: *Constantinople (now Istanbul) c. 1839.*

every 33 miles and, as this took at least an hour each time, progress was slow:

> I find it very difficult in travelling through this country to write a journal, or pursue any occupation requiring attention; for on arriving and taking possession of my room, the smoke is no sooner seen to rise from the chimney than the apartment is half filled with Turks, who, with the most friendly intention, bring their pipes and sit down, saying everything that is kind and hospitable, and watching every motion of my lips and hands. I can scarcely keep my countenance when I see them staring with astonishment at my use of a knife and fork. They watch every piece of food to my mouth; but the moment I look up, their curiosity yields to their natural politeness, and they turn away.

On 19 March he entered the ruins of the famed and fated city of Nicaea. Here, among the broken walls and ruined towers of later buildings, were fragments of sculpture unusually grand and of a peculiar beauty:

> I observed two fragments of basso-relievo, probably part of a frieze, equal to the marbles of the Athenian Parthenon, but much mutilated.

Over one of the two principal gateways to the city was half of an inscription, worn and almost unreadable. The other half, Fellows believed, was on the fallen stone nearby, but it had fallen face down. He gathered a group of men and, for a few pence, had the stone turned over and discovered the inscription as fresh as the day it had been cut:

> The men seeing me refer to a book said, 'The Franks know by their books where all the writing and gold are concealed;' always fancying that we search for inscriptions to find treasure.

The scenery around Nicaea was wild and romantic, high hills and outcrops rising to mountains and gorges with waterfalls which reminded Fellows of the Alps. The further south he went the more dramatic the scenery became, and the more beautiful the wild flowers: red, purple and blue anemones; cyclamen; primroses; snowdrops; and yellow, blue and lilac crocuses. Towns and villages, however, grew sparser, maps were inaccurate and the roads deteriorated into dirt tracks and frequently into mere paths which constantly changed direction as swamps made them impassable. The mountains grew higher, snow fell and the wind became so bitter that Fellows' fingers were so cold he could scarcely write:

> Were I disposed to dwell upon personal annoyances, I might here relate our ride of twenty-five miles against a strong wind from the north-east, and getting thoroughly wet through with cold rain, which was succeeded by a heavy fall of snow: darkness came on, and we were compelled for the last ten miles to trust ourselves entirely to the guidance of our horses, being unable to distinguish the stones from the streams, many of which wound down the steep craggy rocks over which we were riding. In this manner we had to cross and re-cross thickets and swamps. But it was in our favour that our horses were approaching home; and at last we found to our great joy, that an object which in the darkness we had fancied to be a curiously shaped rock, was the wall of the citadel of Kootáya. As it was ten o'clock when we arrived, wet through and miserably cold, I asked to be allowed to undress and have tea by myself, instead of in the presence of eight or nine friends of my host; my request was granted, but one or two of the sons were directed to remain with me, that I might not be lonely ... During my toilet I saw that the sons were watching every act and anticipated every wish, except their absence ... how often I wished them away, that I might go to bed!

Kootaya was 6000 feet above sea level. Aezani stood at 8000 feet. There were no signs of Christian Byzantine churches and no signs of later Turkish fortifications, only the walls of the Greeks and the Romans.

Compared with the experiences of Seely or Belzoni, the physical conditions that he encountered were horrendous:

Though not a stranger to high mountain-passes, I have never experienced such cutting cold nor so strong a wind as in this pass of the Taurus range; neither I nor any of my men could ride, and we were obliged occasionally to lie down until the gusts had ceased: the very rocks of marble seemed cut by it, for they stood in shivered points, through which the wind hissed fiercely. We passed much snow, and were visited by a storm of small pieces of ice, of broken forms and transparent; this was succeeded by beating rain and snow as we descended towards the valley ... where in two hours we arrived thoroughly drenched.

Nothing, though, could dampen Fellows' enthusiasm for the antique or suppress his energy. Hearing of some ruins three miles away at the top of a mountain, he turned out again into the storm, but he was not too hopeful. At this height, 'the situation appeared too high and dreary for the living of any age', but he was wrong. Above him on the overhanging rocks were the foundations of walls and, as he climbed even higher, the piled-up remains of a superb city:

On the side of a higher hill is one of the most beautiful and perfect theatres I ever saw or heard of; the seats and the greater part of the proscenium remain; the walls of the front have partly fallen, but the splendid cornices and statuary are but little broken (though) eight or nine venerable walnut trees have done some damage by heaving up the seats ... I walked almost round, in the arched lobby, entering as the people did about two thousand years ago.

The Greeks always built their theatres so that the seats of the auditorium looked out, not as in the Roman theatres to the enclosed walls of the stage, but to a natural backdrop of the most beautiful scenery that the town could show. Here it faced the snow-capped mountains and this, plus the city's remoteness and the wild and windy conditions under which he first saw it, was, for Fellows, overwhelming. But it also brought home a dilemma which faced many thinking Victorians: how to reconcile the pagan beauty of Greek art with the Christianity which destroyed it. In the town's burial ground, he saw some Christian columns, crudely placed:

How much it is to be regretted that the introduction of a Divine religion should have unnecessarily put to flight all the divinity of art! ... In architecture and in sculpture the Cross is a brand always attended by deformity in proportion, and total want of simplicity in ornament.

Fellows was, like Seely, increasingly on the side of the pagan. As his journey continued, he was to see much greater works of art and even more dramatically situated ruins, but none that had such a strong and immediate impact. The town which he correctly identified as the site of ancient Sagalassus was also the first of the ancient 'lost' towns of which he was the discoverer.

The Taurus mountains stop abruptly just before they reach the Mediterranean sea, and on the fertile coastal plain lie the ruins of ancient Perge. The location, compared with that of Sagalassus, could not be more different, and, as the scenery changed, so did the climate. It became warm and spring-like: fruit trees were in blossom, heron and ducks were nesting in the reeds beside the river. Fellows arrived towards evening and set up camp near the ruins:

> At seven o'clock Demetrius returned with his bag of ducks and snipes, and at the same time arrived a present from the neighbouring tents of kymac, milk, eggs, and bread. After my meal I narrowly escaped a tragical adventure. 'Every bullet has its billet'; but none was yet billeted on me.

It was a close thing. One of Fellows' hospitable Turkish neighbours had discovered Demetrius' gun left hanging on a tree. Unused to double-barrelled guns, the man had carefully let down one lock so that he could safely pull the trigger. There was a loud report as the second barrel fired:

> His alarm was natural, and mine would have been as great had I been aware of my danger; the charge entered the ground within half a yard of my feet.

Perge is first recorded in the history books in 333 BC when Alexander the Great was marching along the Mediterranean coast and conquering the cities of Pamphylia although most of Perge's surviving buildings (the theatre, the stadium, the agora, the main colonnaded street and the nymphaeum) are Roman. Fellows thought they were Greek but only the remains of one of the main gates is Hellenistic, of about Alexander's time.

In the first week of April, Fellows was relaxing on the coast amongst the oranges and lemons, figs and mulberry trees of the Turkish town of Antalya. Before the Turks arrived in 1207, the Christians had set out in 1100 from its harbour on the second

Crusade to the Holy Land. The city was still walled, but where there had once been Roman temples and Christian churches, there were mosques and minarets:

> ... in front of the town the bay is bounded by the continued chain of mountains which rise proudly from the sea. I have never seen mountains so beautiful, so poetically beautiful.

Fellows planned to go into the land that lay west along the coast and behind and beyond these mountains; into the ancient country of Lycia. But from Antalya there were no roads at all. The only way was by boat:

> *April 13th* – It is *Friday*; on Friday I attempted to leave England, but in vain, owing to a storm; on Friday I had a wretched voyage on the sea of Marmora; on Friday I packed to leave Constantinople, but was obliged to remain; and now on the same day of the week, at six o'clock in the evening, I am sitting in my boat in the harbour of Adalia waiting for the be-u-tee, or local firman, from the Pasha; it was to meet me on the opposite side of the port, about two hundred yards from the place whence I started, but the boatmen say they dare not go further, and my Friday's voyage is at an end.

It was impossible to proceed without a firman, the written permission to travel, and Fellows had to wait until the following day before the firman arrived and he was able to depart.

Fellows was not a bad sailor, merely a bored one, and he never took to the water without forming a firm resolution to travel in future on dry land. But for the next fifty miles or so the mountains swept sheer into the sea; there were few inlets and even fewer harbours. The whole coastline was rugged and inhospitable, and the only possible alternative to travelling by boat was to ride on horseback along the shore when the weather was calm. This was the way that Alexander the Great had been forced to come, but even here, as there was scarcely any beach, horses and men had to wade through waves shoulder high. The only survey of this part of the coast had been carried out in 1811 and 1812, by order of the Lords Commissioners of the Admiralty, and this was the map and description (written up by Francis Beaufort, Captain of HMS *Frederiksstern*) on which Fellows had to rely.

After five hours' journey and before eight o'clock in the morning, the boat put in at Tekrova, the ancient city of Phaselis:

> I landed, and at once saw the remains of this ancient port. In the same degree in which the ruins of the cities in the interior

have raised my conception of the grandeur, both in scale, design and execution, of the works of the ancients, the vestiges of their ports and harbours diminish my idea of their naval strength or skill.

Phaselis was never really a Lycian city. It was probably founded from the island of Rhodes and was a commercial centre on the main trade highway from Greece, along the coast of Asia Minor to Syria and Palestine. In the sixth century BC it was dominated by the Persians when their Empire stretched from the borders of China to the waters of the Aegean and, although the Greeks had defeated the Persians at Marathon, Phaselis was not liberated until 469 BC. Alexander arrived in 33 BC and was given a golden crown. In return, he kept a small body of soldiers there to help keep away plunderers before he himself continued on his way through the water to Perge. After Alexander's death, however, the city was dominated by the Egyptians until the arrival of the Romans in the first century BC. It passed into Ottoman hands in AD 1158 and declined as Antalya rose.

Despite Fellows' disappointment, the harbours at Phaselis are impressive. There are three: in the south-western one are the remains of a landing stage; in the northern, where the sea has encroached on the necropolis, Roman stone coffins litter the foreshore and are visible in the water; but the most interesting is the smallest central harbour. It was always the busiest and the most in need of protection. As well as the remains of the Roman quay are the remains of the city wall that was extended into the harbour area to form a breakwater, and just beneath the waterline at the end of the breakwater is the pile of stones that must have supported the harbour lighthouse:

April 17th. – We again put out to sea at three o'clock in the morning, and arrived by eleven at the little port of Kákava, where I determined to change my mode of travelling for one less tedious and affording more amusement. The coast we had passed presented from the sea a barren appearance, and even the outline was monotonous in its grandeur. One peculiar feature in the voyage was the effect of the extremely clear water over the white marble rocks, which here form the bottom of the sea. Upon these rocks I saw sea-plants standing at a great depth, spread out and motionless, and the whole watery world was thickly inhabited by a great variety of shell-fish; thus was I permitted, as it were, to visit this kingdom of the deep with its crystal atmosphere.

Once back on terra firma, the steady procession of ruins began

Above: *Fellows'*
drawings of (top) a
pillar tomb and (below)
a sarcophagus tomb.

again: nameless ruins; buildings; cisterns; sarcophagi and tombs. At Antiphellus, as well as the theatre and temples, Fellows saw for the first time a distinct form of sarcophagus, quite different from the Roman. Whereas the Roman coffins had lids that were only slightly ridged, these were almost pointed like a gothic arch and the most splendid of them had inset stone panels like the doors of a wooden house and were decorated with lion heads and raised on a substantial plinth as much as ten feet high. They were, though Fellows didn't yet know it, Lycian and dated mostly from the fourth century BC. The tombs cut into the cliffs bore:

> ... some resemblance to the windows of the Elizabethan age, with their stone mullions. It is remarkable that all the tombs cut out of the face of the rock ... are in exact imitation of buildings of wood, the joints representing wedged ties or dove-tails, and the overhanging cornices being formed like the ends of beams of round trees, producing a picturesque architectural ornament.

These also were Lycian.

April 19th. – At five o'clock in the morning the wind almost carried away the tent; but we were the sooner on our way, and for eight hours travelled over the summits of the high mountains. Even here we frequently found massy tombs crowning the pinnacles of rocks, and innumerable chambers for tombs hollowed out of their hard sides, many having beautiful architectural designs cut in the rock, and others with the entrances most ingeniously concealed.

As there were not even proper paths, a way had to be cut through the undergrowth or the horses had to leap, step by step, down the rocks. In the late afternoon they were back at the coast and the city of Patara. The triple-arched city gate had been built in AD 100 in the time of Mettius Modestus, the Roman governor of Lycia. It still stood proud in the valley of the River Xanthos, but in the theatre, which was closer to the sea, sand had climbed to the height of the auditorium walls and was drifting over the stone seats and eddying onto the stage:

> ... so that the area of it is more than half filled up, and the whole, with many other ruins, will soon be entirely buried and left for future ages to disinter.

On the side of the theatre was an inscription in Greek recording the fact that it had been built in AD 147. St Nicholas, the original Santa Claus, was born in the town 150 years later.

Above: *The overgrown Roman theatre, a sarcophagus tomb and the tall Harpy Tomb at Xanthos as drawn by Fellows in 1838.*

Captain Beaufort had visited Patara in 1811 and recorded the strange, threatening sand conditions, but he had also recorded something that was to be of much greater significance for Fellows. Beaufort wrote:

> Patara is now uninhabited; but a few solitary peasants were found tending the cattle that wandered about the plain. From these people we learned that at a short distance in shore were ruins of far greater extent than those of Patara. They are probably the remains of Xanthus, described by Strabo as the largest city of Lycia, and celebrated for its singularly desperate resistance to the Persian and to the Roman arms.

Beaufort had no time to explore along the River Xanthos, but continued his job of surveying the coast. Fellows, however, was determined, spurred on by the fact that no European had been there before him. Abandoning the packhorses and with only asses to carry the baggage, he began his march up the valley. After eight miles Fellows arrived at the tents of the village of Koonik, and what he saw there was astonishing, even for him:

> The ruins are wholly of temples, tombs, triumphal arches, walls and a theatre. The site is extremely romantic, upon beautiful hills; some crowned with rocks, others rising perpendicularly from the river, which is seen winding its way down from the

woody uplands, while beyond in the extreme distance are the snowy mountains in which it rises ... I regret that I have not had time, and do not possess sufficient talent, to examine completely the objects here, which alone afford inducement to the man of taste to visit this country, even from distant England. The remains appear to be all of the same date, and that a very early one. The walls are many of them Cyclopean. The language of the innumerable and very perfect inscriptions is like the Phoenician or Etruscan, and the beautiful tombs in the rocks ... are also of a very early date.

It was Fellows' first experience of Lycian writing. It was also his first experience of perhaps the best sculpture in Lycia and some of the most beautiful pieces to be found anywhere in the Graeco-Roman world.

I have attempted a sketch of the most beautiful of the tombs, and I add the description by pen to make my drawing more intelligible. It is a sarcophagus, entirely of white marble, standing on the side of a hill rich with wild shrubs – the distant mountains, of the silvery grey peculiar to marble rocks, forming the background.

This sarcophagus tomb was similar to the tomb he had seen at Antiphellus, except that here there was a sculpted frieze at the base and sculpted panels on the roof:

On the top, or hog's-mane, is a hunting scene; some figures are running, others are on horseback galloping, with spears in their hands and mantles blown by the wind, chasing the stag and wild boar, which has turned to attack its pursuer; the whole of the figures, although in a small frieze, are well formed and finished ...

Upon one side of the roof is a group in which a warrior, carrying a shield, is in the act of stepping into his chariot, which is of the early simple form, with wheels of four spokes only, and is driven by a man leaning forward, with his arms stretched out holding the reins and a whip or goad: four beautifully formed horses, prancing in various attitudes, are drawing the car.

On the side of the tomb ... under two lines of the peculiar characters of this town (perhaps Lycian), is a group of figures ... the principal figure ..., clothed in rich folded drapery, with short hair, sits in the attitude of a judge, with one arm somewhat raised; before him stand four figures: the first is mutilated, but appears similar to the second, who has long

Below: *The Tomb of Payava at Xanthos, before it was dismantled and taken to the British Museum. The name Payava, which Fellows could not read, is on the band of Lycian script round the middle.*

bushy hair, confined round the head, and looking like a wig; his attitude is that of a counsellor pleading for the others; the loose robe falls gracefully from one shoulder, and is thrown over, so as almost to conceal one arm; two other figures, differing only in having hair shorter and the arms hanging down, stand apparently waiting the decision of the judge.

The writing, which Fellows couldn't read but correctly guessed was Lycian, reveals the name of the owner of the tomb as Payava. The sculptured scenes represent his victories in life and, carried in triumph in his winged chariot, a hoped-for immortality in death. We now know that it dates from the first half of the fourth century BC, when the art of Lycia was beginning to show the influence of Greek sculpture. It is the largest and most beautiful Lycian sarcophagus tomb, and of great significance:

> It is not surprising that so beautiful a tomb should have been broken open in all parts; but as each chamber is now exposed, I trust that it may not receive further injury.

Close to the theatre was another form of tomb that Fellows had not seen before, a pillar tomb, unique to Lycia. On a stepped base stands a square monolithic pillar of limestone, 9 feet wide and over 20 feet high, on top of which is a stone funerary chamber with its sides decorated with panels of sculpted marble:

> ... the head is that of a female with the Greek cap and hair, the breast is exposed, and the body, which terminates with the trunk, has wings and a tail like a pigeon's; from under the wings comes a bird's claw, clasping the legs of a child which is carried in the bosom of the figure ... The figures are all flying from the centre of each group and upwards.

The whole monument is some 30 feet high and dates from about 480 BC. Throughout the site, scattered through the undergrowth, were other tombs: rock tombs; sarcophagus tombs; pillar tombs; some with their sculpture still intact. One was the Lion pillar from the sixth century BC, the oldest at Xanthos, with its relief of a reclining lion with a small bull between its paws, and there were others where the panels had slipped to the ground and broken. In the collapsed walls of the city were fragments of more sculptures: lions; warriors; horses; chariots; cocks fighting; and, where temples had fallen, the remains of more friezes, dancing figures with flying drapery:

> This temple, standing upon the brow of a hill, and six or seven others which may still be traced along the same cliff, must have produced an exquisitely beautiful effect.

Above: *The Lion Tomb, the oldest in Xanthos, being excavated by British sailors in 1842.*

It was in the vicinity of this ruined temple that Fellows was later to make his greatest find of all.

What Fellows had discovered was, as he had hoped, Xanthos, the Lycian capital: a city which, according to Homer, had sent troops to fight in the Trojan War; a city that had maintained its independence until 545 BC when it was attacked by Harpagus, Commander of the Persian king Cyrus; and a city that had fallen to Alexander the Great in 333 BC and which was again destroyed when attacked by Brutus in 42 BC. Under Mark Antony and the Emperor Vespasian, however, Xanthos recovered and became part of the Christian Byzantine Empire until the invasion of the Arabs in the seventeenth century.

Xanthos, unlike some of the other Lycian cities, shows buildings and artefacts from all periods of its history: from the pottery sherds of the eighth century BC, excavated on the acropolis, to the recently uncovered Byzantine basilica. In Fellows' time, the sherds and basilica were still underground, waiting for the archaeologists' spade, and they were to remain underground for another hundred years. But Fellows knew the work of the

Above: *The Roman Gate to the city of Xanthos, built to commemorate the Emperor Vespasian.*

classical authors and he also knew that what made Xanthos unique was the sculptured tombs. He also knew that he had discovered a civilisation that, until now, had only been known from books.

On 13 May Fellows was back at his starting point at Smyrna, rejoicing that he had escaped serious accident in a journey of 1000 miles; completely changed in his initial prejudiced attitude to the Turks; thrilled by all that he had seen and determined to return 'to accumulate information and materials for future study'. Two years later, on 14 February 1840, he was back:

> ... in this now almost unknown part of ancient Greece (where) ... even the language of a considerable portion, abounding with inscriptions, has hitherto almost escaped the observation of the philologists of Europe.

Before he left England he had approached the British Museum and asked them to apply to the British Foreign Secretary, Lord Palmerston, to obtain a letter from the Turkish Sultan which would allow him to bring back some examples of any works he might find. He hoped that the permission would arrive at Rhodes shortly after his proposed second visit to Xanthos as, this time, he planned his tour in reverse. He started at the head of the Xanthos valley and worked his way downstream, searching for new Lycian sites on his way to the city of Xanthos and the sea:

> At the next village we again forded the river, and gradually rising from the valley for about five miles, arrived at two or three mills, turned by the copious streams which descend from the mountains behind the ancient city, the ruins of which had attracted me to this place. It is called in the maps Pinara, but from the inscriptions I discovered it to be Tlos ... its splendid and appropriate situation would alone point it out as the site of a Greek city.

Tlos, unlike most of the other Lycian sites, was still inhabited. At the highest point of the citadel was the palace of the local Aga. At its base, surrounding the theatre and the baths which Fellows correctly identified as Roman, were the ploughed fields of the peasants. The theatre, like the theatre at Xanthos, was built in AD 150, from funds supplied by a wealthy Lycian merchant, Opramoas of Rhodiapolis. It is even more lavish than the one at Xanthos, with seats not only of marble but supported on lions' paws and, amongst the tumbled stones of the stage, the remains of cornices, masks and other designs beautifully and still incisively carved. It was the most expensively finished of all the theatres that Fellows had seen and was an indication of the importance of the city when it was a member of the Lycian

Right: *The 4th-century BC Lycian tombs carved in the mountainside at Tlos with the 19th-century AD Aga's palace on top. The Bellerophon carving is on the big house tomb in the centre of the picture.*

league. But of an earlier and more interesting Lycian city, were the remains of the tombs carved out of the citadel rock. Here, carved above the door of one of them, is a relief of one of the legendary heroes of Homer's *Iliad*, Bellerophon on his winged horse Pegasus fighting the fire-breathing monster the Chimaera in the mountains of Lycia. The sculpture:

> ... shows all the beauty of simple line and exquisite proportion of figure, and is sufficiently legible to be of the highest interest to the antiquarian and student of ancient mythology and history.

The earliest rulers of Tlos claimed descent from Bellerophon, who, as a royal exile from Greece and with the help of the horse Pegasus given him by Neptune and Minerva, had:

> ... conquered both man and beast in various combats in Lycia, over which country he afterwards became king, before the time of the Trojan War. Among his other conquests, in this very valley, he slew a wild boar which had destroyed the fruits and cattle of the Xanthians, but for his services he received no reward. He therefore prayed to Neptune that the fields of the Xanthians should exhale a salt dew, and be universally corrupted. This continued until Bellerophon, at the inter-cession of the women, again prayed to Neptune to remove the effect of his indignation. It was on this account that the women of the Xanthians were held in such high esteem, that their children ever after were named from their mothers rather than their fathers – a custom which afterwards prevailed generally over the whole of Lycia.

Fellows had no doubt that the date of these sculptures was the same as the Lycian inscriptions he had seen at Xanthos:

> ... but I have again sought in vain for a single letter of that language in this city.

It is there, however, missed by Fellows, buried under brambles in the theatre: an inscription in both Greek and Lycian.

The city of Pinara, wrongly sited on Fellows' maps at Tlos, was, in fact, some eight miles further downstream and on the other side of the river in perhaps the most spectacular of all the Lycian city sites. Unvisited before Fellows' arrival and still little known, the feature which makes it so extraordinary is the citadel: a natural hill, 1500 feet high, sheer on all sides and, on the side facing the rising sun, honeycombed with hundreds of simple tombs cut from the rock. The only way that the tombs could have

been constructed was by workmen hanging by rope from the top of the cliff face. There is no path and no other way that they could have been visited:

> Beneath this cliff lay the principal part of the extensive and splendid city of Pinara. Two other places, at different elevations, were also covered with massive buildings, and on either side of these were tombs scattered for a considerable distance, many of them of the gothic-form sarcophagus, and some sur-

rounded by columns ... the door of the tomb, which was small, was highly finished, representing frame and nails, and on the panels handsome ring-knockers, all cut in the marble rock. For the purpose of pillaging the tomb, this door had not been moved side-ways in its groove (the usual manner of opening them), but a small hole had been broken in the rock at the side. Putting my head into this, I found the tomb had been finished within, and that the bones of at least two ancient Greeks lay scattered on the floor.

In the porch of another tomb were shallow reliefs showing views of an ancient city, probably Lycian Xanthos, and over the gothic façade of another rock tomb, the horns and mane of a bull were cut like a crest:

> Herodotus, in describing the different nations joining the army of Xerxes, relates that the people of Bithynia carried two Lycian spears, and had helmets of brass, on the summits of which were the 'ears and horns of an ox'.

All about the city were Lycian sarcophagi, some plain and simple and undecorated, others carved in imitation of the construction of the Lycian houses of wood. All of them had a gaping hole, smashed by the treasure hunters.

Strabo records that Pinara was one of the most important Lycian cities. Like Tlos, Xanthos and Patara, it sent three representatives to the Lycian league; it had a fine temple; one of the finest of all the theatres; and St Nicholas was bishop here. The city was too remote, however, too far from the river and from Xanthos and, by the eighth century, it was dead.

> While rambling among the ruins, a peasant brought me ten copper coins, all extremely small, but all Greek, found by himself in a few yards of soil which he had cultivated around his hut. I gave him five piastres, and was soon the possessor of above fifty on the same terms; many of them are probably valueless, but their being all from this place gives to them an interest; for this city is yet unknown to Europeans, and no coins are possessed by any of the museums.

He left Pinara on 15 April, and two days later was back in Xanthos:

> ... my favourite city – the first in which I became acquainted with the remains of art of the ancient Lycians, and in which I hope to find still more, embodying their language, history and poetic sculpture.

He spent four days puzzling over the ruins. They were much more extensive than he had imagined. The tombs extended over miles of country he had not seen before and, in the undergrowth that would take months to clear, there were great Cyclopean walls blended, he thought, with the Greek; but he remained puzzled.

History assists us little ... Of its earliest people we have more correct information from the poems of Homer and the works of Herodotus; each author almost claims this district as his native country, and both seem to have been well acquainted with the poetic legends of its first inhabitants. They tell of Europa's visit, and of her sons possessing the country; and some of the most beautiful parts of the *Iliad* recount the history of the Lycian heroes, Sarpedon and Glaucus. The exploits of Bellerophon, and the tale of the children of King Pandarus, are related at length; the Chimaera, and the natural peculiarities, beauty and fertility of the country are frequently extolled.

I am inclined to consider almost all the works I have termed Lycian as belonging to this age and that immediately subsequent; many of the peculiar sarcophagi and obelisk-monuments, and much of the rock-architecture, sculptures, and the language, as also the coins ... belong to this period. None of these represent any subject which can be called Byzantine, Roman, or even connected with the known history of Greece.

From their extant works of art, Fellows was able to make an accurate distinction between what he calls Ancient Lycians, those who existed before the invasion and destruction by the Persians in the middle of the sixth century BC, and those Graeco-Lycians who followed.

Below right: *The Inscribed Pillar Tomb at Xanthos with its inscriptions in both Greek and Lycian, drawn by Mr G. Scharf, who accompanied Fellows in 1843.*
Below: *Lycian writing as copied out into his journal by Fellows.*

⍓B⍟Ɨ⋏⍟: Ⅴ O
P⍌:M⍟⋏ ⍓ Γ P
Ɨ⍪PFPT ⍟:M⍓
Δ ⍓:⍓ΓƗ⋏⍟ME
⍓+BE:+XΓP⍌
⋏P:J⍓IPT⋏ E

One of those Graeco-Lycian monuments was the Inscribed Pillar, a funerary monument, badly broken but different from all the other monuments in that it was covered with Lycian script. Fellows spent two difficult and tedious days at the top of a ladder copying it and noticed that the characters on the upper portion of the monument were larger and wider than those at the bottom, 'thus counteracting the diminution by distance as seen from the ground'. It was yet further evidence of the aesthetic sophistication of the Lycian sculptors.

Of potentially greater importance, however, was the fact that on one side of the monument there was also an inscription in Greek; the first time that the two languages had been found in conjunction. It was badly weathered and difficult to read, but Fellows was able to make out that the text referred to a king of Lycia and hoped that, by comparing the Greek text with the Lycian, it 'will probably add to our knowledge of the latter'. Unfortunately, apart from confirming the name of the king as 'Kerei' and providing a construction date of sometime between 430 and 410 BC, the Lycian script (actually two different scripts) has remained largely undeciphered, almost 150 years later.

In the rocky valley to the north of the city were tombs that Fellows had missed on his first visit. One, now known as the sarcophagus of Merehi, was similar to the sarcophagus of Payava with its lid sculpted with battle scenes. Another, the oldest sarcophagus tomb of all, carried a sculpture of lions devouring a bull. And he looked with new eyes at the pillar tomb close to the theatre, the tomb with the flying figures. Since his last visit he had been in correspondence with an expert in Rome, who had given him an interpretation of the mysterious iconography:

The winged figures on the corners of the tomb you have discovered in Lycia, represented flying away with children, may with every probability be well supposed to have a reference to the story of the Harpies flying away with the daughters of King Pandarus. This fable we find related by Homer in the *Odyssey*, lib. xx, where they are stated to be left orphans, and the gods as endowing them with various gifts. Juno gives them prudence, Minerva instructs them in the art of the loom, Diana confers on them tallness of person, and lastly Venus flies up to Jupiter to provide becoming husbands for them; in the meantime, the orphans thus being left unprotected, the Harpies come and 'snatch the unguarded charge away'.

The interpretation fitted. Juno, Venus and Diana were clearly recognisable and, though the other gods were more worn, the

Above: *Fellows'
drawings of the
sculpture on the Harpy
Tomb at Xanthos.*

Harpies, those strange spirits of the wind who carried people off
to their deaths, were clear at each of the four corners of the tomb.
Strabo said that Pandarus was king of Lycia and was even
worshipped as a god at Pinara. Could this be the tomb of Pandarus himself? It was, and still is, impossible to say. Fellows
named the tomb the Harpy Tomb. 'This monument, I trust, may
ere long be deposited in our national Museum.'

This hope, of course, could only be fulfilled with the permission
of the Turkish government. When Fellows arrived back in
Rhodes in May 1840, he expected that permission to be waiting
for him. He opened the letter from the British Ambassador in
Constantinople, Lord Ponsonby, who wrote: 'The Porte objects
to the extent and to the *generality* of the demand, and I am much
afraid I shall not be able to obtain what you want ...'

Fellows was forced to return home, but the subsequent publication of his journal by John Murray, the same firm that
published Belzoni and Burckhardt, galvanised the British
government into applying to the Turks again. In October 1841,
news came to the British Museum that permission had been
granted and the letter was in the hands of the British Consul in
Smyrna. Fellows was asked by the Museum to provide plans and
descriptions of the objects to be brought back to London, but
Fellows, aware that other sculptures might come to light in the
process of removal, offered to go back to Lycia in person and at
his own expense and guide the operations.

Fellows' offer to the British Museum was accepted by letter
on 15 October and, within thirty-six hours, he was sailing from
Southampton to Malta. It was in Malta that, on 30 October, he
learnt that the man selected by the government to carry out the
operation was Captain Graves of HMS *Beacon*. He also learnt
that the government had failed to provide any funds:

This omission of placing funds in the hands of the Captain of
the expedition was the first impediment I encountered; but
knowing that the necessary expenses would be small, being

merely for tools, trifling presents to the peasantry, or the occasional hire of their cattle, I offered to provide the funds.

The second impediment was that the permission supposedly waiting in Smyrna turned out to be no permission at all, merely some letters acknowledging the fact that the British government had requested some stones and that the Turks had judged it expedient 'first of all to take some information respecting the stones in question'. The expedition seemed doomed to failure even before it had started, 'but I saw a ray of light.'

Fellows' concern was for the removal of the marbles from Xanthos. What he discovered was that Lord Ponsonby, in his request to the Turks, had included some carved stones from the fortress of Bodrum. As that castle was still in use and the walls would have collapsed if the stones had been removed, it is not surprising that the Turks had decided to stall and 'take some information'. Fellows re-applied direct to the Turkish authorities in Smyrna and was brought the reply that, as the Bodrum request had been withdrawn, and as, at Xanthos:

> ... the antiquities above mentioned are lying down here and there, and are of no use, (His) Excellency shall make no objection to the Captain's taking them away.

HMS *Beacon*, with its load of spades, crowbars and pickaxes poised for action, was nearing the Lycian coast on Boxing Day 1841. A few hours before putting ashore, Fellows was informed that neither the Captain nor any of his surveying officers would be part of the expedition but that it would be led by his First Lieutenant, a man who had never visited the country before and had only recently joined the ship. It scarcely augured well.

There were twenty in the party and the immediate task was to transport food and supplies by dinghy the nine miles up the river to the city:

> The River Xanthus is one of the most powerful, wild and unmanageable streams I ever saw: the volume of water is very great, far exceeding that of the Thames at Richmond; the stream rushes probably at the rate of five miles an hour.

It was impossible to row the boats: men had to jump overboard to keep them on course. Finally they had to attach ropes to them and haul them up, with only a cox and one other man left in the boat to avoid fallen trees and to probe continuously with a long pole for sandbanks and shallows. It took four long days and astonished the locals who gathered everywhere on hillocks to watch. And they were in for even greater astonishment:

Our evenings were not without amusement; the sailors soon made bats and balls, and cricket was perhaps for the first time played in Lycia; at all events the wonder expressed by the living generation showed that it was not a game known to the present inhabitants.

The immediate object of the expedition was to remove the bas-reliefs from the Harpy Tomb and the sculpture from the Horse Tomb – the tomb of Payava, 'but I expected to find much more, and I was not mistaken.'

Fellows had noticed, on the brow of a small cliff near the city gateway, the foundation of what he believed was a temple. Two sections of sculptured frieze found in the bushes in 1840 had strengthened his opinion and he determined to look for more. In the avalanche of stones that littered the precipice in front of the cliff, he found two more portions of frieze, and then:

> The 9th of January was Sunday, when all the men after service generally rambled about, and it often happened that it was the most prolific day for discoveries. In endeavouring to catch a scorpion, I crept into a hole among a pile of large blocks of white marble, and to my great joy saw above me, upon the underside of a stone, an Amazon on horseback, and a fine naked figure with a shield, the whole as white and perfect as when first sculptured.

The great stone blocks, weighing from 1 to 8 tons each, were prized out of the earth. They had formed the base not of a temple but a monument, and the marbles were the monument's decoration. In the next few days, 3 free-standing marble figures were discovered and over 40 sections of frieze. When reassembled back in Britain, they proved to be perhaps the most remarkable of all Fellows' discoveries at Xanthos. It was, Fellows argued, the victory monument of Harpagus, the commander of the Persian King Cyrus, whose destruction of the city in c. 545 BC was recorded by Herodotus:

> When Harpagus led his army towards Xanthus, the Lycians boldly advanced to meet him, and, though inferior in number, behaved with the greatest bravery. Being defeated and pursued into their city, they collected their wives, children and valuable effects into the citadel, and there consumed the whole in one immense fire. They afterwards, uniting themselves under the most solemn curses, made a private sally upon the enemy, and were every man put to death. Of those who now inhabit Lycia, calling themselves Xanthians, the whole are foreigners,

eighty families excepted; these survived the calamity of their country, being at that time absent on some foreign expedition.

This was further evidence for Fellows' observation that the remains at Xanthos were both Lycian (or pre-Harpagus) and Graeco-Lycian, the 'foreigners' mentioned by Herodotus. Further, from study of the frieze, Fellows argued that it depicted the destruction of Xanthos and even 'the removal of the emblems of Persian royalty into the conquered city':

> I do not think it improbable that we have in Herodotus a recital of the events recorded in these friezes ... we must bear in mind that the conquest was made about a hundred years before the time of Herodotus. I cannot but attribute the erection of this structure to the followers of Harpagus, commemorating his victory and serving as a tomb for his heroes: its erection during the lifetime of some of the conquerors would probably not be later than 500 BC.

He went even further. The sculptures were of such a high standard and so similar to those on the Acropolis in Athens that they 'lead us to suppose that Pericles, wishing to adorn Athens, sent to Asia Minor for workmen' – that, in other words, these particular marbles of Xanthos and the Elgin marbles from the Parthenon were by the same hand. Modern scholarship would not agree, usually dating the monument to about 370 BC and referring to it simply as the monument of the Nereids.

> The pleasure and excitement of these discoveries were entered into even by the sailors, who often forgot the dinner hour or worked after dusk to finish the getting out of a statue: indeed, great care was needed to prevent their being in too much haste to raise up the figures, for while the marble was saturated with the moisture of the earth, the slightest blow chipped off the light folds of the drapery.

Fellows devised plans for the removal of the sculptures from both the Horse and the Harpy tombs but they were dismissed as unfeasible and Captain Graves gave orders that neither tomb should be touched. Furthermore, he ordered that no stones should be taken downriver until proper supplies were brought from Malta. This, Fellows realised, would mean a whole season's work lost, plus the risk of visitors damaging the stones and, worst of all, the possibility of the Turkish authorities changing their minds:

> I took a solitary walk of some hours before I could decide upon my course of action. I need not say that I was annoyed ... I

Above: *Reconstruction (1850) of the Nereid Monument. It has recently been more accurately reconstructed in the British Museum.*

decided upon my plans. We had two carpenters who had hitherto worked with the men; these I employed solely in constructing crates and cases for securing the stones as soon as they were found.

This solved the problem of keeping the stones protected. Sculptures built into the walls of the Acropolis were lowered 200 feet down the rock by long ropes; the bas-reliefs of the Harpy Tomb, despite the Captain's orders, were prized off the sarcophagus' walls, with the coffin lid precariously propped up with stones to prevent it crashing down when the reliefs were extracted; work began on the Lion pillar and then, finally, on the most difficult job of all:

> The gunner informed me one morning at half-past eight o'clock, that they were going to pull down the Horse Tomb. I begged that he would delay for an hour, as I wished to mark with lines and numbers the various cracks and stones upon the middle story, and to map them accurately, as I felt sure it would fall in pieces as soon as the weight of the top was removed. This I did, and left the men to proceed with this monument also, for the removal of which I had suggested plans, differing altogether from those now adopted. My feelings were the same as with respect to the Harpy Tomb, and I did not interfere, except to request them to clear away previously all stones from around, and afterwards to preserve any fragment which might fall. The means adopted appeared to me to be more sailor-like than scientific; the men placed slings and cords over the top, which probably weighed ten tons, and making blocks fast to the neighbouring rocks, *hauled* the top off. As I anticipated, the centre fell in pieces, but the sculptured parts did not receive more injury than they probably would have done from a more scientific operation. The whole may be easily restored, and will again form one of the most elegant and interesting monuments I have ever seen.

There were additional problems. There was malaria; a boat bringing fresh supplies capsized offshore and two men drowned; another man, lost in the sandbanks of the river, came on to camp by foot, leaving his horse tethered overnight:

> On the following day Wilkinson went himself, and found only the saddle, a part of the bridle, and one hoof; the whole of the animal having been carried away and devoured by wolves. The marks of the blood and struggling of the horse pointed out the scene of its destruction.

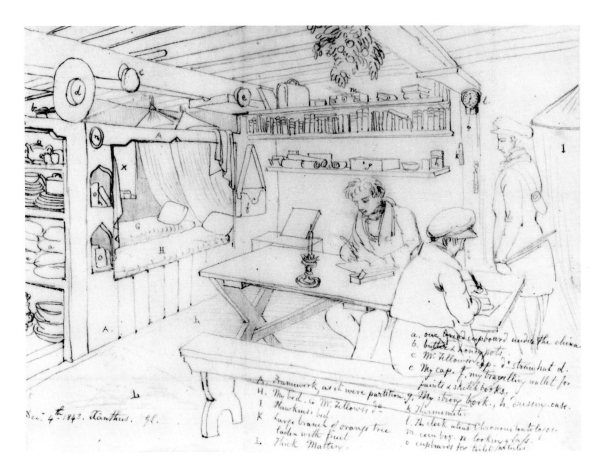

Within the drawing, handwritten annotations include:

a. our...cupboard under the china
b. butter & honey pots
c. Mr Fellows...
e. My cap. f. my travelling wallet for...
...prints & sketch books.
g. My strong book, h. dressing case.

Dec 4th 1843. Xanthus. gb.

A. framework, as it were partition.
H. My bed. G. Mr Fellows do.
i. Hawkins' bed
K. large branch of orange tree
laden with fruit
L. Thick Matting.

k. Thermometer.
l. the clock above Chronometer telescope.
m. compass, n. looking glass.
o. cupboard for toilet...

Above: *Scharf's
drawing of the house he
shared with Fellows
and Hawkins at
Xanthos in December
1843. Fellows is facing
front, writing at the
table.*

On 3 March HMS *Beacon* was off the Xanthos estuary with Fellows and his team on board, reluctantly leaving behind them the fruits of nine weeks' labour – 82 cases of marbles to be sent for from Malta. Seventy-eight cases were picked up in June and the other four, the sculptures from the Horse Tomb, the next year.

Fellows was knighted in 1845 'in acknowledgement of his services in the removal of the Xanthian antiquities to this country'. He was reimbursed for his expenses by the British Museum; he married, twice, and retired to farm in the Isle of Wight. He died in London on 8 November 1860, aged sixty-one.

The marbles are now all on display in the British Museum with the Nereid Monument, the most elaborate of all Lycian tombs, restored and reconstructed and in a room of its own. However, as Lieutenant Spratt, one of the navy rescue team, wrote at the time as he watched the dismantling of the Horse Tomb:

We had to regret the down-fall of the tomb of Payava (or 'winged-chariot tomb') as the most beautiful of the Xanthian monuments, feeling that if it could not be transported without mutilation to England, it had been better left where it stood, the ornament of the fallen city, and an object of pilgrimage to the Oriental traveller. Its remains can convey no idea of the original elegance of this splendid sepulchre.

Chapter Five

THE TEMPLES OF KING SOLOMON
Karl Mauch at Great Zimbabwe

And King Solomon made a navy of ships ... And they came to Ophir and fetched from thence gold, four hundred and twenty talents, and brought it to Solomon. So King Solomon exceeded all the kings of the earth for riches and wisdom.*

Karl Mauch was born in Würtemberg, Germany, in 1837. His apparent discovery in southern Africa of King Solomon's mines and a home of the Queen of Sheba was to excite the imagination of Europe for over half a century. In the long term, it was to lead to one of the greatest social, anthropological and political controversies of all time.

Mauch landed on the east coast of southern Africa in 1865, intending to explore, write, map the landscape, test the soils and analyse the rocks. As a result he became the first man to produce a complete map of the Transvaal and, in the Bechuanaland Protectorate in 1866, one of the first white men to discover gold. It gave him a problem:

I had before me the alternatives either to take advantage of the discoveries and become unfaithful to my former plan, or else decide to carry on with my explorations and so to neglect my pecuniary interests.

He opted to continue his explorations: he was temperamentally more suited to the role of lone scientist in the bush than corporate businessman in the boardroom, and, perhaps more important:

* First Book of Kings 9: 26–8.

... every attempt to dig for gold would bring one into mortal collision with the owners of the land, the warlike Matabele.

Mauch's decision changed the entire course of his life. Whilst the coastal areas of south Africa and some parts of the hinterland were already settled by the British, the Dutch and the Portuguese, further inland lay a vast, unexplored territory that tradition associated with the lost Biblical land of Ophir, source of Solomon's fabulous treasure. It was to this land that Mauch was inexorably drawn.

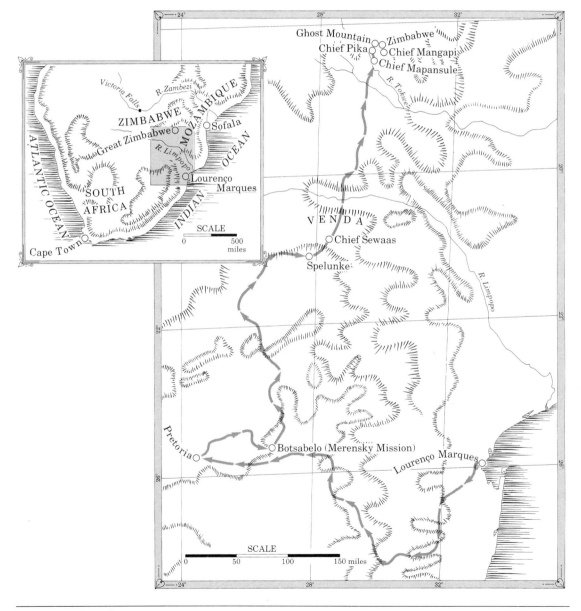

The Biblical account of King Solomon's 'Mines' appears in Chapter Nine of the First Book of Kings, Verses 26–8, but on the geographical whereabouts of the land of Ophir it is silent. Over the years, fuelled by travellers' tales of the Arabs who were trading along the East African coast as early as the ninth century, Solomon's name became linked with southern Africa, and it was here that Milton placed it when he wrote *Paradise Lost* in the 1660s:

... thought Ophir, to the realm
Of Congo, and Angola farthest south ...

But the first written references to gold mines in southern Africa, and of the existence of a great ruined city, date from a century earlier. In 1552, the Portuguese Joao de Barros had written:

There are other mines in a district called Toroa, which by another name is known as the Kingdom of Butua ... and these mines are the most ancient known in the country, and they are all in the plain, in the midst of which is a square fortress, of masonry within and without, built of stones of marvellous size, and there appears to be no mortar joining them. The wall is more than 25 spans in width ... This edifice is almost surrounded by hills, upon which are others resembling it in the fashioning of the stones and the absence of mortar, and one of them is a tower more than 12 fathoms high ... The natives of the country call all these edifices Symbace.

Above: *Karl Mauch (1837–75).*

An even earlier account appears in a letter written by Diego de Alcacova to the king of Portugal in 1506:

And, Sir, a man might go from Sofala to a city which is called Zumubany which is large, in which the king always resides, in ten or twelve days, if you travel as in Portugal.

This, by modern calculation, might well bring a traveller from the coast of Mozambique inland into the vicinity of Great Zimbabwe.

Mauch was originally unaware of these descriptions. In his journal he writes that he first heard of the existence of ruins in 1867 and that he determined to visit them after their general location was described by a local man in 1868, and thereby:

I shall make it the highest duty in my profession to add honour to the name of the German nation.

He planned to make his journey with the Reverend Dr Alexander Merensky, head of a German religious mission. Merensky, as a

Christian, was fascinated by the possibility of discovering the lost land of Ophir and, as early as the 1860s, was talking of Solomon and Sheba and even 'ruins with Egyptian antiquities'. Mauch was predisposed to believe these stories as he himself had noted the Semitic facial characteristics of some of the local blacks:

> ... similar to the children of Israel, a similarity that one later finds as well among the Makalaka (Shona) and Banyai (Batonga). To what does this point?

Mauch, now having 'read much about the presumed site of Ophir', considered the most likely location for the ruins to be in the region between the Limpopo and Zambezi rivers. He set out on 3 July 1871, alone. Merensky, because of a raid on the mission, was unable to go with him and anyway considered Mauch's proposed route:

> ... definitely dangerous. I have advised him to travel through Bampedi country, but he went further to the east towards the Baramapulana, who have to be greatly feared as a result of the Boer war. I fear the worst.

Mauch himself, however, had already anticipated the worst. The four years that he had spent travelling in unexplored regions had taught him what to expect. The black tribes, as well as being hostile to one another, could be hostile to a white man. The land itself could be harsh and the heat intolerable; there could be a danger from wild animals, from snakes; the mosquito brought fever. There could be a shortage of water; a lack of food:

> Our hunger was at times so terrible that one day we had nothing else to eat but our sandals of buffalo leather.

And eating local plants was not always a sensible option:

> I collected a considerable number of the hard-as-bones beans, boiled them for a long time and, although they would not become tender, I began to relish them and left part of them to my companions who then eagerly began to devour them. But only a few minutes later we began to vomit violently – a fairly merciful punishment for our imprudence. This taught me never again to test in such a manner the medicinal reaction to an unknown plant.

Mauch planned his expedition with great care and precision, and, in his account, usually so Germanic in its matter-of-factness, betrays an unexpected sense of humour:

I could not very well follow the demands of elegance or fashion, not even the demands usually required for man to clothe himself according to the season. I had to consider it far more practical to travel with one suit only, probably for several years.

The suit was made of leather and had roomy pockets. He had a leather cap, thick leather boots studded with nails and thick flannel underwear:

This costume was certainly well-wearing, but with the proverbial African heat, its weight was at first insupportable. By and by one gets accustomed to it and though one is inclined to call the weight of the clothing a mistake, it is however compensated by various advantages. The leather garment is made so loose and comfortable that there is a layer of air between it and the body which nearly always retains the same temperature, be it hot as at noon or cool as at night. Moreover, the surface is smooth so that, in case a naughty buffalo or a short tempered rhinoceros should suddenly force the wanderer to seek his safety in flight through dangerous thorn-bushes, only a few points of contact are offered on which could occur any of those well known rectangular tears the like of which we can observe in ordinary clothing material when we want to push quickly through rose-bushes or blackberry bushes. Another, not to be disdained advantage I must mention: those small animals which thrive amongst filth and against which even the cleanest African tribes cannot win, find no turn-ups wherein to establish their breeding places.

He carried an umbrella to protect him from the sun and a woollen blanket to keep him warm at night. For food and defence, he carried a gun 'that must be able to kill an elephant as well as a rabbit' and which, when the bullets ran out, was sufficiently adaptable to fire glass beads. He also carried a powder horn, a long knife, and a revolver because 'it impresses the primitive natives greatly when being demonstrated'. He looked, he thought, like Robinson Crusoe.

Yet his most important equipment were his astronomical and meteorological instruments, both to find his way ahead and to calculate the quickest route to the coast if he had to flee: a sextant, two compasses, a pocket watch, a barometer, a thermometer and a magnifying glass. For sampling rocks he also took a hammer. These instruments he always carried on his person; other articles – his books, files, sewing kit, pincers, medicines and trade goods for buying food or favours – were carried by the African porters he had with him. Just how many porters he had at any one time, Mauch was never quite sure; porters were a constant source of irritation and their sudden burst of activity that delayed his departure was a portent for the future:

The one had not yet prepared his snuff, another had first to consult his prophetic woods, bones, shells and roots; the third had to hand over for the duration of his absence the care of his wealth, which consisted of one solitary goat, to his half-brother who lived nearby; a fourth one had begun a love-affair and wanted to present some beads to his beautiful one, as a farewell gift for which, naturally, he had to take recourse to me; my interpreter had promised a lump of lead of a certain size to his friend but had forgotten it at home; furthermore, all of them had not yet eaten and drunk.

But Mauch was a hostage to fortune:

In these circumstances one has to exert one's patience so as not to assume on one's face the wrong expression and to hold one's hand fully open so as to hand out presents. The people know I have need of them, that they are indispensable to me.

By the end of July, travelling north-north-east, Mauch had reached the region called Spelunke, the home of Chief Lomondo:

... an uncouth fellow with a complete animal-like expression on his face. While his eating-tools had perfectly been developed behind his extraordinary thick lips, his already low forehead was hidden by a once red cloth. His demeanor completely fitted that which one was able to read from his animal features. He would make a perfect creature to play the role of a cannibal, and I could hardly doubt my interpreter's pronouncement that in fact he was one.

Another's day march and he was the guest in the kraal of another chief, Chief Sewaas:

Here he sits, not using a mat, with his behind directly on the manure – cutting a peculiar figure. His full-moon face is rather greasy but half covered by his beard. All around and from underneath his headcovering – a soldier's cap adorned with some rooster feathers – hang artificially curled locks which are richly smeared with grease ... Constantly cheerful, happy, joking with his companions, his tongue never took a rest and through the strong development of saliva and as he often knocked his tongue against his teeth I was not infrequently exposed to a fine, drizzling rain. Often he offered me some snuff

Opposite: Marble relief of the God Dionysus, relaxing in the ruins of the Roman theatre at Perge, Turkey.

Right: *The northern harbour of the Romano-Lycian city of Phaselis. In 1838, Charles Fellows noticed 'a couple of large sarcophagi which lay on the beach and appeared to have been washed out by the violence of the sea'.*

Below: *The theatre of the extensive and splendid city of Pinara. Set into the base of a small hill, Fellows found it 'in a very perfect state'.*

Below right: *At Antiphellus, Fellows wrote: 'The form of the sarcophagus found here is peculiar to the district*

of Lycia. The shape of the lid or top somewhat resembles the pointed gothic arch.' The stone is also carved to resemble the wooden beams of Lycian houses. This example from the fourth century BC is one of the best preserved in Turkey.

Opposite: *Rock-cut 'house' tombs and a pillar tomb on the hillside near the Necropolis at Xanthos, Turkey, dating from the fifth century BC.*

Top right: *Ruins of the Acropolis at Great Zimbabwe as seen from the air.*

Centre right: *The 'royal' enclosure in the Acropolis. The door is the only original to survive. The daga floor was so badly excavated in the late nineteenth century that most evidence of occupation was lost.*

Bottom right: *The Great Enclosure or House of the Great Woman, which Mauch first saw on 5 September 1871. He became convinced that it was built by order of the Queen of Sheba.*

Left: *The conical tower inside the Great Enclosure. Probably a symbol of royal authority, it was built by Africans c. AD 1400.*
Below left: *Decoration on the wall of the Great Enclosure. The stone beams protruding from the top of the wall (which go down into it) were probably intended to give greater strength to a wall built without mortar.*
Overleaf: *Tikal, in Guatemala. The crowns of the temples rise above the trees of the jungle. 'I entered the house on top and saw in the distance, one-quarter to one-third of a mile off, two other pyramids even higher than the one I was in.' (Alfred Maudslay, Easter Sunday 1881)*
Inset left: *Temple I, the temple of the Great Jaguar, built c. AD 700.*
Inset right: *Stela no. 9 in the ceremonial heart of Tikal, the Great Plaza, showing a Mayan priest. Early classic, Maya date 9.2.0.0.0. (AD 475).*

Right: *The central
Acropolis at Tikal
with, in the distance,
Temple V, almost 200
feet high and engulfed
by the jungle.*

from a box which formerly had served for the storage of tinder-caps. I preferred to light my small pipe, however, so as to paralyse the aroma of his perspiration by means of strong clouds of smoke.

Mauch had no great love for his fellow white men, especially the Afrikaners of Dutch extraction, whom he regarded as lying, lazy and ignorant. His 'love' for the blacks, however, got even less the more he got to know them:

> During the day-time I am plagued by the black, two-legged rabble that in its proud stupidity thinks itself superior to the whites. They beg for anything they see and if it is not given to them voluntarily, they just grab it.

And there was no relief at night:

> A hell of vermin begin to torture me and a complete menagerie could have been established. Lice, fleas, cockroaches, sand-fleas, spiders, etc. compelled me to transfer my resting-place into the open so as not to be scratching or rolling over the whole night through.

By 10 August, Mauch, constantly irritated and frustrated in his progress by demands to socialise, drink local beer and eat maize porridge, finally reached the Limpopo river, the present border between South Africa and Zimbabwe. As the entire area was completely unmapped, Mauch had to chart his own course, relying solely on his instruments:

Wednesday, 16 August 1871
6.30–7.30 One hour at two and a half miles an hour. East-north-east. A low rand to the left.
8.00–9.00 One hour at two and a half miles an hour. North to the Nuanetsi (river, a sand bed of about 200 paces width with very little water ...)
Midday. 59 Degrees 44 minutes. Error plus 22 seconds. Therefore latitude 21 degrees 29 minutes 22 seconds south.
During the observation I was suddenly hit on the back of my head by a burning log, so that the glowing embers shot past on both sides. One of my men who was fetching water mistook me for a large carnivore and made a lucky throw.

By 23 August he had reached the banks of the River Tokwe. He had no more additional information about the whereabouts of the ruins but, from Merensky's information, he estimated that they were about another fifty miles north. The country became very wild, with huge bare granite outcrops packed tightly together; the heat was insupportable and the porters mutinous. There were now nine of them, plus his 'useless and lying' interpreter, and thirty-one hangers-on, all of whom had to be watered and fed.

Ten miles away he could just see the site of the kraal of Mapansule, an important chief of the Banyai tribe, by the faint outline of trees on a granite crop. He decided to head straight for it, forcing his porters ahead through hunger and feeding them only after they'd carried his goods. The plan backfired. An hour before sunrise on 26 August the men got up and, laden with bows and arrows, moved off to shoot guinea fowl. They didn't return. They had taken with them some cloth and some tobacco.

Mauch, alone, gathered his remaining goods close to himself round the fire and waited for daylight. He kept watch all day, afraid to move. By evening, as nothing untoward had happened, he felt safe and fetched water from a spring. He was gone only a few moments but when he returned one of his packages had been ripped open and his complete store of beads stolen:

> I had everything to fear here, not only the loss of my goods, but also the loss of my life, either through poisoned food or by arrow. Thus I find myself alone as keeper of my possessions, on guard day and night, capable of moving only for 100 paces.

He could not flee west for fear of being killed by hostile tribes; east were cannibals ('I would make a fine roast for Moseila'); and south 'they would certainly pay me with murder.' Mauch was trapped:

> As the second night followed the first my position was desperate and it was therefore not surprising when the thought occurred to me to lay hands on my own life before I would succumb after slow torture.

There was still the way north, to Mapansule, however, and beyond him the home of a mysterious white man called Adam Render, who, rumour had it, was a German hunter who had abandoned his wife and children in south Africa to marry two local women. As Mauch was contemplating what to do, rescue came suddenly in the form of seven young men who arrived to escort him to the very place he was planning to go – to Chief Mapansule. Within five minutes he was again on the march:

> W, then NW. High kopjes (hills) emerge in great irregularity up to 1000 feet above the plain; now as bare bell-shapes, then as broken and wonderfully wooded mountains from which clear waters descend in plenty; fertile soil in which maize

stalks grow to extraordinary height and circumference; individual springs at the foot of immense boulders, shaded by tall water trees with splendid dark foliage ... Footpaths crisscrossing themselves furnished proof of a numerous population, though one could not see their huts which they build high up between broken boulders.

Mapansule's kraal was on the highest peak in the region, but Mapansule himself was a disappointment. Instead of a young, strong, vivacious leader, Mauch met only a little old man half hidden under a home-made cloth of birch bark. They had no conversation as Mauch no longer had his interpreter: they sat and looked at each other until Mauch got bored.

What Mauch had regarded as rescue by Mapansule was, in fact, capture, as Mapansule, to gain status amongst his fellow chiefs, planned to keep Mauch as his 'white captive'. Mauch found himself in an even more desperate situation than before:

Should I agree, I condemned myself to a pitiful life, should I disagree I risked the double danger of losing my life, but as, in any case, it was already in the balance, everything, even the most improbable had to be tried.

He wrote to Adam Render, asking for help. Mauch did not approve of Render, believing he had disgraced the German nation by 'sinking to the state of a kaffir by marrying two kaffir women'. The desperate situation, however, called for a desperate remedy and Render turned out to be a much more likeable man than Mauch had been led to believe. He prised Mauch from Mapansule's grasp by placating the chief with a gift and hurried Mauch to the neighbouring village of Chief Pika, three hours' march away. This was to be Mauch's home for the next nine months.

Mauch's kraal was on a ledge half-way up a steep mountain, safe from raids by animals and people and looking out over some of the most beautiful countryside in southern Africa. The most exciting development was that:

... according to the natives, white people had once lived in this country.

The Makalaka or Banyai people (a group of the Shona tribe) had only moved into the area some fifty years ago. They had discovered tools such as:

... a piece of iron which ... could have been a miner's pick. They affirmed with conviction that they would not have been able to make such things.

Mauch began to investigate, climbing the mountain to a higher terrace where, concealed by trees and undergrowth, he was shown broken clay pipes and piles of slag which indicated that iron had once been smelted there:

> Poor as these remains are, the information of the blacks that these stem from whites is, nevertheless, very important.

Conversation over a beer with the chief and his sons revealed more exciting pieces of information:

> ... the presence of quite large ruins which could never have been built by blacks. Could these be the ruins of the Banyai for which I have been looking?

There was also talk of a mysterious pot with four legs that walked about on the summit of the nearby Ghost Mountain. No native had actually seen it because he was too afraid to go and look. The pot was apparently aggressive. In the past, one old man had gone mad seeing it, another had his hair shaved off and a third, who pushed his hand inside it, lost his fingers when the lid clamped shut.

On 3 September 1871, accompanied by Render and Pika's sons, Mauch started to climb Ghost Mountain. As they approached the summit the blacks' fears increased. Mauch offered them his gun for protection but even after the two whites had rested on the summit, the blacks were reluctant to come nearer:

> Though the view was magnificent, that was not what we were looking for and there was no trace of the pot. It was a myth.

But there was something much more exciting. On the mountaintop itself were some half-filled pits which, Mauch thought, was further evidence of white activity. Then:

> Suddenly the thought occurred to me that from here one ought to see the ruins which had been mentioned during our conversation yesterday, and to my great joy someone pointed out to me in an ESE direction, at a distance of about 8 miles, a hill on which ... were largish walls that had been built by whites. 'Bravo' I exclaimed, 'that is what I have been seeking since 1868. What luck! And how unexpected! – Only a few days before, occupied with serious thoughts of death, and to-day standing before the most brilliant success of my travels. God be praised!'

Mauch couldn't go to the ruins immediately: it was impossible to know whether the local people would be friendly or hostile, so it was decided that he and Render should investigate the area for the ostensible purpose of hunting. Mauch, eager for every snippet of information, spent the following day asking questions:

I obtained very little information regarding the ruins during the evening's conversation, but what I was told was so astonishingly incredible that I did not wish to listen to more of it and rather preferred to rely on my eyes, and chance.

They set out on 5 September early in the morning, approaching the ruins by a roundabout route so as not to alert the people of Chief Mangapi, who owned the land. After two and a half hours' walk they reached a small hill from the top of which they could see, on the summit of the hill opposite, something that might have been a wall. It was rather disappointing. For another half hour they walked along a little valley at the foot of the opposite hill, which was about 400 feet high. The blacks regarded it with awe:

A long line of tumbled-down stones guided us and in places one could still recognize the former shape of a wall. The stones are granite and about double the size of our bricks. On three sides of the oblong they are smoothly cut, the fourth, facing inwards, has been left unworked. Nowhere is the wall higher than 3–4 feet and it has usually fallen down or is covered. The western slope of the rocky mountain is likewise covered with similar stone fragments. Nothing further could be noticed, but that these probably had been walls of a fortification.

So as not to break with custom, Mauch sent a messenger to the chief, whose huts he could see on the top of the hill. As he waited for the man's return he explored further: a short distance away he saw what looked like a round building:

Left: *Mauch's sketch of Great Zimbabwe, showing the Acropolis hill and the Great Enclosure in the right foreground.*

Presently I stood before it and beheld a wall of a height of about 20 feet, of similar granite bricks. I did not have to look for an entrance long, for very close by there was a place where a kind of foot-path, which apparently is used quite frequently, led over rubble into the interior. Following this path I stumbled over masses of rubble and parts of walls and dense thickets, and big trees prevented me from gaining an overall view from any point. Several attempts to obtain such were in vain and, finally, I stopped in front of a tower-like structure which was built quite near to the opposite side from which I entered. It stood there apparently quite undamaged. Altogether it rose to a height of about 30 feet. The lower 10 feet are cylindrical with a diameter of 15–16 feet, the upper 20 feet are conical with a diameter of about 8 feet at the top; completely similar kind of building with trimmed granite bricks without any mortar, but with bonding according to the art of building. In vain did I look for an entrance or a walled-up opening, in vain did I try to discover the reason for this structure.

Was this the place the Portuguese de Barros had written about in 1552: the 'square fortress built of stones of marvellous size with no mortar joining them ... of a tower more than twelve fathoms high'? In the King Solomon Bible story (I Kings 6:7–22):

And the house, when it was in building, was built of stone made ready before it was brought thither ... The door for the middle chamber was in the right side of the house: and they went up with winding stairs into the middle chamber and out of the middle into the third. So he built the house, and finished it; and covered the house with beams and boards of cedar ... And the whole house he overlaid with gold ...

Mauch's cursory view of the ruins was interrupted by the arrival of Chief Mangapi himself, who led Mauch up the hill to his huts:

As this was only a casual visit to initiate the establishment of friendship, we hardly mentioned the ruins in our conversation. Suffice it that I obtained visual sight of their existence and permission to return again in a few days' time.

Four days later Mauch was back at the site, but Mangapi wanted to talk and beg powder and gunshot:

He did not want to grant my wish to visit (the ruins) the following day, giving as an excuse the fact that my short visit looked to him more like espionage. Although quite correct, I could not very well admit this.

Mauch was forced to spend another long day with Mangapi:

> It seemed to me as if a year of my life was disappearing. Absolutely nothing to do but sit and listen to the chatter, to drink freshly brought beer, to eat goat's meat and to sleep, without being allowed to have a look at the country.

Mauch eventually got back to the site on 11 September. He didn't stop at the 'round edifice' in the valley but went immediately to the ruins on the hill, excited by the stories he had been told by the blacks:

> There was supposed to exist a tin bowl filled with various things and a great quantity of beautiful white linen was supposed to be hidden at a certain place. At another place, it was said, large iron rods were to be seen, then again, inscriptions and, further, drawings of birds' feet and carved heads of children, etc etc. Small wonder that I presented the chief, who had promised to show me all, with many beads which should now be thrown down this kloof or on to that crag as sacrifice. He left everything to me and my companions while he himself rested once again and showed great fear of going any further. So I went through a narrow entrance between boulders into the interior of the ruins. After prolonged wandering over and between rocks and rubble, after troublesome and dangerous pushing through dense undergrowth in which a shrub-like nettle played not a minor role, I came to the definite conclusion that these ruins must be the fallen remains of a very strong fortification of earlier times. I noticed some very narrow corridors (hardly 2 feet wide) formed by 15–20 feet high walls still standing, as well as another covered one which leads into the ruins below a large boulder, but it is partly in ruins, partly walled up. The cross-beams are of trimmed stone and, indeed, of a peculiar, easily split, mica slate. Wood appears to have been used only exceptionally. Most of the walls join one another and the outer wall in a curve. This (outer wall) is best preserved on the southern slope and is 30 feet high over a length of about 120 feet and, from the bottom to the top, 12 to 6 feet thick. It is built on the extreme edge of a mighty rock precipice so that only sufficient room is left for one man walking barefoot or for a baboon to proceed along the foot of the wall. It is especially remarkable how strongly this wall had been built without any mortar and that it is succumbing only very slowly, in spite of wind and decay.

Mauch noted that protruding from the top of one of these walls were long thin rods of stone, 4 foot 6 inches in diameter and

Above: *Decorated beam and soapstone bowl discovered by Mauch in the Acropolis.*

Below: *Mauch's sketches of the decoration on the walls of the Great Enclosure.*

about 10 feet high. He guessed they were altogether about 20 feet long and served to strengthen the wall, although one rod was decorated. This rod and a small soapstone dish were the only two 'relics' that he found. He drew them in his notebook. Other relics, he thought, had either been stolen or had been hidden in caves:

> In some places it is evident that walls have been built in front of caves by the Kaffirs according to their sense of art, for they have no notion of the regular laying of stones or of bonding. They even think that the walls were built at a time when the stones were still very soft, otherwise it would have been impossible for the whites who built these walls to form them into a square shape!

Mauch climbed back down the hill to the great round enclosure in the valley, a distance of about a quarter of a mile. The two structures, the hill fort and the enclosure, seemed to be linked by buildings, but they were too overgrown for Mauch to be sure.

The great enclosure ruin is described by Mauch as a 'rondeau'. It consists of a great circular wall about 24 feet high and varying from 8 to 12 feet thick. It is constructed of unmortared stones similar to the ruin on the hill and has the characteristic protruding rods. Mauch found that the entrance to the rondeau was through a single low doorway. Inside the enclosure was a jumble of tall trees and fallen masonry, apart from the 30-foot-high conical tower which was apparently perfectly preserved:

> An ascent to the summit by means of creepers which grow all over it, taught me that it is not hollow from the top but filled with small stones, and on none of its sides could a walled-up entrance be discovered. That it, actually, was the most important object is shown by some nearby decorations and attempts to reinforce it. For it stands between two very high walls which are only 10 feet apart. A narrow path of access, coming from N through one of them, shows alternate double layers of grey or white granite and black phonolite, that is, on either side of the access but only covering a length of 6 feet.

Mauch sketched the two examples of decoration. Again, there were Biblical echoes (I Kings 7:17): '... nets of chequer work, and wreaths of chain work'.

Mauch was forced to postpone any further investigation as Chief Mangapi wanted further conversation. Mauch returned to the hilltop but, on the way, discovered a curious arc-shaped object made of iron, which he considered further proof 'that a civilised nation must once have lived here'. Mauch questioned Mangapi:

No further information about the 'when' and 'how' could be obtained. The name of the hill with the ruins is Zimbabye or, possibly, Zimbaoë. The former is the name given to it by the local Makalakas or Banyais. It is without doubt that these are the ruins sought by Merensky.

Mauch could only guess at the age of the ruins; that they were very old was shown by the fact that builders had not learnt how to make mortar. He also guessed that the ruins were probably 'merely an imitation of buildings known in former times'. He sought further information from the locals but they were, at first, reluctant to talk. However, he did find out that ceremonies had been held in the hill ruins until comparatively recently, and that the enclosure ruin in the plain was called 'mumbu huru' or 'The House of the Great Woman' or 'Great Wife'; that is, the queen's house or palace. Confirmation came from an unexpected source, from a man living with his family in isolation from his neighbours and regarding himself as not belonging to any of the local tribes. The man's name was Bebereke and he described how, a long time ago, after a successful harvest, people would gather at the hill ruins and the high priest would sacrifice to Mali (or Mambo, the father, God) two oxen and a cow, make libations in a secret cave and return to the people crying out how God had made everything right for them. The people would reply by playing cymbals and drums and blowing horns:

> The man from whom I received this information is one of the sons of the last High-priest Tenga, who had conducted the ceremonies about 30 to 40 years ago, but (who) had been attacked one evening by his enemy Mangapi (father of the present chief) and had been murdered in a treacherous manner, without any of his sons receiving the information as to where various objects, needed for the sacrifice, had been hidden.

Mauch believed that the story he had tried to investigate of the great and fearful walking pot was, perhaps, the surviving folk memory of the ceremonies that Bebereke had described. Even more important, the ceremonies linked the ruins with the Bible:

> The similarity of these sacrifices to those ordained in the Israelitic cult is unmistakable. The basis is actually there though much is lacking in details ... Relying on this, I believe that I do not err when I suppose that the ruin on the mountain is an imitation of the Solomonic Temple on Mount Moria, the ruin on the plain a copy of that palace in which the Queen of Sheba dwelled during her visit to Solomon.

Proof of the correctness of this surmise was to be had in the name that Bebereke and others gave to the rondeau – The House of the Great Woman. There was no greater woman than the Queen of Sheba, to whom Solomon gave 'all her desire' as well as 'his royal bounty' before she returned 'to her own country, she and her servants' (I Kings 10:13).

But why had Sheba had built, in this African 'colony', copies of Solomon's temple in Jerusalem? Mauch surmised that when she had stayed with Solomon she had been converted to Judaism and commemorated the fact by building replicas in her own territories. But how had she been able to build something so technically difficult? The obvious answer, Mauch thought, was that she had been helped by the clever Phoenicians. The Zimbabwe ruins:

> ... conform best with known Phoenician buildings. Natives and Arabs would have built differently and the Portuguese already had knowledge of the existence of the ruins.

Although Mauch's presence at the ruins had led to 'unpleasant suspicions', even outright hostility, he was determined to see them again, make an accurate drawing of the House of the Great Woman and, if at all possible, find further confirmation of his theory. However, six months passed before he felt safe enough to risk it. He set out on 6 March 1872, again guided by Render:

> No sooner was the rocky drift of the Tokwane crossed than war-cries were heard from the opposite mountainside, the war trumpet was sounded and the call to arms given with the order to descend upon us. An exchange of unfriendly remarks took place during which the indignant enemies became aware of the fact that we were well armed and therefore would be dangerous enemies. Because of this their call to arms was countermanded and permission for free passage given. We would most certainly have sent them home with bloody heads, had an attack taken place, for the mission which we pursued was too important for us to allow it to be stopped right at the beginning. We soon reached the foot of the mountain ...

When they reached the ruins, Render climbed to the hill ruins to cause a diversion to keep Mangapi busy, whilst Mauch, armed with revolver and sketchbook, crept through the long grasses towards the enclosure. While the grass kept him safely hidden it also hid the layout of the ruined buildings:

> ... the ruined walls were hidden to such an extent by trees, thorns, nettles, creepers, shrubs, grass and dry branches, that I had to do the sketch without accurate measurements.

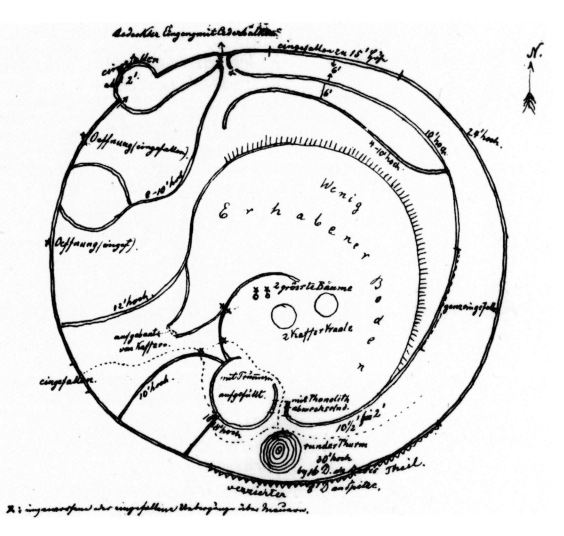

He also had to do it quickly to prevent further trouble by being late at Mangapi's. As he left the enclosure, he had time to hack off a splinter of wood from the lintel of the enclosure entrance:

> I suppose ... it must be cedar-wood. This would be a dead, though very telling witness to the fact that these ruins are an imitation of Salomo's buildings.

Whilst Mauch talked to Mangapi, Render sneaked off and took further wood samples from the lintels in the hill ruins. They were the same wood as Mauch had discovered in the enclosure. For Mauch, all the evidence that he had found, both visual and verbal, seemed to prove the ideas that he had first heard from Merensky five years before. Doubt, surmise and speculation became certainty:

Above: *Mauch's plan of the Great Enclosure. The main entrance* (top) *faces the Conical Tower* (bottom). *The lines inside the enclosure are stone walls which, unknown to Mauch, once linked daga huts that have since disappeared.*

It can be taken as a fact that the wood which we obtained actually is cedar-wood and from this that it cannot come from anywhere else but from the Libanon. Furthermore only the Phoenicians could have brought it here; further Salomo used a lot of cedar-wood for the building of the temple and of his palaces; further: including here the visit of the Queen of Seba and, considering Zimbabye or Zimbaoë or Simbaöe written in Arabic (of Hebrew I understand nothing), one gets as a result that the great woman who built the *rondeau* could have been none other than the Queen of Seba ... Indeed, to make such a great discovery was now my fate! The Lord be praised!

He summarised his theories in his journal:

Today I dare to close this account with:
  The Queen of Seba is the Queen of Simbaöe,
  Psalm 72,10 – The Seba mentioned there is Simbaöe,
  Math. 2,11 – Of the three Kings the one from here, the others
        from Arabia and India
  The reported pot is possibly an Ark of the Covenant.
  The ruins are copies of Salomo's temple and palace.

And Ophir, he concluded, was the port of Sofala (on the coast of present-day Mozambique) where 'the oldest navigating peoples exchanged their home products against those of the interior', against the gold of Zimbabwe, 250 miles inland. Mauch never saw the ruins again:

This visit is likely to cause more ill-feeling and any further visit could become dangerous, and as the next work there would consist of clearing the ruins in order to make archaeological discoveries ... I have to be content with the knowledge that this visit to the ruins was also my last one.

Given the difficult conditions under which Mauch first saw Great Zimbabwe and the harsh conditions under which he was allowed to inspect them, as well as the state of the ruins themselves – overgrown and, in part, modified by recent use – his plans and descriptions are surprisingly accurate. But he saw the ruins, of course, through the eyes of a European brought up in the Judaeo-Christian tradition, at a time when the primary function of archaeology was to 'prove' the authenticity of the Bible, and against a political background of the European scramble for Africa, a scramble to which the Germans were latecomers. Mauch wanted to discover Great Zimbabwe and was predisposed to believe that it was Ophir. He had written in a letter four months before he reached the ruins:

I shall make it the highest duty in my profession to add honour to the name of the German nation ... The discovery of the ruins of Ophir would be a point which would have to be envied by other nations.

His ideas were to prove much less reliable than his site plan.

One of the first men to visit the ruins after Mauch was Willi Posselt in 1889. He came at the same time as Cecil Rhodes' Pioneer Column was establishing control over the area for the British South Africa Company, and he left an important description of the site: important because it describes a feature of the ruins missed by Mauch, the carved soapstone birds in the ruins on Zimbabwe hill:

> There (near Andizibi's hut) in an enclosure which served as a cattle kraal, I saw four soap stones, each carved in the image of a bird and facing east; one stone shaped like a millstone and about nine inches in diameter, and a stone dish, about eighteen inches in diameter, with a number of figures carved on the border. The 'bird' stones were planted in an old ruined wall within the enclosure.
>
> I examined the best specimen of the four 'bird' stones, and decided to dig it out; but while doing so, Andizibi and his followers became very excited, and rushing round with their guns and assegais, I fully expected them to attack us ...

Above: *A soapstone bird from Great Zimbabwe.*

Andizibi was soon reconciled:

> I was able to tell Andizibi that I had no intention of removing the stone, but that I was quite prepared to buy it. This evidently pacified him, for I was not molested further.

Posselt returned the next day and exchanged two of the bird stones for some blankets, but, as the birds were perched on five-foot-long pedestals, they were too heavy to carry. He cut them from the pedestals, taking one away and hiding the rest for collection in the future before returning downhill to the Great Enclosure. It was still covered with trees and bushes and he was only able to enter the ruin by climbing the great circular wall and lowering himself down the other side on creepers. It was not a fruitful exercise:

> I could not find any trace of human remains or any implements, nor was the hope of discovering any treasure rewarded with success.

Posselt didn't return to collect his birds. They were found, along with others, two years later by Theodore Bent. The Pioneer

Top: *The Great
Enclosure
photographed c. 1890.*
Above: *The Conical
Tower, photographed
by Bent in 1891.*

Column, now established in Mashonaland, had asked the Royal
Geographical Society in London to provide an experienced man
who could properly examine the Zimbabwe ruins and other ruins
that were being discovered in the area. Bent, antiquarian and
traveller, was the Society's nominee. He arrived with Mrs Bent,

who took photographs, and R. M. W. Swan, who did the surveying. Bent cleared the undergrowth from the Great Enclosure sufficiently for Swan to make an accurate plan. He also dug around the base of the conical tower and in the process, by removing the soil, destroyed all evidence by which later archaeologists might have been able to date the tower.

Swan developed a new theory for the origins and layout of Zimbabwe: like Stonehenge it was astronomically based and, developing his theory even further, was built sometime around 1100 BC. Bent, on the other hand, was more careful. He steered well clear of Mauch's extraordinary suggestion that Zimbabwe was the home of the Queen of Sheba and assiduously avoided linking Zimbabwe with Ophir. Nevertheless, despite the fact that, apart from fragments of Arab or Persian beads and glass, his finds of stone, metal and clay were 'African', he confirmed Mauch's belief that Zimbabwe was ancient and non-black in origin:

Above: *Representation of a 'conical tower' on a coin from Byblos, used as evidence of the link between Great Zimbabwe and Arabia.*

> It would seem to be evident that a prehistoric race built the ruins in this country ... a race like the mythical inhabitants of Great Britain and France who built Stonehenge and Carnac, a race which continued in possession down to the earliest dawnings of history, which provided gold for the merchants of Phoenicia and Arabia, and which eventually became influenced by and perhaps absorbed in the more powerful and wealthier organisations of the Semite.

The man who gave most credence to the Solomonic theories (and gave them a spurious scientific basis) was a journalist with a taste for the ancient, R. M. Hall. With the help of W. G. Neal, an unsuccessful miner and treasure hunter, Hall published *The Ancient Ruins of Rhodesia* in 1902 and was soon appointed the ruins' curator. He cleared the site of the remaining undergrowth and dug to a depth of four feet through accumulated deposits of what he thought was useless native rubbish. He found what Bent had found: dishes of soapstone; clay pots; stone phalli; iron tools like axes; weapons like metal arrow heads; other iron articles like nails and bells plus the Persian porcelain and Arab beads. He also found what Bent hadn't and what he himself was secretly seeking: gold. He claimed to have found £4000 worth, an incredible amount that would have meant almost a thousand ounces.

Hall was the first of the investigators of Great Zimbabwe who was a local resident. He immediately recognised that many of his finds were similar to artefacts still in regular use in the neighbouring villages of the Karanga and Rozwi, but, in spite of this and again like Bent, he is:

... forced to admit that the theory of the successive occupations of Rhodesia by Sabaeo-Arabians (Shebans), Phoenicians, and Arabs has, so far as researches have been made, exceedingly strong claims for acceptance.

In support, he quotes at length the ideas of Professor Keane, Fellow of the Royal Geographical Society, who placed Ophir, the Queen of Sheba's capital, in the Yemen:

> ... ruins of Yemen show striking analogies with those of Rhodesia, while the numerous objects of Semitic worship ... found at Zimbabwe ... leave no reasonable doubt that the old gold-workings and associated monuments of this region are to be ascribed to the ancient Sabaeans of South Arabia and their Phoenician successors.

The man who shattered the theory and caused a major row with Hall, which simmered bitterly for years, was the young archaeologist David Rendall-McIver. Shortly after Hall's arrival at the ruins, McIver was sponsored by the British Association to go to Great Zimbabwe and was the first archaeologist, in the modern sense, to work at the site. He was a pupil of the great Egyptologist Sir Flinders Petrie and, although at Great Zimbabwe for a little under two months, he was able to turn the

Right: *The Acropolis c. 1890, showing ruined walls and African kraals.*

theories of Hall and his supporters on their heads. He was the first man to look at the ruins objectively, free of subjective prejudice and previous ideas; he was the first man to use the two dating methods pioneered by Petrie in Egypt, one, whereby an object's age could be dated according to its development when related to other objects of the same kind (usually shape and sophistication of manufacture) and, two, dating an object of unknown date by the position in which it is found compared with an object of known date; and he was the first man to regard homely objects like the iron axes as of equal importance with the more exotic, like glass beads.

The stated main aim of his dig was 'to determine its approximate date by means of trial excavations'. He deliberately dug a trial trench in the enclosure ruin in order to compare his results with Hall's. The trench cut through a section of a floor made of local cement or 'daga'. Hall stated that the layers of construction proved that the enclosure had been occupied over many years by a succession of peoples. McIver showed that this was wrong, that the layers were caused merely by the method of floor construction and virulently attacked Hall who:

> ... might have been saved from his very serious misconception had he observed the excavator's primary axiom and dug to

Left: *The main entrance to the Great Enclosure before restoration in 1911 to a more 'Arabian' design.*

bed-rock before riveting his conclusions ... he stopped at the
cement and rubble ... And yet it is only ... *below* the cement
and rubble that the question of whether there was more than
one occupation, or more than one period in the building can
be legitimately raised.

And what McIver found beneath the daga floor was exactly the
same kind of African object that he found above it:

> The pottery from this lowest level is that which Mr Hall calls
> Makalanga, and which is, in fact, exactly like modern Kaffir
> pottery ... It is impossible therefore, to resist the conclusion
> that the people who inhabited the 'Elliptical Temple' when it
> was built belonged to tribes whose arts and manufactures
> were indistinguishable from those of the modern Makalanga
> (Shona).

McIver dates the Great Enclosure as not earlier than the fourteenth or fifteenth century and believes that the enclosure was
an African royal residence, the 'great Chief's Kraal', and that
the mysterious conical tower was a ceremonial symbol of that
royal authority. According to him, the hill ruins or 'Acropolis'
was a fortress that guarded a sanctuary of some kind and the
birds found there possibly represented the tribal totem. In conclusion, he pointed out that Great Zimbabwe was the largest but
not the only ruin of its kind in the country, that it was the
centre of gold distribution and not gold mining and that it was
constructed solely by Africans and without any outside help:

> These dwellings ... are unquestionably African in every detail,
> and belong to a period which is fixed by foreign imports as in
> general mediaeval.

The difference between McIver and Hall is the difference between
archaeology and antiquarianism; between science and romance;
between the twentieth century and the nineteenth. It was the
difference between the professional and the amateur; the man
with an international outlook and the provincial. Ultimately it
was to polarise black and white.

By 1906, McIver had solved the riddle of the ruins that Mauch
had discovered just thirty-four years before, but he knew that
not everyone would accept it. He ended his report:

> ... many no doubt will bewail that a romance has been
> destroyed. But surely it is a prosaic mind that sees no romance
> in the partial opening of this new chapter in the history of
> vanished cultures. A corner is lifted of that veil which has

shrouded the forgotten but not irrecoverable past of the African negro. Were I a Rhodesian I should feel that in studying the contemporary natives in order to unravel the story of the ruins I had a task as romantic as any student could desire. I should feel that in studying the ruins in order thereby to gain a knowledge of the modern races I had an interest that the politician should support and that the scholar must envy.

Rhodesian politicians, of course, didn't see it that way. Nor did the people whom they represented. The miners and farmers settling the area had a vested interest in believing the fact that whites had lived, worked and profited in the region once before. The King Solomon and Queen of Sheba story had given an apparent legitimacy to white colonial rule. The colonists were not now going to give up that legitimacy or the stories. Solomon and Sheba sank into the collective deep of white Rhodesian consciousness. The myths were taught as history in schools; Rider Haggard's novel *King Solomon's Mines*, which drew largely on Great Zimbabwe, was popular if not actually required reading; and tourist posters depicted a phantom Queen of Sheba coiling around the conical tower like the genie out of Aladdin's lamp. Movies showed white rulers conducting strange ceremonies, watched and worshipped by crowds of blacks in Cecil B. De Mille-style profusion – with suitable commentary:

Above: *Travel poster showing a white Queen of Sheba receiving a native gift – presumably gold – at the entrance to the Great Enclosure.*

> The caravan of Solomon leaves the desert oasis and hastens on its way to Ophir. The dancing girls bend and sway in rhythm before the lovely guest and the ancient king, whose mines are somewhere in the hinterland of Africa. Did the messengers of Solomon arrive in this valley to collect the riches from the great fortress of stone? Did this priest hear their coming? Beneath the Conical Tower a figure reveals itself. What does this movement signify? Is a sacrifice about to be made?

In the last days of the white regime in the 1970s, political broadcasts on Rhodesian television still poured doubt on the African origins of Great Zimbabwe:

> Zimbabwe was not built by either whites or blacks. Zimbabwe was built in approximately AD 570 long before blacks or whites were here. It was a virtual replica of the temple of the Moon Goddess in Southern Arabia, which was built about 750 BC. The people who built it were Semitic. They were brown in colour and were evidently the Sabaean people who were a mixture of Arabs and Jews. The Queen of Sheba was Queen of the Sabaeans.

Not only the whites, but the blacks doubted their history as well. In the 1930s the Shona independence movement used Great Zimbabwe as prime evidence of blacks being exploited by white rulers.

Since 1906 the ruins have been investigated by numerous archaeologists and anthropologists. All of them have refined as well as supported McIver's hypothesis. In 1926, J. F. Schofield analysed the building methods and concluded that the walls were 'the finest and latest architectural achievement of that Bantu civilisation'. Anthony Witty, in 1958, was able to date the walls according to their style of construction, the oldest being the most primitive in the hill ruins and the latest the wall of the Great Enclosure, probably the difference between 1100 and 1450 and contemporary with the building period of the medieval European cathedrals. In 1929, Gertrude Caton-Thompson tunnelled under the conical tower to prove that it was solid; solved the problem of the strange, short and winding walls inside the Great Enclosure by showing that they linked long-vanished daga huts; and confirmed an African origin:

> ... examination of all the existing evidence, gathered from every quarter, still can produce not one single item that is not in accordance with the claim of Bantu origin ...

The local authorities hated her for it. In 1952, carbon dating on wood from the hill ruin showed that the construction could not be earlier than the year 700 and, given the fact that the wood could have been lying about for years before it was used, probably much later. The wood was local mopane and not cedar as Mauch had thought, whilst the birds (far from being imported versions of Egyptian birds as suggested by some early investigators) are most likely to be stylised representations of a bird that still visits the ruins, the crowned hornbill.

It is still not certain which African tribe built Great Zimbabwe, but it is most likely to have been one of the local tribes, the Lemba, the Rozwi or the Shona. A study of the Venda tribe, close associates of the Lemba, gives some idea of how Zimbabwe looked and functioned. The Venda now live in northern Transvaal, 200 miles from Zimbabwe, but, as at Zimbabwe, their village huts are still built of daga, have thatched roofs and are linked by serpentine walls. The village chief lives 'on the mountain', which is in fact a small eminence just away from the village centre but which is linked to it by a narrow, winding path lined by stone walls: a tiny version of the winding path that climbs the hill at Great Zimbabwe, through rocky outcrops into the sacred enclosure. Here the chief, always sitting so that his head is higher than all the rest, takes counsel with his elders, and here the villagers still crawl along the path on their bellies to pay the chief elaborate and ritual homage.

At the height of its prosperity, Great Zimbabwe probably had a population of about 10,000 people. It was a trading city: an economic base for the region, trading in gold, amongst other things, with its African neighbours, with the Arabs and, later, with the Portuguese. It was a religious centre and it was the residence as well as the burial place of chiefs; the soapstone birds might mark their graves on the hill. The high priestly sacrifices described to Mauch had nothing to do with the Jews but were to do with the traditional practices of calling on chiefly ancestors to intercede with God, or 'Mali', in times of collective trouble.

Great Zimbabwe declined as a major centre during the eighteenth century and was abandoned, probably sacked, in about 1830. When Mauch arrived in 1872 it was only partially in use as a cattle kraal by the recently arrived Chief Mangapi. Today it is a national monument, as well as a national symbol of black African achievement, well-kept and cared-for, although the rebuilding of the entrances between the walls in 1911 by Corporal Wallace of the British South African Police gives it a spurious 'Arabian' air, in keeping with the sentiment and theories of that time.

Mauch left Pika's village for the last time in May 1872 and, after several attempts, finally reached the coast. Disillusioned,

Left: *Venda village showing huts built of daga, similar to the remains of huts found at Great Zimbabwe.*

despairing, hating whites as well as blacks and physically ill, he set sail from Africa, never to return. His hopes, however, remained:

> May future expeditions, supplied with better means than I had at my disposal, contribute to a greater interest in those regions than has been the case until now. The country between the Limpopo and the Zambesi contains so much of value, old and new, that any further neglect would amount to injustice. I for my part, consider myself lucky to have been called, as it were, to be a pioneer, and I hope that the results of my eight years of travelling, carried out with such meagre means, may be the cause of greater inspiration for more intensive exploration of the country and the exploitation of its valuable products.

At home in Würtemberg, he was unable to settle. During a delirium, probably caused by a recurring bout of malaria, he fell from the window of his house and died shortly afterwards. He was thirty-seven. On his memorial are written the words: Discoverer of the Ruins of Zimbabye.

Chapter Six

PYRAMIDS IN THE JUNGLE
Alfred Maudslay
in Guatemala

I was naturally anxious and expectant on this my first visit to a Central American ruin, but it seemed as though my curiosity would be ill satisfied, for all I could see on arrival was what appeared to be three moss-grown stumps of dead trees covered over with a tangle of creepers and parasitic plants ... We soon pulled off the creepers, and ... set to work to clear away the coating of moss ...*

Alfred Maudslay arrived at the ruins of the 'lost' Mayan city of Quirigua in January 1881. The only description of the site had been written forty years before, by the American traveller John Stephens. Between the years 1839–42, Stephens had visited most of the abandoned cities built by the Mayan civilisation in Central America. His book *Incidents of Travel in Central America, Chiapas and Yucatan*, illustrated by his English colleague Frederick Catherwood, was a bestseller and for the first time drew the world's attention to the early civilisations of the western hemisphere. Stephens and Catherwood were part of the 'heroic' period of archaeological discovery, when attention was focused on the discovery of new sites, new cultures; but now there was a new attitude. In place of the preoccupations of those early explorers was the concern to study, in proper scientific detail, those sites already located. Maudslay played a major part in that process, and the day he reached Quirigua in the footsteps of Stephens and Catherwood was the turning point:

* A. P. Maudslay, *Archaeology*, vol. II, from *Biologia Centrali-Americana*, vols. 55–9 (London: R. H. Porter, 1889–1902).

As the curious outlines of the carved ornament gathered shape it began to dawn upon me how much more important were these monuments, upon which I had stumbled almost by chance, than any account I had heard of them had led me to expect. This day's work induced me to take a permanent interest in Central-American archaeology.

Above: *Alfred Percival Maudslay (1850–1931) at work in a Mayan building at Chichén Itza, Mexico, 1889.* Right: *Stela K at Quirigua, photographed by Alfred Maudslay – one of the monuments 'upon which I had stumbled almost by chance' and which he cleaned with a hairbrush.*

What had begun, according to his own account, merely as a journey to escape the rigours of an English winter turned into fifteen years of meticulous and painstaking scientific analysis undertaken in the most difficult and unpleasant physical conditions. It was to lead to a breakthrough in understanding one of the world's most colourful civilisations. It also led to the 'discovery' of two of that civilisation's most splendid cities, both unknown to Stephens and Catherwood.

Alfred Percival Maudslay was born in London on 18 March 1850, the seventh of eight children. The family firm, Maudslay, Sons and Field, made large marine engines for, amongst others, the Admiralty. When he was thirteen he was sent to Harrow:

> At the entrance examination I was placed last but one in the school, for strange to say there was found one boy who knew less than I did.

He went to Cambridge at the age of twenty-two and then spent five years as a junior colonial official in the South Pacific. It was not until he was thirty-one that chance introduced him to what was to become his life's interest and work. In December 1880, he set sail alone from London for Guatemala in the steamship *Bernard Hall*:

> The principal object of my first journey was not geographical or antiquarian research, but a desire to pass the winter in a warm climate. I had made no previous study of American archaeology, but my interest had been roused by reading Stephens' account of his travels and I started for Guatemala in the hope that I might reach some of the ruins so admirably described by him.

Maudslay landed at Livingston, the Atlantic port of Guatemala, in early January 1881:

> ... and thence travelled in a very rickety steam-launch up the Rio Dulce to the village of Yzabal. Here I hired mules and rode a distance of about eighteen miles over the Sierra de las Minas to the cattle ranch of El Mico which is within a mile of the village of Quirigua and, after a day's rest, started, accompanied by some villagers, to visit the ruins partially examined by Catherwood.

Catherwood was the first man to have recorded a visit to the site when, in 1840, he spent a day there while Stephens was in San Salvador. He reported stone monuments and hieroglyphs and regretted the fact that he had time to make only two drawings.

Right: *This map shows the route of Maudslay's first visit to Tikal, in 1881.*

It was these monuments that had attracted the attention of the British Consul in 1855. Hearing that Britain might be left out in the race for museum exhibits, the Consul proposed that some of the monuments should be put on a raft in the Belzoni style and floated downriver for shipment to London. He was backed in the enterprise, as Fellows had been, by the Foreign Secretary Lord Palmerston, but, fortunately for the Guatemalans, the stones proved too heavy.

Starting from the ranch, which stands amongst pine-woods six hundred feet above sea-level, an hour's ride brought us down to the edge of the plain through which the river Motagua flows. Here the path ended in some native plantations and we then followed a track newly cut through the undergrowth by some villagers who had been sent ahead of us and, in another hour we came to the ruins ... Overhead and all around was a dense tropical forest; the undergrowth was so dense that we had difficulty in finding any of the monuments and even when within touch of them, so thickly were they covered with creepers, ferns and moss that it was not easy to distinguish them from dead tree trunks. However, we pulled off the creepers and then scrubbed away the moss with some rough brushes we made out of the midribs of the palm leaflets and, as the sculpture began to show up, I sacrificed one of my ivory-backed hair brushes out of my dressing bag to clear out the more delicate carving of the hieroglyphics.

Maudslay, on this first visit to the site, was able to stay only three days, one of which was rained off by a tropical storm. What he had seen, however, astonished him. Five stone monoliths, freestanding and between 12–25 feet high, and two curiously carved stone animals:

> The upright monoliths are all of the same general character, ornamented with carvings of human figures and tables of hieroglyphics ... The heads are sculptured in high relief and are usually surmounted by carved feathered head-dresses. The ears are very large, bent forward, and pierced for large ear ornaments. The body and dress are carved in lower-relief and are covered with the most intricate and elaborate ornament in which small human faces and grotesques frequently occur.

The carved stone animals, or what he could see of them half-buried in the earth, were even more intriguing:

> I could not make out what animals they were intended to represent, but both of them have curved claws and indications of armour like an armadillo. Each one has a human head, apparently the head of a woman, between its jaws ... On the sides of all the monuments are well-carved tables of hieroglyphics and other groups of similar inscriptions ... They certainly do not give one the idea of writing but their arrangement and position are such that they can hardly be merely capricious ornament, and I think they must have some symbolic meaning.

Some of the monuments were reasonably well preserved, others were damaged by tree roots or by the constant drip from water off the trees overhead. But how many monuments were there?

> So dense was the undergrowth that, although we were encamped round the base of one of the standing monuments it was only on the third day that I caught sight of another monument which lay within a few feet of my camp-cot buried beneath the decaying trunk of a huge tree ... (so) I was not

Right: *Stela E at Quirigua, an 'upright monolith ornamented with carvings of human figures and tables of hieroglyphics'. Maudslay, despite the problems of heavy equipment and lack of light, took excellent photographs.*

altogether happy with my search, as I felt sure that there must be other monuments unknown to the villagers hidden away in the thick undergrowth.

Although perhaps at one time the area supported a vigorous agriculture, the jungle now covered everything. The local villagers referred to the site as 'Los Idolos', the idols, and knew nothing more. Maudslay had no way of knowing who had built the ruins, when they had been built, what, exactly, they were – whether temple, religious site or city – nor what the hieroglyphics meant. He took some photographs and left. He crossed the Guatemalan border into Honduras on his way to the Mayan site of Copán and toured the ruins there with a copy of Stephens and Catherwood as guide. Stephens had been so impressed by these ruins that, hoping to return and excavate, he had actually attempted to buy them for fifty dollars.

What struck Maudslay most, however, was not the site's excavation potential but the sculptural detail of the standing monuments. They had a 'decided likeness in dress and ornaments' to what he had just seen at Quirigua, but to be able to compare them properly, to study them and try to draw conclusions from them, he needed to have an accurate likeness of them side by side. Catherwood's drawings were in no way detailed enough. To draw, free-hand, such large, minutely detailed, unfamiliar and often stained and damaged sculpture was impossible.

With the recent invention of the dry-plate process, providing factory-made negatives which could be developed on the spot, photography was now comparatively easy, despite the weight and bulk of the apparatus. However, with the density of the forest cover and shadows cast by the depth of carving, getting the correct exposure was difficult, as Maudslay discovered. Even when the exposure was accurate it was still not possible to record the wealth of detail.

It was the unexpected magnificence of the monuments which that day came into view that led me to devote so many years to securing copies of them, which, preserved in the museums ... are likely to survive the originals.

He took some more photographs, underexposed, and moved on to Guatemala City and Cobán, where his friend Mr Sarg doubled as Consul for both the Americans and the Germans. Maudslay had met Mr Sarg on the boat over:

He is very civil and his assistance will be most useful to me in Guatemala. He excites me by an account of a newly discovered and undescribed ruined city near Flores which is said to be as fine as Palenque.

Sarg was now using his influence to make the journey of his English friend to this 'city' in the interior as easy as possible. Indeed, his friend was to need all the help he could get:

Cobán may be called the limit of civilisation in this direction ... To the north the country is very little known and all the published maps are inaccurate.

The preparations took a week and the journey was to take about seventeen days, much of it through forest that was virtually uninhabited. Sarg had taken on the responsibility of hiring mules

and 'mozos' – Indian porters – to carry Maudslay's food and equipment a distance of 150 miles as the parrot flies. The expedition left the site on 31 March 1881:

> ... about eight o'clock with Carlos as attendant on his horse: I on a good mule and a horse with pack ... For some distance the road passed among the detached and precipitous limestone hills which are the feature of the country around Cobán. The track got worse and worse as we proceeded and the packhorse floundered about over the slippery rocks.

Maudslay was not the kind of explorer who kept a diary for future publication, but he did on this occasion keep a notebook. On the first day out, a makeshift meal gave him a bad headache and made him sick; the road got worse and washing, if possible at all, was in the river. Nights were spent either in the open, in the house of the occasional rancher or even in the public ranch, the mud and straw hut put up by the government for travellers:

> *Saturday 2nd April*
> As the public ranch had the dead body of an Indian in it, we put up in the shanty of the Alcalde. After dark the friends of the dead Indian assembled, the music struck up and they danced and feasted until morning. I kept to a diet of cornflour and raw eggs but did not feel much better.
> *Sunday 3rd April*
> It was with great bother that we could collect the mozos the next morning and get them off. Their packs are light – 50–

70 lbs – but they have to carry food for a week and we have to take maize for the animals, but some of the mozos are mere boys and I have doubts about quick travelling. One failed to turn up so we started eleven strong.

Maudslay's experience with his mozos was no better than Mauch's with his porters in Africa or Belzoni's with his labourers in Egypt:

Monday 4th April
I ventured on some tinned beef for dinner – the first meal I had eaten for many days.

Tuesday 5th April
The streams were as numerous as ever and the bridges as bad – leading my mule over one of them which looked passable though unsafe, I heard a crack just as I was on the side and turned round to see my mule with his feet hanging just above the water and his body wedged between two loops of the bridge. The centre log had given way. I scrambled up to him and managed to loose his girths. The poor head struggled a good deal at first and was then tolerably quiet whilst Carlos and I got poles and levered one of the logs aside and dropped the mule down into the stream and then, with some little difficulty we got her up the bank. I had an awful vision for a moment of journeying the rest of the way on foot.

The road, which was sometimes through open country, sometimes through scrub and sometimes through dense forest, was no more than a mud track skirting fallen trees and impassable altogether in the rainy season.

Ever since his days at Cambridge, Maudslay had wanted to experience the sights and sounds of a tropical rain forest. He found it strange, hostile and beautiful:

We often passed under the most splendid giant mahogany trees and now and then saw perfect fountains of yellow orchid playing from the trees and, in the undergrowth, numerous species of graceful palm ... For the last few days we have constantly heard the howls of the howling monkeys and sometimes passed them under the tall trees on which they were desporting themselves – the males howling as if their lives depended on it and the ladies keeping up a gentle grunting accompaniment. I never cared to shoot them although the Indians appreciate them much as food.

There were wild turkeys, strange long-tailed parrots, snakes and macaws. There were also some much smaller animals:

Whilst riding through the forest I suppose we had disturbed a wasps' nest for both Carlos and I were stung. I opened a bottle of liquid ammonia which I kept in my saddle bags in case of snakebite or scorpion and I suppose owing to the knocking about and the high temperature, on loosening the stopper nearly the whole of the contents flew up into my face. I dropped the bottle and stumbled along the road gasping for breath, blinded and choked by the ammonia and it was some minutes before I could breathe freely or open my eyes … I bathed in the river and then passed a most unpleasant night as fleas, mosquitoes, sandflies, horseflies, ants and every other form of noxious insect seemed to abound. It is hotter than we have felt it yet and (I have) a rash which has troubled me for some days.

They had been travelling nine days and had met almost no one. To avoid the heat of midday, the expedition broke camp at six the next morning. On this occasion, Maudslay rode ahead of his mozos on the assumption that as there was no water supply on the road they were 'unlikely to loiter'. At eleven o'clock they arrived at Sacluc, the principal town of the province of Petén. It consisted of a few dozen houses made of wattle and plaster with thatched roofs and had a population of about 600 people, all of them Indinos. In this remote region, the writ of the government in Guatemala City scarcely ran. There was a great deal of smuggling and murder. A few days before Maudslay's arrival the customs officer was killed, and, shortly before that, the local 'mayor'.

They reached the bank of the Flores lake:

As the lake was so smooth we named 4.0 p.m. as the hour of starting and after much bother got off at six in a bad canoe. In all, eight mozos, then we stopped at a village a little further along the lake for eight more mozos, but although they were all ready they refused to start and more delay and bother.

Finally, with a larger canoe, they began the journey up the lake. It was a moonlit night; the lake was still and the dark forest surrounded it on every side. Maudslay tried to get snatches of sleep as the mozos rowed. They reached the far end of the lake at past midnight and camped till morning. The ruins were now only thirty miles away. The water supply was appalling:

Full of tadpoles and innumerable insects. I boiled it and let the filth subside. I possibly swallowed the germs of many fevers. Diarrhoea all day.

There was no water for washing and, as they penetrated deeper into the jungle, there was scarcely any water at all, just a few inches in the bowl of a hollow tree; they collected the milk of four coconuts:

> The only food for the mules is 100 feet up in the canopy of the forest. Every evening Cruz makes this climb. Twice he has fallen. These men are accustomed to setting up camp one night at a time and moving on. After a short rest, we made for the ruins and the Indians lost their way. However, after some hunting, we came to traces of stone houses then to court after court with houses in different state of ruin surrounding them. I chose one in better state of preservation than the rest for my dwelling and then went in search of others.

Maudslay arrived at Tikal on Easter Sunday 1881. He was only the second foreigner to reach there, but what was eventually to prove the most extensive, important and certainly the most impressive jungle 'lost city' in the world was almost invisible:

> Everything of course was covered with forest and large trees were growing on the steep sides of the pyramid which supported the highest house.

At the base of the pyramid Maudslay found a number of sculptured stones:

> But very much damaged and weatherworn and other stones like large tombstones without any carving and a number of circular stones about the same size and much of the same appearance as the circular altar at Copán but as far as I could see, unornamented.

Maudslay began to climb the pyramid. Even today, with the pyramid restored, the climb is not recommended for sufferers of vertigo. It is a dangerous climb up a flight of steep stone steps at an angle of approximately 50 degrees sheer from the jungle floor, and for a height approaching 120 feet. There is no handrail, just a chain cemented into the stonework at foot level to haul yourself up or to steady you on the way down. In Maudslay's day the steps were worn and broken and covered with earth and rotting vegetation. There were only protruding tree roots and creepers to hold on to: it seemed a choice of being pitched to death if the creepers snapped or, if his movement dislodged the buildings above him, of being crushed to death instead. Maudslay managed to escape incident:

> (I) entered the house on the top and saw away in the distance, a quarter to a third of a mile off, two other pyramids even higher than the one I was on.

Covered by colossal trees were two others. It is still one of the world's most extraordinary views, the plumed and crested tops of five pyramids, boats riding on a sea of forest as far as the eye can see. Maudslay felt, as Stephens and Catherwood had felt when they saw the much lower pyramids of Copán, 'an interest perhaps stronger even' than when viewing the pyramids of Egypt. But this was a sight that Stephens and Catherwood never saw:

> Every house I entered had square doorways with beams of sapote wood across the top and all were built of stone and plaster. In the house at the top of the pyramid the beams were elaborately carved but too much eaten away to trace the figures … On the whole I must own to being much disappointed. The forest was over everything. The work of clearing would be much more than I could do and there appeared to be very little hope of taking satisfactory photographs. No doubt I was on the site of a very large city, larger than anything mentioned by Stephens but although the houses were large and numerous there was little sign of carving or ornamental work, and my mozos told me that I had seen the best there *was* to be seen. I returned to my house rather downhearted.

The ruins of Tikal had been rediscovered by the outside world in 1848 when they were chanced upon by Colonel Mendez, Chief Magistrate of nearby Flores, and Governor Tut. Tut and Mendez made only a cursory exploration. Mendez marked the ruins as belonging to the Guatemalan government – since Stephens' attempt to buy Copán and the growth of interest from European museums, ruins had become valuable – and returned to Flores to write a report for the government. This report, along with its illustrations, was not published until it found its way, via the German envoy in Guatemala, to the Berlin Academy of Science, which printed it in its journal in 1853. Tikal was now known to the world, but for a while the world took scarcely any notice. The first European visitor did not arrive until 1877 when a Swiss called Dr Bernouilli, who was on a botanical expedition, 'discovered' the ruins and removed several of the carved beams

Right: *Maudslay's drawing of a lintel at Tikal, showing the 'serpent bird'.*

of sapote wood which, at one time, were such a feature of the site. During the removal process the natives cut down the beams, shortening and damaging them as well as defacing the surrounding stonework. The beams are now in the museum in Basle, but Bernouilli died only months after leaving Tikal.

In the Mayan language the name 'Tikal' means 'the place where spirit voices are heard' and Teobert Maler, the archaeologist who made extensive surveys of the ruins twenty years after Maudslay, wrote:

> The Mayas believe that at midnight ... their ancestors return to earth and, adorned as in the days of their glory, wander about in the forsaken temples and palaces, where their spirit voices are heard in the air. Therefore all important ruins in this land are regarded as enchanted, *encantadas*, and timid people do not like to sleep alone in their chambers.

Maudslay set up camp:

> All the mozos had fled back to the plain being frightened to sleep in the ruins because of the 'Spirits of the House' but I got some of them to bring water which had to be fetched some distance, and was very bad and dirty, and got some of them to work to clear the two inches of dirt and loose plaster from the floor of my house and then made myself pretty comfortable.

Maudslay's 'house' was typical of the surviving houses at Tikal.

Left: *The Maudslay camp at Tikal – outside the buildings and away from the spirits.*

Because of the growth of trees and shrubs it was difficult to judge how the upper part of the house was shaped, but the lower walls were about 3 feet thick and, inside, rose to about 8 feet high. Because the Mayan architects had not mastered the construction of an arch, the roof came to a narrow point like an interior gable. It meant that the rooms could never be more than 5 or 6 feet wide and had, in Maudslay's words, 'more the appearance of long passages than rooms'. Across the vault were sapote wood beams:

> These may have been built in as supports but were possibly used for the same purpose to which I put them, namely to hang hammocks to ... Carlos and the commandante prepared to string their hammocks to the trees outside being also I think a little frightened of ghosts in the house. However, after hearing a tiger (jaguar) prowling about a little too close to them to be comfortable they too strung their hammocks in the house. There were certainly strange noises in the night but they were nothing worse than the howls of the howling monkeys.

The following day, Easter Monday, the mozos returned and began to clear the scrub in front of the house:

> I found them terribly idle doing nothing when one's back was turned and inclined to be impudent. Evidently very little work to be got out of them. Leaving some to clear the first big pyramid house I went on to the other and scrambled to the top. The house contained more carved beams very much eaten. I then got a ladder made to get up part of the side of the house and obtained a good view – then returned to breakfast. At one o'clock set to work again. All the mozos on pyramid no. 1 and the men worked better. I worked at carved stones – scrubbing them with soap and water. Dinner and bed.
>
> *Tuesday 19th April*
> Nothing much to tell of – cloudy and a little rain early – then fine. Mozos worked at the ruins – slowly. Carlos found another carved stone and I went with him to see it, but he could not find it again in the forest so left mozos to look for it. In the afternoon went for a ramble and scrambled up other pyramid. The ruins are very extensive indeed. The mozos found the carved stone again and I am to see it tomorrow. I am disgusted with the mozos they are so lazy.
>
> *Wednesday 20th April*
> Went in the morning with Carlos to see the other sculptured stone and after many twists and turns came to it and found it very much damaged. Carlos says it is not the same which he

saw before. This one stands in the courtyard of a small house. The stone is carved on both the top and the sides. The mozo who is a most disagreeable duffer vowed that it was the same and that he knew of no other. Returned and took some photos of plaza then walked to the highest ruined pyramid passing some larger houses than usual. Then climbed the big pyramid.

Thursday, 21st April

Slept very badly – dyspeptic. Took some measurements of casa no. 1 in morning. Very dull day – waited long for good light – at last took some photos.

Right: *Maudslay's plan of the central ruins at Tikal. Pyramid-temples A and B face each other across the Great Plaza.*

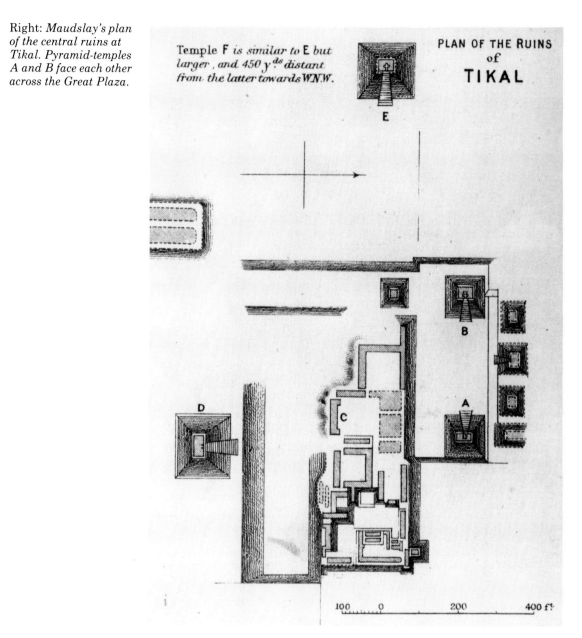

After five days' work clearing what was, in fact, only a minute part of the city, Maudslay was able to take measurements and make rough plans. The five great pyramids were grouped together in 'what was evidently the most important part of the city'. The houses on top of the pyramids were, he believed, temples:

> There is no trace of any idol or object of worship in these buildings but I cannot doubt their being temples such as those so often mentioned by the Spanish conquerors ...

The dimensions of the pyramid measured were 168 by 184 feet at the base and 112 feet from the slope to the base of the temple. The temple itself, which he wasn't able to measure, was about another 50 feet. (The Pyramid of Cheops is 460 feet high.)

> The whole town had been laid out on a rectangular plan and wherever there are differences of elevation the ground has been terraced and the slopes faced with carefully-laid squared stones. Some houses are in a fair state of preservation ... but the buildings can be seen in every stage of decay and are often merely overgrown heaps of squared stones.

After cleaning, the carved stones in the plaza revealed the familiar figures in profile with large feathered head-dress and elaborate ornament, but the stone crumbled to the touch.

Maudslay took some final views of the cleared ruins in the late afternoon light and packed up ready for an early start the next morning:

> In shifting the dry plates just before going to bed I have great fear that some of the views I had taken were spoilt. I had told the boy to let the camp fire burn low and when there was nothing of a flame, only smouldering embers, I set to work inside our house with the red lantern. But, just as I had taken six of the plates out of the slides a sudden flare of light came through the open door. I yelled to the boy and tried to cover up the plates – the light only lasted a moment and then died out again and the boy told me that it was caused by a dry leaf of the tree falling on the embers. I hope the plates are not much damaged.

Fortunately for posterity, they weren't.

> The great discomfort in the exploration of these ruins is the want of water. Every drop we used had to be brought a distance of about a mile and a half, from a small overgrown muddy lagoon not more than 150 yards wide; and this water was so thick and dirty that I never drank any of it without first boiling it and then passing it through a filter ... Yet I could not impress upon my workmen the advantage of boiling the water and letting the mud settle, and as a consequence, many of them were attacked by fever and my visit had to be somewhat shortened. Luckily the fever did not seem to be of a very severe kind, and a few doses of quinine soon pulled them round ... But I failed to find a satisfactory explanation of how water was supplied to the large population which must formerly have inhabited the town.

Below: *Altar 5, one of the finest at Tikal. It shows two priests, bones and a skull set inside a calendar round.*

In the central plaza, Maudslay had found some pits in the ground. Were these subterranean reservoirs? Or storage containers for food? He couldn't tell but he was asking the right questions.

As Maudslay left the site on 23 April 1881, all he knew for sure was that the ruins were remarkable and, he guessed, not as old as the civilisations of the East; but he was determined to find out more. What had begun as a holiday for an English gentleman of leisure had turned into something quite different.

After a summer spent in England he was back in Guatemala in December 1881. He spent an uneventful week at Tikal, continuing to clear the undergrowth – including the creepers and saplings that had grown up in the year he'd been away – and a further five days at Quirigua. Here he had arranged for the local villagers to fell the trees in advance of his arrival. It meant that he could now see those monuments he had been so certain the previous year lay hidden in the jungle, including the largest and most interesting monument of all:

> From a rough calculation I believe this single block of stone to weigh about 18 tons. It is symmetrical in shape, the pattern carved on either side differing only in details. In this case the animal represented is a turtle, but the resemblance is not very easily made out, and in fact, I walked round it time after time and could not think what to make of it. In place of a turtle's head is a huge grotesque human head, with the same out-turned ears and large ear ornaments common to the other figures I have described. The forearm and flipper can be easily

Right: *The giant turtle at Quirigua.*

made out on the left side, but on the right side the flipper is not quite so clear; the two hind flippers are turned up at the back of the animal, and in place of the tail is the life-sized figure of a woman sitting cross-legged and holding a mannikin sceptre in her hand. This sceptre occurs in several other monuments, and is more like the children's toy of a monkey on a stick, which one sees sold in the streets, than anything else I can think of ...

On his previous visit to Guatemala, Maudslay had met a man called Edwin Rockstroh in Sarg's house in Cobán. Rockstroh, at the request of the Guatemalan government, had since been on a survey expedition down the Usumacinta river which, for much of its length, formed the boundary between Guatemala and Mexico. The information he imparted to Maudslay when they met for a second time in Guatemala City set Maudslay's pulse racing. On the left bank of the river, deep in the jungle, Rockstroh had found the ruins of yet another 'lost' city. Maudslay wasted no time in mounting an expedition. In March 1882, with a team of mozos, a guide and two canoes, he set out:

> The ruined town for which I was bound is the lowest point in the Usumacinta ever reached in safety by canoe. It requires considerable skill to guide the canoe safely between the projecting rocks and snags.

The area was virtually unexplored and, apart from woodcutters and occasional Indians, uninhabited. The river was infested by alligators and, for some of its length, made impassable by rapids:

> There were a few rapids today but none of much account ... missed a shot at an alligator ... Several times during the day we had seen traces of the 'Lacandones', or 'Caribes' as my men called them (the untamed Indians who inhabit the forests between Chiapas and Petén), and while stopping to examine one of their canoes, which we found hauled up on a sand-spit, its owner, accompanied by a woman and child, came out of the forest to meet us. The man was an uncouth-looking fellow with sturdy limbs, long black hair, very strongly marked features, prominent nose, thick lips, and complexion about the tint of my half-caste canoemen. He was clothed in a single long brown garment of roughly-woven material, which looked like sacking, splashed over with blots of some red dye. The man showed no signs of fear, and readily entered into conversation with one of my men who spoke the Maya language, but the woman kept at a distance and I could not get a good look at her.

The Lacandon Indians are the surviving Mayans. Later in the day, Maudslay was taken by his guide to visit a Lacandon 'cari-bal' or village that stood somewhere near the river-bank:

> There was no trace of it, however, near the river, so we followed a narrow path into the forest, marked by two jaguars' skulls on poles, and here and there by some sticks laid across the track, over which the Indians had probably dragged their small canoes. About two miles distant from the river we found three houses standing in a clearing near the bank of a small stream. A woman came out to meet us, and received us most courteously, asking us to rest in a small shed. Her dress was a single sack-like garment, similar to that worn by the man we had met earlier in the day; her straight black hair fell loose over her shoulders, and round her neck hung strings of brown seeds interspersed with beads and silver coins, which she said were obtained in Tabasco ... Some especial significance must attach to the wearing of the brown-seed necklaces, for no offers which I could make would induce either man or woman to part with one of them ...

The houses were indistinguishable from those of other Indian tribes and the clearings round the houses were planted with maize, plantain, chilli, tobacco, gourd, tomato and cotton. The Indians' only weapons, as far as Maudslay could see, were bows and stone-tipped arrows. Tethered dogs kept snarling guard. What most impressed Maudslay, however, was the head shape of the Lacandon – 'such a sloping forehead and skull' – which, he was about to discover, was identical to the carved stone heads at the site he was about to visit:

> We continued our course downstream, and camped for the night on the right bank of the river ... the next morning an hour's paddle, with a current sometimes up to five miles an hour, brought us in sight of the piled-up heap of stones which stands out in the river and marks the place where the ruins are to be found. We scrambled up the bank and began to cut our way through the undergrowth in search of the ancient buildings which we found on a succession of terraces rising in all about 250 feet above the river ... It was some time before we could find a house good enough for me to live in, but at last we came upon one at the top of many terraces and steps which was in fairly good preservation and rather wider than any I had seen at Tikal ... In one of the recesses stands a great stone idol, twice life-size. The figure is fairly well carved, and being represented sitting cross-legged with its hands on its knees,

reminded me much of the figures of Buddha. The head, with its grotesque mask helmet and large plume of feathers, is broken off the body and lies beside it. Scattered about in all parts of the house and especially near the idol were a large number of earthen vessels in which some resinous substance had been burned. These I believe had been brought by the Lacandon Indians who, still holding in reverence the temples built by their ancestors, make offerings of incense.

These offerings, Maudslay believed, provided the clue to the story current in Central America at that time (and still fairly widely believed) of a lost city flourishing in the jungle exactly as it was in the days before the Spanish Conquest. Stephens, forty years before, had repeated a story told him by a padre who had himself seen 'a large city spread over a great space, with turrets white and glittering in the sun'. As Maudslay points out, as the country was explored, the 'city's' location was pushed further and further back into the forest:

> ... until it had arrived on the banks of the Usumacinta, and it now must be driven downstream to the impassable rapids.

The story was a myth.

As Maudslay's mozos cleared the trees, the city began to show itself. It was built on a succession of terraces linked by flights of stone steps. The houses had all been once covered with plaster and stucco and, in places, still were:

> The view from the river in the old days of the white terraces and brightly coloured houses with their rows of sculpted figures must have been both picturesque and imposing.

Some of the houses still stood three storeys high, the top storey looking like an extended pigeon loft full of nesting boxes. Inside, the feature that most distinguished the houses from those at Tikal were the lintels, which were made of stone instead of wood. These were most beautifully carved, 'excellent examples of Mayan art', and the most beautiful of all Maudslay determined to carry home:

> I at once set my men to work to reduce the weight of the stone, which must have exceeded half a ton, by cutting off the undecorated ends of the slab and reducing it in thickness. This was no easy matter, as we had not come provided with tools for such work; but shift was made with the end of a broken pickaxe and some carpenter's chisels. By keeping mozos at work at it three at a time in continued rotation, by the end of

Above: *Menché (Yaxchilan). 'The view in the old days of the white terraces and brightly coloured houses with their rows of sculpted figures must have been both picturesque and imposing.'*

Above: *Stone lintel from House G at Yaxchilan, now in the British Museum. It shows a penitent kneeling before a priest and mutilating his own tongue by passing a rope of thorns through it.*

a week the weight of the stone had been reduced by half, and we were able to move it to the river-bank and pack it in the bottom of our largest canoe.

Its subsequent journey was an eventful one. It took great skill and several days to navigate the canoe upstream against the current to land at Paso Real. From here it was carried by Indians overland to Sacluc to be again reduced in weight. From Sacluc it was hauled across the savannah on a solid-wheeled ox-cart, the only wheeled vehicle in the whole of the Petén province, and then slung like a dead pig on a pole and carried through the forest by sixteen mozos to the frontier village on the Guatemala-Belize border and, finally, downriver by canoe to Belize City to be shipped to London and the British Museum.

Maudslay made only two assumptions about his 'lost' city; that the city was smaller but older, given the state of the ruins, than Tikal and that it once flourished as a crossing point of the river. He first called it Usumacinta, unaware that Rockstroh had already named it Menché. Today, still the most inaccessible of all the major Mayan ruins, it is called Yaxchilan. Had Maudslay not arrived when he did, however, it might now be called Lorillard City, for Maudslay, unknown to himself, was in a race to reach the site first.

On the fourth day of his arrival and running short of food, Maudslay sent his men to buy plantains from the Lacandon. They returned with, of all unlikely things, a European visiting card. It read: 'M. Desiré Charnay, Mission Scientifique Franco-Americaine'.

Charnay was leader of an expedition which had been working at Mayan sites in neighbouring Mexico for two years. Having travelled for weeks across difficult country to crown his career by discovering a 'lost' city, he was more than a little peeved to find Maudslay, an Englishman to boot, already arrived. Maudslay, in his turn, was 'not best pleased' at being interrupted in his work by a visitor and a Frenchman. But the Anglo-French rivalry that had existed between Belzoni and Drovetti was almost a thing of the past: politeness prevailed. And there was, in this unlikely meeting of two Europeans in the remote jungles of Central America, something of the meeting of Stanley with Livingstone. Charnay wrote:

We shook hands. He knew my name, he told me his: Alfred Maudslay Esq, from London; and as my looks betrayed the inward annoyance I felt: 'It's all right,' he said, 'there is no reason why you should look so distressed. My having had the start of you was a mere chance, as it would have been mere chance had it been the other way. You need have no fear on my account for I am only an amateur, travelling for pleasure. With you the case of course is different. But I do not intend to publish anything. Come, I have a place got ready for you; and as for the ruins I make them over to you. You can name the town, claim to have discovered it, in fact do what you please. …' I was deeply touched with his kind manner and am only too charmed to share with him the glory of having explored this city. We lived and worked together like two brothers and we parted the best of friends in the world.

Maudslay behaved with the impeccable manners expected of an old Harrovian and Charnay took him at his word and named the site 'Lorillard City' after the name of the tobacco manufacturer backing his expedition. But in private, Maudslay confided to his notebook that, whilst Charnay was extremely civil and had a good stock of provisions and plenty of wine, he found him:

> … a pleasant, talkative gentleman, thirsting for glory and wishes to be Professor of the history of American civilization in Paris, (but) he is just my idea of a French traveller, not of a careful scientific observer.

Charnay did, however, provide Maudslay with the answer to the problem of how to record the detail on Mayan monuments:

> … he immediately set his secretary at work to take paper moulds of some of the carved lintels. It is a very easy process and I wish I had known of it before.

The idea was not new. Both Belzoni and Fellows had taken papier mâché impressions, and the technique was ideal for recording the incredibly minute detail of Mayan carving.

The paper that Charnay had left over he handed to Maudslay and, on 26 March, they left Yaxchilan together. Neither of them were to return.

For the next twelve years Maudslay mounted expeditions throughout the Mayan area of Mexico, Guatemala and Honduras, visiting and revisiting – among others – Copán, Chichén Itza, and Palenque, beginning in 1883 with a return to Quirigua to mould the giant turtle. Maudslay found the papier mâché was ideal for giving detail of carvings in low relief but for the large monuments carved in deep relief something more substantial was necessary. Plaster of Paris was the answer. In one season, Maudslay transported across the Atlantic a quarter of a ton of paper and four tons of plaster of Paris, which he bought in Carlisle for fifty shillings. By the time it had reached Central America it had cost him £50 per ton and he was paying all the expenses himself. In addition, he employed an expert Italian plasterer to make the plaster-casts and Signor Guintini's cast of the Great Turtle at Quirigua was made up of 600 separate pieces.

Maudslay never succeeded in returning to Tikal. The attempt in 1887 to take paper impressions of the wooden beams there was a complete failure. Lack of water, as usual, was the cause. Nevertheless, by the end of his last expedition undertaken with his wife in 1894–5, he had amassed an enormous collection of photographs, drawings, site plans, moulds and casts, as well as published writings from which both he and others could work:

> My aim was to gather together and publish such a collection that would enable scholars to solve the problems of the Maya civilization whilst comfortably seated at home in their studies.

Not only at home. Where Maudslay had led at Tikal, others, later, were able to follow: a succession of explorers, archaeologists, anthropologists, Indians and looters. Indians smashed images on stelae for fear the spirits might harm their crops. Other Indians smashed stelae to sell the pieces to dealers and museums as they still do occasionally, but despite the desecration, central Tikal has now been systematically explored and restored and most though not all of the answers that Maudslay was searching for have been found. Tikal is revealed as a 'city' of enormous size, 'a religious centre with an urban sprawl'. The sprawl, still not fully explored, probably covers some twenty-five square miles and it is here, in clusters, that most of the huts of the population were located. The religious, ceremonial and political buildings were at the city's heart: an area of six square miles, only a tiny proportion of which Maudslay was able to see. Today it contains over 3000 stone buildings – temples; palaces; terraces; platforms; houses; and ball-courts for games – plus 200 stone monuments, stelae and altars, collectively 'the greatest creation of Mayan civilisation', and constructed without the help of metal tools or pack animals. Most of these buildings date from the period of the classic Maya, the peak of their civilisation from about AD 550 to 900, but they are built around or on top of older structures. The beginnings of Tikal go back to 600 BC, possibly earlier.

Maudslay complained that, apart from the carved wooden lintels, he found no artefacts. Archaeological excavation has since revealed an enormous amount of objects of all periods, from pottery figurines dating back to 200 BC to bowls, masks and figurines of shell, obsidian and jade of both the early and late classic periods. These objects – and in particular the painted decoration of scenes and figures on the bowls and vases – reinforce the picture of a society hinted at by the decoration of the stelae and altars: people obsessed by the concept of time.

The population of Tikal, at its height, has been estimated at 70,000. How was this large population fed? Maudslay, as he pushed his way through the jungle at Copán, thought that at one time the area could have been extensively farmed. He was right: at Tikal there is evidence of intense cultivation: of terraced fields with all the traditional Indian crops, like the ones Maudslay saw round the huts of the Lacandon Indians at Yaxchilan; plus animals, fish and even 'kitchen gardens'. The pits that Maudslay found in the plaza at Tikal, which he thought might be for water storage, were more likely pits for storing food but he was right to wonder how, in such a parched region, water could be stored. The answer has been provided by the discovery in central Tikal of vast underground reservoirs.

However, not all new information has come from archaeological excavation. Of equal importance has been the reading of the Mayan glyphs, a long, slow, tedious and still incomplete process. Stephens and Catherwood recognised the importance of the glyphs and copied them, but the stelae were not the only source of the written Mayan language. In 1831, an eccentric English aristocrat called Lord Kingsborough recognised in the Bodleian Library in Oxford a manuscript of Mexican picture-writing. It proved to be the best of only three manuscripts which survived destruction by the Spanish. It was not until 1863 when, in a library in Madrid, another manuscript was discovered that there was some indication of what the picture-writing meant. This manuscript was written by Bishop Landa, who was the Spanish Bishop of Yucatán in 1566. He showed that the writing was not just 'Mexican' but specifically Mayan and, despite inaccuracies and misinterpretation, he named the signs used in the Mayan calendar. This was the key discovery and, though it took several years, established that glyphs should be read from top to bottom in double columns and from left to right, and that, in the Mayan system of counting, dots stood for units and bars for fives. As early as 1886, Maudslay himself had recognised the formula for the start of many inscriptions:

> One of the many interesting points that I have noticed is that all the inscriptions which I have reason to believe are complete ... are headed by what I shall call an initial scroll, and begin with the same formula, usually extending through six squares

Below: *Four Mayan numerals. From the top, three dots denote three, a bar with a dot above means six, two bars and two dots stand for twelve, and one bar with four dots above means nine.*

of hieroglyph writing. The sixth square . . . being a human face, usually in profile, enclosed in a frame or cartouche.

Maudslay's greatest contribution, however, came from his moulds and casts. These, accurately and painstakingly redrawn and coloured by his assistant Annie Hunter, enabled scholars to see glyphs clearly, and in 1894 led directly to the dates being read on seven of Maudslay's stelae at Copán. In 1905, it led to a correlation between the Mayan calendar and the Christian one.

Whereas we count in hundreds, tens and units, the Maya counted in multiples of twenty and units. They had two calendars, one of which consisted of 13 named months of 20 days each – giving a cycle of 260 days – and which was used for fortune divination. A second calendar consisted of 18 months of 20 days each, plus 5 'unlucky' days, which gave a cycle of 365 days and which, because it charted the changing seasons, was of practical use to farmers. The two calendars coincided only once in 52 years, called, by modern scholars, the 'Calendar Round'. The oldest stela at Tikal, dated in Mayan 8.12.14.8.15, gives it in the Christian calendar a date of 6 July AD 292.

Mayan is the only indigenous writing in pre-Hispanic America, and is of a very primitive kind. It was, as the Maya specialist Dr Ian Graham pointed out, the product of an agricultural people coping with a capricious climate who felt the need of a calendar both to record days and seasons and, at the same time, to attempt to control the climate by honouring the right gods at the right time. It is now known, however, that the stelae were not just public calendars but were erected in public places by public figures, rulers or officials, to commemorate birthdates and historical events. They were erected during the lifetime of the commemorated and have religious and divinical overtones. They were honoured only during the subject's lifetime and, on his death, they were often smashed and placed in his tomb, as if to kill the stelae's influence.

The study of glyphs has now progressed so far that it is possible to read the name of the person commemorated on the stela and to discover several dynasties at Tikal. Stela 4 reveals the name of 'Curl Snout' and the date AD 378. He seems to have been a foreigner from the great centre of Teotihuacan, north of Mexico City. His accession was accompanied by an unprecedented building programme. Curl Snout was succeeded by his son 'Stormy Sky', commemorated on Stela 31. Under him, Tikal rose to the peak of its pre-classic power in about 470 and probably established new dynasties at Copán and Quirigua.

Two hundred and fifty years later it was Ruler A, an ancestor of 'Stormy Sky', who began the great building scheme which reflected Tikal's final power and greatness, giving it the unique set of pyramid temples that were first explored by Maudslay in 1881. Ruler A is mentioned on the stela that commemorates his son, known, prosaically, as Ruler B. The stela records that Ruler B became Lord of Tikal in 734 and that the stela itself was set up in 743. Beneath Ruler B's name glyph are written his honorary titles and his pedigree, beginning with his mother. She is known as 'Lady Bat' from the tiny carving of a bat's head above the profile of a woman's head with a topknot of hair. His father, Ruler A, is represented by a glyph that looks like an opened-out cocoa-pod and gives him the affectionate name 'Cocoa Beans'. He lived, the stela says, into his fourth 'katun', that is until he was over sixty at least.

It was Cocoa Beans who built the two great pyramid temples which face each other across the Great Plaza: Temple I, the Temple of the Giant Jaguar, and Temple 2, the Temple of the Masks. Excavation tunnels recently driven into the Temple of the Giant Jaguar revealed the richest of the many graves to be found at Tikal: a skeleton surrounded by a fabulous collection of jades, pearls, pottery and shells from the Pacific and, on the body itself, 180 pieces of jade jewellery, necklaces, ear ornaments, bracelets and anklets. In contrast, beneath the floor of the rear room of the temple was found a grave that was built well after the erection of the temple, probably about the year 900. It had later been broken into by Mayan Indians of the twelfth century who, as well as the bones of one of their own contemporaries, had left a residue of broken incense burners and copal, the sacred incense gum. It was this same kind of gum and pottery sherds that Maudslay himself noted had been left by the Lacandon at Yaxchilan.

It was in the dark interiors of these temples, hundreds of feet into the sky, that Mayan priests would observe the stars or intercede with the gods of the rain, sun, wind and corn, nourish the gods by bleeding themselves and, in their pain, hallucinate. From here, too, on sacred days, the priests would come out of the temple, out over the great plaza with its brightly coloured buildings and thousands of people milling below, and make sacrifice, a human sacrifice, perhaps in the same way as the Aztecs did 500 years later: a flint knife in the chest and the body tossed down the steep steps to the ground and the crowd over 100 feet below. In this way, the ordinary Maya would be bound by awe and obedience to their rulers.

Above: *Stela 4, 'Curl Snout', from Tikal, dating from AD 378.*

Some time after the year 900 the Mayan civilisation collapsed. The Maya returned to the jungle they'd come from and where, in small communities, they still are. Maudslay, who had correctly gauged that the collapse had come well before the Spanish Conquest, had his own theory as to the cause:

> When and why the valleys of the Usumacinta and Motagua were deserted by the Mayas there is no evidence to show ... Famine and pestilence, civil strife, and the attacks of warlike neighbours have all been suggested as the causes, and all may have contributed to the result, but there is some reason for giving preference to the last.

Add earthquake, the collapse of centralised government and the decline in trade and the theories still debated today are complete. Confirmation for any of them (or any combination of them) has still to be found.

Maudslay's active fieldwork ended in 1894, but his interest in the Maya, and in helping others to research the Maya, continued throughout the rest of his life. Gradually his achievements were acknowledged, and due honours bestowed. His casts and moulds were rescued from museum basements and displayed at the British Museum in the Maudslay Room, the only time that a living scientist had been honoured in this way. He retired to Somerset and then, finally, to Mornay Cross in Herefordshire, where he died in January 1931 aged eighty. He was one of the few explorer archaeologists to die peacefully in bed.

> Only one attempt, as far as I could learn, has ever been made to navigate these rapids, and that was by two wood-cutters who, after a very festive evening, boastfully started in a canoe for the village of Tenosique. The canoe arrived in safety, but neither of the men were ever seen again; as I further learnt that they had with them a keg of that awful compound known as native rum, it would be hard to say whether they were killed by the water or the spirit.

Chapter Seven

SPIRITS OF THE CANYON
Richard Wetherill in the Four Corners of the USA

The number of skeletons found at one level and in one place would suggest a sudden and violent destruction of a community by battle or massacre. Many of the skulls are broken, as well as the ribs, and the bones of the arms and legs. In the back-bones of two different skeletons we found the ends of spear points imbedded; in one case the break in the bone was partially healed, showing that the person must have lived for some time after the wound was inflicted.*

Richard Wetherill was a cowboy. His ranch was in the Mancos Valley in Colorado near the 'Four Corners', the only point in the United States where the boundaries of four states meet: Colorado, Utah, Arizona and New Mexico. It is a land of flat-topped mountains and deep canyons, of desert and rock, and inhabited by Indians: the Ute, the Navajo and the Hopi. White settlers from the east first moved into the area in the 1870s and into inevitable conflict with the Indian tribes, but one family who were on good terms with the Indians was the Wetherills. During the bleak, cold winters the Wetherills ran their cattle on Ute territory, in the rocky, unexplored canyons branching off from the Mancos river, where the Indians themselves rarely went. It was the home of Indian spirits who dwelt in the little ruined buildings which clung high up to the canyon walls. It was here that Richard Wetherill was to discover a culture and a civilisation undreamt of by the white man, of cliff villages unique

* R. Wetherill, in *Archaeologist Magazine* (May 1894).

in the world. It was here that Wetherill was to pioneer the study of archaeology in the south-western United States and here that he was to lose his life.

The Wetherills were a Quaker family from Pennsylvania. Benjamin Wetherill had moved to Fort Leavenworth, Kansas, in 1859 and for a while was an Indian trail agent riding the Chisolm Trail and sorting out disputes between whites and Indians in Texas and Oklahoma. He had five sons – Al, Win, Clayton, John, and Richard, the eldest. In 1876 the family moved further west in search of a fortune in the silver fields of Colorado. In 1880, unsuccessful and almost penniless, their wagons arrived in the Mancos Valley.

Compared with the surrounding barrenness, the country of the Mancos Valley was at this point green and fertile, though the summers could be parched and in the winter the area could be cut off by heavy falls of snow. The ranch that the Wetherills

Right: *The Wetherill Brothers about 1893. Richard is in the middle and around him, from left to right, are Al, Win, Clayton and John.*

founded they called 'The Alamo' and it prospered, with a ranch house, outbuildings, corrals and a smithy. The *Mancos Times* called it 'one of the most beautiful and fertile mountain farms in the west'. Because the family were Quakers they were pacifists and, except for hunting game, they never carried guns, unlike their settler neighbours. They were not hostile to the Indians and the Indians were not hostile to them. The area where the Ute Indians allowed the Wetherills to winter their cattle was in the Mesa Verde, or 'green table': a vast rocky plateau 8000 feet above sea level, riddled with gulches and canyons and dense with pine trees. It was an area of several hundred square miles and an area in which it was very easy to get lost.

In the winter of 1884, the brothers established a camp at the base of Johnson Canyon to watch the cattle. To pass the time they searched the canyons for signs of the Indian ruins that had first been noticed by a geologist searching for gold in 1874. The cliff dwellings were usually high up in the canyon walls and at first it was difficult to make out what was Indian dwelling and what was natural formation of the rock. But, as their eyes became accustomed to the terrain, the houses began to show themselves; houses full of abandoned Indian relics, pots and stone tools. The brothers took many relics back to the ranch and these were sent by their father to a bookseller in Denver. It was during one of these expeditions that Richard Wetherill was told by a Ute Indian called Acowitz of a secret and sacred place, deep in the canyon, bigger than any they had already seen.

On 18 December 1888, Richard Wetherill was in the company of his brother-in-law, Charlie Mason. They were searching for strays and it was snowing. From one of the deep gullies in the side of Cliff Canyon they climbed on horseback to a vantage point on the top of the mesa. There, looking up towards the head of the canyon, they saw the most extraordinary sight. In the canyon wall opposite was the mouth of a giant cave, filled with buildings. It seemed like an entire city. Fine masonry houses piled on top of one another in terraces; towers reaching to the cave roof; strange, circular pit-like buildings going into the earth; doors, windows and every available space filled and protected from the snow by the giant overhang of the cliff. Al Wetherill thought that he had caught a glimpse of this place a year before in 1887:

> I stood looking at the ruins in surprised awe. I had hoped to find some unexplored dwellings – but this discovery surpassed my wildest dreams. I gauged the steep walls of the canyon

Right: *Cliff Palace at Mesa Verde before restoration. 'This discovery surpassed my wildest dreams.'*

against my tired legs and the ebbing daylight and turned slowly away. They would wait – they had waited for hundreds of years for the moment of discovery.

They named the place Cliff Palace and then rode round the head of the canyon and found a way down over the cliffs to the level of the buildings. For the next few hours they went slowly from room to room. Wooden beams still protruded from ceilings, plaster still clung to some of the walls; skeletons lay on the floor:

> It appeared as though the inhabitants had left everything they possessed right where they had used it last.

There were corn cobs, a stone axe, and broken pots. Mason came to believe that the Cliff Palace had withstood an extended siege and witnessed the final tragedy of its mysterious inhabitants:

> All of the joists on which floors and roofs were laid had been wrenched out. These timbers are built into the walls and difficult to remove, even the little willows on which the mud roofs and upper floors are laid were carefully taken out. No plausible reason for this has been advanced except that it may have been used for fuel.
>
> Another strange circumstance is that so many of their valuable possessions were left in the rooms and covered with clay of which the roofs and upper floors were made, not to mention many of the walls broken down in tearing out the timbers. It would seem that their intention was to conceal their valuables so that their enemies might not secure them; or perhaps the

people were in such despair that property was not considered.

There were many human bones scattered about as though several people had been killed and left unburied. Had Cliff Palace been abandoned . . . and the timbers used in other buildings, all movable articles of value would have been taken away instead of being covered, and much of it broken and destroyed unnecessarily.

It seems to me that there can be no doubt that the Cliff Dwellers were exterminated by their more savage and warlike neighbours, the men being killed and the women being adopted into the tribe of the conquerors, though in some instances migrations may have become necessary as a result of drought or pressure from outside tribes.

Future archaeologists were to show that drought and natural disaster was a more likely explanation than siege and slaughter.

With just a few hours of daylight remaining, the two cowboys split up to see what else they could find. Mason found nothing, but Richard Wetherill, riding north, made the second great discovery of the day; sheltered by the cliff overhang of another canyon wall and almost hidden by fir trees was another large ruin, not as big but even better preserved than the Cliff Palace itself. 'Spruce Tree House' was to prove to be the best preserved dwelling in the whole of the Mesa Verde.

Wetherill did not enter the building that night but went searching for it the next day with Charlie Mason. In the maze of snow-covered canyons, each one looking the same, they couldn't find it. They completely lost their way and found, instead, yet another major ruin – the 'Square Tower House', again sheltered by an overhanging cliff, a dwelling with seventy rooms and the tower built against the canyon wall: the tallest structure they had seen.

What the two men had discovered in two days was the remains of a civilisation that had existed in North America centuries before the arrival of Columbus. For Richard Wetherill, it was a turning point. From now on he was to spend his summers at the ranch and his winters searching for ruins; the search was to become his life's work.

Within days, Richard's brother John and three companions were back in the ruins searching for artefacts. They stretched a canvas over the top of one of the round subterranean rooms and lived there for a month. They had no idea that they were in fact living in a 'kiva' – a sacred room devoted to religious ceremonial. In the weeks that followed, as they moved from room to room digging into the piles of accumulated earth and fallen stones, they found stone tools, tools of bone, kitchen implements and broken pottery. And as they dug deeper they came across whole pots, white with distinctive black markings, baskets, shells, beads and pieces of cloth. At the back of the cave, where the roof was too low for houses, was the turkey house and the communal rubbish dump. Here the cowboys came face to face with the 'cliff dwellers' themselves:

> These mummies were not embalmed but they simply dried, from the corpse having been buried in ground so dry that complete decomposition did not take place.

Long hair still hung over the dried skin and bone. Even the eyes were still in place, only the spark of life was missing.

It soon became obvious that digging in the ruins could be profitable, artefacts could be sold. The first collection of 'Cliff Dweller' relics was offered to the Denver Historical Society for 3000 dollars and eventually bought by them. The following December the Wetherills returned. As Charlie Mason wrote:

> Our previous work had been carried out to satisfy more our own curiosity than for any other purpose but this time it was a business proposition.

One of several new ruins they discovered was one that they named 'Fortified House'. It was situated just under the lip of the overhang of the canyon wall:

Right: *John Wetherill in Cliff Palace at Mesa Verde. Note the graffiti.*

Some walls along the ledge on which the house is built were undoubtedly put there for defensive purposes. This house did not yield much until one day John found by measurement that there was space near the centre of the building for a small room to which no entrance could be found, so he made one through the top. The room was small, not over five or six feet square, but in it were five skeletons, about a dozen pieces of pottery, several baskets, the finest we had ever seen, also a bow and a dozen arrows, all nearly perfect, except the bow.

One of the arrows had an agate tip and all were lying across the heads of the five bodies. Bowls were placed between the skulls and on the feet of one of the skeletons was a pair of moccasins.

The bow was the heaviest one we had ever found and it was well wrapped with sinews. Part of the string remained: it was made of twisted sinews and was larger than a slate pencil and he who could draw one of those arrows to the head with such a bow must have been a powerful man.

The owner of the bow was probably the man whose skeleton was larger than any of the others and clothed in a buckskin suit and cap that seemed almost new.

The diggings continued and the artefacts were removed to the ranch, where they were put on display in a small museum. During the summer, as the word spread and the interest grew, people began to come to the ranch to see the relics and to ride the thirty-mile round trip into the Mesa Verde to see the sites.

Compared with the scientific methods of excavation that Alfred Maudslay was employing at exactly the same time on the sites of the Mayan Indians over 1000 miles south, the methods of the Wetherills were little different from those of Belzoni, and did as much damage. They were the methods of the pot hunter, the looter. But like Belzoni, as their knowledge increased, so their excavation techniques improved, even though their appeals for help from the Smithsonian Institution and the Peabody Museum at Harvard were rejected. Although the brothers saw the sale of artefacts as a way of financing their digs, all the four collections that they made from the Mesa Verde ended up in museums. To be accused by later archaeologists of vandalism hurt. Al Wetherill wrote just before he died in 1948:

We never destroyed, nor permitted destruction of any of those buildings nor their contents, feeling that we were the custodians of a priceless heritage. Those who came as tourists were aware that we would allow no damage nor wanton pilfering, and not many of them were the type that would.

Below: *Pottery bowl from Mesa Verde, decorated with a hermaphroditic figure, c. AD 900.*

By March 1890, Richard Wetherill, by his own reckoning, had found and investigated all the ancient Indian ruins in the Mesa Verde. There were 182. The following summer, 1891, there arrived from Sweden Baron Gustaf Nordenskiold. He was twenty-three years old, an explorer and a scientist, and, with the Wetherills' help, the first to make a proper scientific investigation of the ruins. From Nordenskiold, Richard Wetherill learnt the value of digging with a small trowel instead of a large spade. It was Nordenskiold who helped Wetherill realise that the subterranean rooms that he called 'estufas' were not water or storage tanks but the same kind of ceremonial rooms found in the modern pueblos of the neighbouring Hopi Indians and which the Hopi called 'kivas'. The exact age of the ruins, however, remained a mystery. Spanish priests who had crossed the region in the eighteenth century on their way from Mexico to the missions of California had neither seen the ruins nor mentioned them. Nordenskiold, counting the growth rings of a tree sprouting out of a wall at Spruce Tree House, showed that the walls were at least 162 years old, giving them a date no later than 1739, although he thought they were much older and only appeared new because protection from the elements and the dry air had preserved them so well. Charlie Mason wrote:

> In making these collections we learned much of the Cliff Dwellers' life. They were agriculturalists and raised crops of corn, beans and squashes, and kept tame turkeys. Their corn is a yellow dent with some red ears, not at all like the corn grown by the Navajos. Their beans are similar to the beans of the Mexicans: the squashes were of good size.

The apparent association with Mexico brought the assumption in some quarters that these ruins, and others soon to be found in the region, were built by the Aztecs, whose capital Tenochtitlán (now Mexico City) had been destroyed by the Spanish in 1521. The assumption was wrong. What we now know is that the buildings and the artefacts of the Mesa Verde date, for the most part, from the twelfth and thirteenth centuries, from the last period of the Pueblo Indian culture, an indigenous stone-age culture that began in the region at the time of Christ but which ceased to develop around 1250 when, for some unknown reason, the buildings of the Mesa Verde were abandoned. One of the last dateable timbers found at Mesa Verde shows that the tree was cut and used in 1278.

In 1892, the brothers made their last collection from the ruins of Mesa Verde for the Colorado state display at the Chicago

World's Fair in 1893. It was here that Richard Wetherill met the brothers Talbot and Fred Hyde. They were heirs to the Bab-O soap fortune and, for the next decade, were to finance Richard's archaeological expeditions.

Grand Gulch lay 100 miles to the west of Mesa Verde in the neighbouring state of Utah, in country even more remote and dangerous than the Mesa Verde itself. It was not until the late 1880s that the first white men to reach there had returned with photographs of cliff dwellings like those in the Mesa Verde canyons. As the artefacts ran out at Mesa Verde, Wetherill suspected Grand Gulch might provide an alternative source of supply. He wrote to Talbot Hyde in early 1893 and proposed an expedition. However:

> This whole subject ... is in its infancy. The work we do must stand the most rigid inspection and we do not want to do it in such a manner that anyone in the future can pick flaws in it.

In the same letter he outlined a system of recording, drawing plans, and photographing each house excavated and a system for logging every article found on what he called a 'form of work':

1	2	3	4
Number of house or ruin	Number of article	Name of article	Number of room

5	6	7	8
Number of section	Depth	Number of floors if any	Remarks

Every article to be numbered with India ink and fine pen with tube paints white, red or black. Plan of all houses and sections to be made on paper or book, to be ruled both ways.

Richard Wetherill was a pioneer archaeologist. Without any scientific background, self-taught and with only experience and example to guide him, he aimed to do work that would stand comparison with the work of the professional archaeologists back east and would be accepted by them '... since the value of these things consists largely in the scientific data procured'.

The headquarters for the expedition was established at Bluff City, a small desert town of less than 1000 people. Grand Gulch was three days' ride away, across territory that was unmapped and without roads:

It is the most tortuous canyon in the whole of the south-west, making bends from 200 to 600 yards apart almost its entire length for fifty miles ... (it) is from 300 to 700 feet deep and in many places towards the lower end the bends are cut through by nature making natural bridges. Ingress or egress is very difficult. There being not more than five or six places where even footmen can get in or out.

But the effort was to prove worthwhile. From an address as strange as it was geographically accurate, 'First Valley, Cottonwood Creek. 30 Miles North of Bluff City', Richard Wetherill wrote to his patron Talbot Hyde with great excitement on 17 December 1893:

Our success has surpassed all expectations ... In the cave we are now working we have taken 28 skeletons and two more in sight ... and a thing that will surprise the archaeologists of the country is the fact of our finding them at a depth of 5 and 6 feet in a cave in which there are cliff dwellings and we find the bodies *under* the ruins, three feet below any Cliff Dweller sign. They are a *different* race from anything I have ever seen.

It was the first appearance on the archaeological scene of the Basket Maker People:

They had feather cloth and baskets, no pottery ... The whole thing is truly wonderful.

The cliff dwellings, as at Mesa Verde, were situated high up in the canyon walls under a cliff overhang and facing the sun. The amount of Cliff Dweller material that the Wetherills took from them was prodigious; 200 articles from a cave here, nine mummies from a cave there, many of them quite remarkable:

Whether it is a specimen of surgery or not, I have not yet determined, but I think it is. It is a very old man cave dweller. He was cut in two at the loin and abdomen, or rather the skin is, and sewed together again with a string at least an eighth of an inch in diameter, with stitches one half-inch apart. It seems most horrible to me. The face seems to indicate pain. The hands are clutched on the cut upon the stomach.

But extraordinary, even ghoulish, as this Cliff Dweller material was, its immediate scientific function was to provide a comparison with the new and unfamiliar material of the Basket Maker People:

In these caves in Grand Gulch are cliff houses as well as the burials of the cave dwellers. We get a perfect idea there, and we can easily separate the two classes of people ... The rock of the caves could easily disintegrate and would in time form a foundation for the cliff dwellers to build upon, but this is not always the case. When the Basket People dug out their bottle-shaped rooms, the tops, of course, were all on a level with the surface, and they covered them in such a way that it could not be detected. The C.D., in some cases, built over them not knowing they were there. In others that were open, the C.D. used to throw rubbish in ... The Basket People and C.D. both made feather cloth ... The feathers are from the turkey. The B.P. used the caves more as a burial ground than anything else. Some of the caves have evidence of being temporary camping places for these people ... They are a larger race than

Left: *Excavated Cliff Dweller pots, and human Basket Maker skulls and bones, from Cave 7 at Grand Gulch. 'Our success has surpassed all expectations.'*

the Cliff Dwellers. I have measured none of them, but I know from comparison, as I have now handled more than one hundred of each.

In later letters Wetherill wrote:

They made no pottery nor fine arrow points like the C.D. but all large spear points. The C.D. had bows and arrows but the B.P. race had no weapon but the atlatl and spear ...

In these pot holes of caches are found the bodies of all ages and sexes – sandals upon the feet – human hair, gee string, cedar bark breech cloth. Beads around their necks. All wrapped in a blanket of rabbit fur – of a weave similar to the feather cloth. Then they are (also found) in a mummy cloth or sack cloth such as the Peruvians used. This is made from yucca fiber and good cloth it is. Over the head is a small basket – flat – about 20 inches in diameter, usually found in good condition; Apaches make a similar one today ...

The sandals were not all square toed but differed from the Cliff Dwellers in this way: Basket Maker ... much finer than the usual Cliff Dweller.

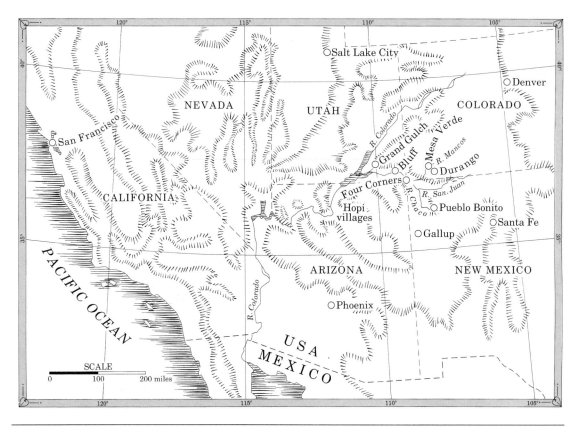

Richard Wetherill, the cowboy with a shovel, had now become the ethnographer drawing comparisons between modern Indian tribes and their prehistoric ancestors. In his method of excavating surface areas first and carefully progressing downwards to the layers underneath – and comparing the finds on the principle that the deeper ones are older – he was an archaeologist practising the modern technique of stratigraphy.

Excited by what he had found, he wrote to Talbot Hyde on 1 October 1895:

> I am going into New Mexico for a little while to see if I cannot find some more accessible ruins where I can put in this winter and find a different character of relics.

Wetherill was heading for a place, if hearsay could be relied on, that contained prehistoric Indian ruins even finer than those at Mesa Verde and Grand Gulch. The place was called Pueblo Bonito and the ruins were in the Chaco Canyon, some 120 miles south of The Alamo ranch and the same distance north-west of the old state capital of Santa Fe, though no white man living seemed to know exactly where. Wetherill, however, was not the first white man to go there.

The state of New Mexico had been Mexican territory until annexed by the United States in 1846. Three years later the Washington government sent an expedition into the area to 'pacify' the local Navajo, and a member of that expedition was a young lieutenant called James Simpson, the first man to map the area called the Chaco and give a description of the ruins of Pueblo Bonito:

> The circuit of its walls is about thirteen hundred feet. Its present elevation shows that it has had at least four stories of apartments. The number of rooms on the ground floor at present discernible is one hundred and thirty-nine.

He estimated that at one time there had been about 650. Cliff Palace in the Mesa Verde had only 217. He added that the country in which the ruin was situated 'presented one wide expanse of barren waste'. The next white visitor was William Henry Jackson, who took the first photographs of the ruins in 1877 and described Pueblo Bonito as: '... the largest and in some respects the most remarkable of all (the ruins). Its length is 544 feet and its width 314 feet.' Jackson noted from the ground plan and the different ways that the masonry walls had been laid that the pueblo had not been built all at one time but had been added to over the years.

Wetherill left the ranch in mid-October 1895 in the company of his future wife. The Palmers, father, mother and daughter Marietta, were a Quaker family who travelled the mid-west giving musical entertainments. They had just driven their wagon 700 miles to The Alamo ranch to see the ruins at Mesa Verde and, despite the lack of food and water in the desert and the threat from the hostile Navajo, were keen to see anything else. Wetherill invited them to join him on his winter expedition and they set out with two wagons pulled by four mules, three saddle horses and supplies for two months, which included barrels slung beneath the wagons for water. With the help of a Navajo guide they entered the Chaco after six days' ride across the open desert. It was over 6000 feet above sea level, windy and bitterly cold, but there, on the canyon floor, lay the great crescent of North America's biggest prehistoric ruin: Pueblo Bonito, or 'beautiful village'. They stayed a month, examining the ruins of Pueblo Bonito, Pueblo del Arroyo and Chetro Ketl, and doing a little digging. Wetherill reported to Hyde:

> Not having anything important on hand this winter, I have taken the opportunity to visit the ruins of New Mexico. Those of Chaco Canyon being the greatest in New Mexico and almost unknown. Everyone so far having tried to get relics there making a total failure of it. For that reason more than any other I wished to examine them. I was successful after a few days search in finding relics in quantity. The ruins there are enormous. There are 11 of the pueblos or houses containing 100 to 500 rooms each and numerous small ones, how many I do not know but there must be more than 100. I stayed there until I had gotten 40 pieces of pottery ... Grass and water is plenty, wood is scarce. A wagon can be driven to the ruins in five or six days from our ranch ... I will send you a map and description of different regions in which it will pay to work.

The Chaco Canyon has been described as the 'primitive Athens of America, the largest, most thriving and progressive center of human life on the continent, north of Mexico'. Fifteen miles long and up to a mile wide, it lies in the centre of a vast arid desert of sand, rock and mesa. The only local inhabitants are the Navajo who live in small, isolated 'hogans' – domed huts built of sticks and mud. At one time, however, the canyon supported a thriving community: a group of villages and townships, places to live, work and worship, which were connected by a network of roads and which contained some of the most spectacular masonry buildings that the Indians ever built.

Opposite: *Mesa Verde, Colorado, USA. Spruce Tree House, first seen by Richard Wetherill and Charles Mason on 18 December 1888, the same day they found Cliff Palace.*

Right: *Cliff Palace at Mesa Verde is the largest known cliff dwelling in the south-west United States. It dates from c. AD 1250, the last period of the Pueblo Indian culture. The cliff cave in which it is built is 60 feet high, 90 feet deep and measures 325 feet across the front. It consists of over two hundred rooms.*
Below right: *The Balcony House, Mesa Verde. The house walls are plastered with adobe and traces of painting still survive. The circular building in the foreground is the kiva, the sunken chamber used for ceremonials.*
Opposite: *Pueblo Bonito, Chaco Canyon, New Mexico. This stone building was excavated by the Hyde expedition in 1897.*

Opposite: *The beauti-fully constructed curving wall of the temple at Machu Picchu which Bingham called the royal mauso-leum, 'one of the finest examples of masonry I had ever seen'.*

Right: *The valley of the Urubamba river, Machu Picchu, Peru. 'One is drawn irre-sistibly onward by ever-recurring surprises through a deep, winding gorge, turning and twisting past over-hanging cliffs of incred-ible height.' (Hiram Bingham, July 1911)* Below: *'When asked just where the ruins were, he pointed straight up to the top of the mountain.' The mountain in the middle distance is the Huayna Picchu (the little Picchu).*

Opposite top left: *Wat Chang Lom, Si Satchanalai, Thailand. Brick elephants, similar to the elephants at Ellora, support the temple terrace.*
Opposite top right: *The pagoda of Wat Chang Lom, built to a revolutionary Thai design c. AD 1290 by King Rama Gamhen.*
Opposite below: *Wat Chedi Chet Theo, a royal mausoleum built c. AD 1350 by Rama Gamhen's grandson Lü Tai. 'I cannot find a single soul who knows ... about the history of this ancient city. I must wander alone among the pagodas and try to conjure up in my mind the kind of men who built them and why they fell into ruins.' (Reginald Le May, 1924)*
Left: *The ruined Wihan (assembly hall) of Wat Maha Tat, the great temple of the Sacred Relic. The oldest of the Satchanalai temples, it was built c. AD 1200. The pagoda is traditional Khmer in style.*

The first inhabitants were the Basket Maker People, who came into the area in about the year AD 500 and built their pit houses similar to those found throughout the south-west. They built circular pits about fifteen feet across, with sandstone slabs lining the walls and with a roof of beams covered with soft, sandy soil rising above ground level and supported internally by four free-standing posts. A complete Basket Maker village was discovered in 1926 at Shabik'eschee on top of the mesa, but, sometime between the years AD 500 and 850, the Basket Maker People moved into the canyon bottom where pit houses have been discovered under the present remains of Pueblo Bonito. At the same time there began a shift from pit houses to above-ground structures, rows of single living-rooms paired with storage rooms at the back. By AD 950, the Pueblo began to take on its present characteristic crescent 'D' shape, with rooms added at ground level and then rising to three and even four storeys high, a vast apartment house of 800 rooms with, at its height, a population that has been estimated at between 2000 and 5000 people. But Pueblo Bonito was just one site – the area probably had a population well in excess of 10,000 people.

Like the people of Grand Gulch and Mesa Verde, the Chacoans were not just hunters but farmers, growing beans, corn and squash. But they were also weavers, potters of extraordinary skill, jewellers in turquoise and, above all, architects. As well as the beautiful masonry walls of the houses, once covered with adobe, there are the great kivas, the vast circular sunken halls that developed from the pit houses of the early Basket Maker People and which could accommodate up to 500 people for major ceremonials. They were sacred places where the spirits of ancestors who dwelt underground could escape into the air and light of the world through a small hole in the ground, the 'sipapu'. This sense of the spiritual aspect of the natural world pervades the entire way of life of the Pueblo Indians, even to their rubbish dumps. These are found throughout the Chaco, ash piles on which the Indians placed broken pots, broken implements, even the sweepings from their houses so that everything goes back to nature – the Pueblo idea of what is good in the world. In the modern Pueblos of the Hopi, the dumps, like their kivas, are still sacred places. No white man is allowed to walk on the dumps and Hopi prayers are offered there on days of great ceremonies.

Although the Pueblo Indians had no metal, no wheel, and only developed pictographs in place of writing, their culture and achievements might be compared with their near contemporaries, the Maya, who also had no metal, no wheel and no

Opposite: Buddhist attendant, nearly two feet high, stoneware c. AD 1300 from the kilns of Si Satchanalai. 'The King, sovereign of the Kingdom, as well as princes and princesses, men as well as women ... without exception, without distinction of hierarchy or sex, practise with devotion the Buddhist religion.'

writing but built and crafted superbly. The key to survival in the Chaco, as at the Mayan Tikal, was water, but in the year AD 1035 there was a great drought which lasted for six years. Instead of destroying the community, it was the spur to expansion. Around the year AD 900, the inhabitants of the Chaco had begun to construct a system of dams and channels which could catch the vital storm water that fell on the mesa tops and divert it to irrigate their fields. The construction of the townships was a direct result of these new irrigation systems; the people were banding together for survival. When the water began to fail, the Chaco became the hub of a road network which spread forty miles across the desert in each direction, linking outlying townships and along which could be taken and traded not only water but goods and food.

In the south-west of the United States, even a small change in the climate can be catastrophic. A beam of wood recently dated to AD 1125 probably marks the start of the end of the building programme at the Chaco. Again as with the Mayan site at Tikal, it was probably not disease or invasion that finally drove the inhabitants out but a gradual lessening of the water supply and, with it, the supply of fuel and food that depended on it. By AD 1150 most of the Chacoans had gone. People arrived from the drought-hit Mesa Verde but they too were gone by AD 1200. The Navajo did not arrive in the area till about AD 1400; so where did the Chacoans go? Are their descendants the Hopi of the Hopi villages of Walpi and Oraibi which Wetherill visited in 1895? The Hopi themselves believe that they are.

After Richard Wetherill's initial trip, Talbot Hyde sponsored the first proper expedition to the Chaco in April 1896. It was led by a 23-year-old student archaeologist from Harvard called George Pepper, who had been recommended to Hyde by the American Museum of Natural History. For Richard Wetherill, the most experienced explorer in the south-west, it was a galling demotion.

The wagon train left The Alamo ranch in April and pitched camp in the shadow of Pueblo Bonito's north wall, where two of the Pueblo's rooms were used for stores and another as a photographic dark room. Trenching immediately began, at Pepper's suggestion, on the rubbish dumps, but finds were disappointing: discarded sandals; pottery sherds; bits of rope and animal bone. Later archaeologists were to regard these finds, indeed all finds, as significant clues to the residents' customs and way of life, but the Hyde expedition were expecting to discover bodies. They moved to rubbish dumps on the south side of the canyon and at once discovered thirty skeletons. Wetherill wrote:

Seven o'clock in the morning every man was at his place when I was in camp. They worked until noon, nooned one and a half hours, then worked until 6 p.m. ... Each one knew what was expected of him and where and how to work; failure in this meant loss of their job, as also being late more than two mornings.

The workmen were Navajo – Hostyn Klipe, Thomas Padilla, Alihipa, Tenehiagi and Chis-chilling-begay, and they worked hard under Wetherill's supervision:

I felt that the success of the expedition depended upon my efforts. Therefore every moment I had was spent with them giving instructions and placing room numbers upon articles except when doing photographic work, trading for mutton etc. I measured nearly all the rooms, and gave all finds personal attention. My rule was to be up at five-thirty every morning except Sunday.

In August, Wetherill found one of the largest caches of pottery ever discovered in the United States. In a corner of one of the rooms of Pueblo Bonito, buried under the drifted sand that had to be carefully spooned out were more than 150 bowls and jars, all perfect and, in a neighbouring room, were arrows, bird effigies, strangely carved wooden staves and over 4000 pieces of turquoise. By the end of the season in September, they had cleared thirty-seven rooms – and Wetherill was in desperate financial straits:

My circumstances now are such that I am free to do work, as I have lost all the property I had and this work is all that I am fitted to do. It has been the cause of loss but I can build up a better reputation for careful honest work.

He had also rumbled George Pepper:

Mr. P's records are O.K. also but I know the man better than you ever will. Therefore I know I will receive no credit from him unless I were in his presence. Since he is the head of the expedition I ought not to expect it, of course, but it is my right just the same.

When Pepper wrote up his report on the Hyde expedition, twenty-four years after it had taken place, there was no mention of Richard Wetherill at all.

In the fall of 1896, Wetherill, after his unfortunate experience with Pepper, returned to the place where he could be his own boss again, to the Grand Gulch. He wanted to do 'good scientific

Right: *House floor of Room 61 at Pueblo Bonito, under excavation by Navajo workmen. 'I measured nearly all the rooms and gave all finds personal attention.'*

work as good as though the Museum (the American Museum of Natural History) was represented'. This time the expedition was larger and better equipped. There were fourteen people, each with specific duties ranging from cooking, feeding the stock, making weekly trips for supplies to Bluff City, digging, recording and storing, plus forty animals:

> Twenty-seven to thirty were packed all the time with from 100 to 250 (pounds) each. No grass whatever was found. The animals subsisted on the grain fed them with the tops of brush which they picked ... many were very weak and thin. We had several extra ones on the way down to use in case of accidents which proved of frequent occurrence. One animal fell off a bridge and broke its neck. Another fell off the trail where it wound about a ledge going into the cañon and was killed instantly. Another fell off a cliff with the same result. Two gave out completely and were abandoned ... Another animal when near Bluff fell about 20 feet with a pack and could go no further, making a total loss of nine horses.

The party camped in the Gulch in the shelter of the overhanging cliffs. Wood for the camp-fires came from the scrub oak which grew on the canyon floor; water, as the stream in the canyon bottom was almost dry, came from melted snow. The weather was bitterly cold and, inside some of the caves, working conditions were often appalling:

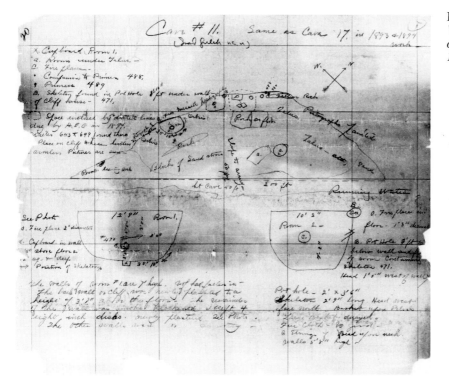

This cave we did not work. Could not stand the filth and dust raised by shovelling.

The cook was up to make breakfast by 4 a.m. and work continued all day until dark. Everyone was aware that a blizzard could cut them off from supplies for weeks on end. Most of the caves explored were near the canyon floor but others, twenty feet or so from the canyon rim and sheltered by the rim rock, could only be reached from the canyon top. This was done by dropping a rope over the ledge down to the cave and down which a man gradually went, supported, for safety, by a second rope that was attached to his waist and held by his companions overhead. It was a perilous job, but it wasn't the only peril: the Gulch was not in the territory of friendly Utes but of the Navajos.

The expedition had not, this time, been financed by the Hyde brothers but by a rich Harvard student called George Bowles and his tutor C. E. Whitmore, who both went out on the dig. Towards the end of the expedition, the two Harvard men vanished. A search of the maze of canyons produced nothing except an Indian with a message. The white men had been kidnapped by the Navajos and were being held to ransom. The sum demanded was to be paid in silver dollars and, if the money was not paid immediately, the white men would die. It took three days for Richard Wetherill to round up the money and hand it over in a sack and another day before Bowles and Whitmore were able to ride back into camp, unharmed but shaken by four threatening nights on the summit of Moqui Rock. For the two men from back east, their adventure out west had proved more than they'd bargained for. And for the only woman on the expedition, 19-year-old Marietta Palmer – who had just become Mrs Richard Wetherill – it was a bizarre honeymoon. Not every bride willingly shares a tent with the desiccated bodies of prehistoric Indians in order to protect them from dampness.

As well as locating and excavating new caves and new houses, including one of the largest of them all in the south-west at Kiet Siel, the expedition found numerous pictographs on the canyon walls and especially under the natural bridges:

> The painted ones of the Basket Maker with the later ones of the Cliff Dweller cut or incised in the rock without paying attention to the previous one.

But what they mean, we don't know. There is no Rosetta Stone to tell us and modern Indians don't know – or aren't saying.

Of Basket Maker material alone, the expedition produced over 500 examples. But the Basket Maker culture was not taken seriously by the 'real' archaeologists. It was dismissed as a device invented by Wetherill to boost sales of his artefacts and it wasn't until 1914 that independent proof was forthcoming to show that what Wetherill had suggested was true.

The Basket Maker People were the forebears of the Cliff Dwellers, a semi-nomadic race living mostly on the mesa tops where they developed agriculture. They had no bow and arrow but hunted with a short spear thrown with the help of an arm-lengthening device called the atlatl. They had no knowledge of pottery but made baskets so fine that, by dropping hot stones into a basket of water, they could even boil water and cook in them. This way of life lasted until the seventh century AD, not only in the area of Grand Gulch but at Mesa Verde and elsewhere as well. After AD 1200 they moved off the mesa tops and permanently into the caves, becoming what are now identified as the Cliff Dwellers, the Pueblo Indians. The only physical difference between the two groups is that the Cliff Dwellers had flattened heads, as a result of strapping their babies to hard wooden cradle boards, and the Basket Maker People didn't. Together they are known by the Indian name 'Anasazi' – the Ancient Ones. It was a name the Indians were to give Richard Wetherill. Wetherill wrote to Talbot Hyde on 7 May 1897:

The expedition we have just returned from has been a great success but the Cliff Dweller material is practically exhausted as well as the Basket Maker in that region.

He offered the whole collection to the Hydes for $5,500 – to be divided equally between himself and Bowles. The Hydes planned to give the material to the American Museum of Natural History but felt the price was too high. After a lapse of nine months, Wetherill wrote again:

Mr Whitmore and Mr Bowles both wrote me that they had become involved in some serious trouble whereby a little ready money would relieve them. They decided to sacrifice the collection if they could and are now willing to take $1,500 for their share, of course that means cash but $1,250 is an enormous loss it seems to me ... I fancy I need the money as bad as either of them but anything less than that will do me no good. I want it to save the ranch as it is mortgaged but the main thing with me is to know that the amount is coming from somewhere. I am in receipt of several offers for parts of the collection but think it should be held together.

In January 1898, the collection was shipped to New York:

One barrel by express ... This barrel contains 169 sandals, 18 jar rings, 44 baskets and material for making three ears of corn, two bags of corn and one package of corn and beans. Two bunches of herbs. Two feather blankets, three pieces of feather blankets. One feather shirt. One bunch cedar bark rope. Two bunches cedar bark tinder. Five pieces mountain sheepskin. One piece buckskin. One buckskin string. One buckskin bag containing agurite. Four pieces cotton blanket. 23 bunches turca material, in all 361 numbers. This is the small material. ... Have shipped box containing princess and all her belongings just as we found her ... Tomorrow will ship box containing four mummies, a lot of bones, basket and a few skulls.

In a postscript to his letter of 16 February:

My interest in this collection is to be paid to Mrs R. Wetherill, except $1,000 which you can have sent to me by express, provided you find the collection O.K. and the sale goes through. You see I am horribly in debt through my efforts to help all. The result is I am thrown now entirely on my own resources which are nil.

The Alamo ranch was a continuing problem. It not only had to provide a living for the eight members of the Wetherill family,

Below: *Jug decorated with spiral design c. AD 1100, from Chaco Canyon.*

but had to make a profit to pay off the mortgage. Al took over the day-to-day running of the ranch whilst Richard, working the farm in the summer, hoped to raise additional income from the sale of the artefacts he gathered during his expeditions in the winter. In the spring of 1897, Wetherill was back in the Chaco Canyon. Despite his request to Talbot Hyde to be put, this time, 'on a different footing', he wasn't: he remained as Pepper's subordinate. It was not a happy time. Already deep in debt, Wetherill was owed 444 dollars in back pay by the Hydes, and it was not immediately forthcoming. Marietta, who had come to the canyon to support her husband, had to return to The Alamo, pregnant. Water, as for the Chacoans themselves, was either non-existent or, in the summer rains, cascaded over the clifftops and formed into muddy rivers that flattened tents, carried away equipment and then, almost as suddenly as it came, seeped and dried away. And there was trouble with the Indian workers:

> Two men worked to the room or as many as could to advantage, because there were so many eyes to see and less liability of them stealing. So much rivalry existed that they would tell upon each other if anything was taken.

Several things were taken, however:

> One good turquoise was lost from R-38 this year. I could not get to see it. Most likely it will turn up this winter. Only a small number were stolen the year before, among which was the fine pendant that Hosaleepa has, and the small hematite bird that I have. Mr Robinson saw me purchase it. The Indians claimed it came from elsewhere. Turquoise beads taken by the Indians can be gotten for very little, but I should not value them except from the fact of their coming from the workings ... Nothing else was taken by the Indians, as they place no value on other things.

Most serious of all were rumblings of trouble to come. At the end of his letter to Talbot Hyde on 24 October 1897, Wetherill wrote:

> All work in Arizona in ruins is prohibited. New Mexico is waking up to that point also.

And seeing that time was running out, he was not happy with what the expeditions had so far achieved:

> I'm not fully satisfied with the past work at Bonito as I see now where we could have added materially to data. Small things which might help to determine the race of the tribes or stock who lived there.

Such as the discarded sandals and rope in the rubbish dumps.

In the spring of 1898, Richard Wetherill left The Alamo ranch for good and headed for the Chaco:

> I had to get into something to make a living and had decided on this point for a store. I had a good stock of goods amounting to a little over $1,200.00. I had a house planned and work started on it when Mr Pepper arrived. The work has continued until now the house is about ready for occupancy. The store has taken much more of my time than we thought it would, but that is more on account of space. The new building will be so arranged that my wife can do most of the trading, giving me time to carry on the expedition work.

The goods were traded with the Navajo in return for Navajo blankets to be sold in New York. Wetherill also helped build up the Navajo's sheep flocks and provided them with Mexican silver dollars to be turned into Navajo jewellery – and the digging continued, for this and another year. At its end in 1899, after four seasons, it had cost the Hydes some 25,000 dollars and resulted in the excavation of more than half of Pueblo Bonito's remaining rooms and provided more material than from any other site in North America up to that time. It also put on the map the archaeology of the south-western United States and showed that prehistoric civilisations were not limited in the Western hemisphere to Central and South America alone. But in the autumn of 1900, the Hyde expedition was ordered to stop work pending investigation by government and state officials into charges of 'spoilation and destruction' at the Chaco Canyon.

The investigation began in spring 1901 and the charges, including the 'selling of artefacts', were dismissed, but the Hyde expedition was forbidden to continue. At the same time, Richard Wetherill's file for homesteaders' rights was also dismissed and the Chaco Canyon was recommended as the site of a National Park. The relationship between Wetherill and the Hydes ended and in the bureaucratic in-fighting which followed the investigation, Wetherill was caught in the cross-fire as rival interests – government, state, business and Indian – squabbled over the future preservation of the canyon and the surrounding area. Richard was accused of continuing to dig illegally. Washington was informed by the government commissioner:

> The more I know of Richard Wetherill the more I am convinced he is a man without principle. He boasted to me that he was known as the 'Vandal of the South-west', which at the time I did not accept seriously but have since learned was a matter of some pride with this man.

The Indian Commission accused him of mistreating the Indians and stealing from them. It could be argued that any stealing was the other way round. One man who owed Richard Wetherill money was the Navajo Chis-chilling-begay. On the evening of 22 June 1910, Wetherill was riding back to the store through the Chaco Canyon, half a mile below Pueblo Bonito. He was with another cowboy, Bill Finn, rounding up stray cattle. At a bend in the canyon, a shot rang out, and then a second and a third. Wetherill was killed instantly.

Despite Chis-chilling-begay's plea that he hadn't meant to kill the white man and that Anasazi was his best friend, he was indicted for murder and served three years for voluntary manslaughter. Wetherill's homesteading rights were approved two years after his death. He is buried in the Chaco Canyon.

Richard Wetherill, for so many years dismissed as a cowboy looter, is now recognised as a man who contributed more than any other to the discovery of the Indian civilisations of the south-west United States. In 1903, still searching for knowledge, he had written modestly to Talbot Hyde:

> I hope in ... time to learn a little about this region that may be of value to someone who will know how to use it.

Chapter Eight

LOST CITY OF THE INCAS
Hiram Bingham in the Peruvian Andes

He insisted that as I was a 'Doctor', a Ph.D., and a government delegate to a scientific congress, I must know all about archaeology and could tell him how valuable Choqqequirau was as a site for buried treasure and whether it had been, as he believed, Vilcapampa the Old, the Capital of the last four Incas.*

Hiram Bingham was an American. Born in 1878, he had been educated at Yale University and, at the age of thirty-four, was back at Yale as Assistant Professor of Latin American history. In February 1909 he was returning to the United States from a conference in Chile when his journey was interrupted in Cuzco, in the Peruvian Andes, by the Prefect of the Province of Apurimac, the Hon. J. J. Nuñez.

Nuñez had recently led an expedition of local landowners, lured like their Spanish ancestors by the thought of gold, to an Inca ruin called Choqqequirau, 10,000 feet up in the Andes mountains. They had failed to find gold, but Nuñez and his colleagues were preparing a second expedition and they asked Bingham to join them.

My protest that he was mistaken in his estimate of my archaeological knowledge was regarded by him merely as evidence of modesty.... Archaeology lay outside my field and I knew very little about the Incas except the fascinating story told by Prescott in his famous *Conquest of Peru*.

* H. Bingham, *Lost City of the Incas* (New York: Duell, Sloan and Pearce, 1948).

Prescott's famous history was published in 1847, the first full-
length account of the Spaniard Francisco Pizarro's remarkable
conquest of Peru in 1533. Pizarro, with a ragamuffin army of just
168 men, had landed on the north coast of Peru in 1532. Within
weeks, with the help of weapons new to the Indians, he had
physically and psychologically out-manoeuvred a native army of
30,000 men and captured the Inca leader Atahualpa. In return
for a ransom of gold Atahualpa was promised his freedom, but

was cheated, publicly executed and replaced by a puppet leader, Inca Manco. Manco, however, turned on the Spanish, lost a last ditch battle against them and was forced to flee into the mountains. The Spanish Chronicles, the contemporary accounts of the Conquest written in the sixteenth century, record what happened:

> With those who stood by him and their women and servants and all his treasure, which was not small, Manco Inca took refuge in the province of Vilcabamba, a remote part of the Andes. There he would be safe from his enemies the Christians, and would not hear the neighing and stamping of their horses, nor would their trenchant swords anymore slash the flesh of his people.

Inca resistance finally ended in 1572 and Peru became a possession of Spain.

The exact location of the city of Vilcabamba was forgotten but a legend, fostered by greed, began to grow of a vast city of temples, palaces and treasure; of gold, silver and precious stones:

> It seems that in Quechua, the language of the Incas still spoken by the majority of the mountaineers of Peru, Choqqequirau means 'Cradle of Gold'. Attracted by this romantic name and by the lack of all positive knowledge concerning its last defenders, several attempts had been made during the past century to explore its ruins and discover the treasure which it is supposed the Incas hid there instead of allowing it to fall into the hands of Pizarro with the ransom of Atahualpa.

The identification of Choqqequirau with Vilcabamba was first made in 1768, when a Peruvian chronicler reported that a group of people 'attracted by a tradition that there was an ancient town called Choqqequira' reached the site and found it 'a deserted place built of quarried stone, covered in woods and very hot'. A French explorer, Comte de Sartiges, climbed to the ruins in 1834 and was convinced that they were the remains of Manco's city. Now, despite the extreme difficulty of reaching the site, came Hiram Bingham, spurred on by United States' concern for good relations with South America:

> Secretary Root had impressed upon us the importance of developing international goodwill by endeavouring in every way to please the officials of the countries we visited. Accordingly, I agreed to the Prefect's proposal, not knowing that it was to lead me into a fascinating field. It was my first introduction to prehistoric America.

Above: *The Spaniards execute the Inca Atahualpa, from Poma de Ayala's Chronicle c. AD 1600.*

Choqqequirau was to produce both less and more than was expected:

Had it not been for Prefect Nuñez and his very practical interest in Choqqequirau, I should probably never have been tempted to look for Inca ruins and thus find the two cities which had been lost to geographical knowledge for centuries.

The party of explorers set out from Cuzco on 1 February 1909. After travelling fairly comfortably for several days:

...we commenced a descent that for tortuous turns and narrow escapes beat anything we had ever seen. We were about to discover what it means to go exploring in the wild region where the Incas were able to hide from the Conquistadors in 1536 ... the mules and horses trembled with fright as we led them across a mass of loose earth and stones which threatened to give way at any moment ... An hour after dark ... we were still 1,000 feet above the river.

There was a path cut in the face of the precipice that they still had to negotiate. It wound down in loops like a corkscrew. In daylight they would never have attempted it but in the pitch dark they blindly followed the voice of their Indian guide:

At one end of each turn was a precipice, while at the other was a chasm, down which plunged a small cataract which had a clear fall of 700 feet. Half-way down the path my mule started trembling and I had to dismount, to find that in the darkness

Below: *Bingham (in boots) with his Peruvian colleagues.*

he had walked off the trail and slid down the cliff to a ledge. How to get him back was a problem. There was no way to back him up the steep hill and there was scarcely room in which to turn him round. It was such a narrow escape that when I got safely back on the trail I decided to walk the rest of the way and let the mule go first, preferring to have him fall over the precipice alone, if that was necessary. Two-thirds of the way down the descent, the path crossed the narrow chasm, close to and directly in front of the little cataract. There was no bridge. To be sure, the waterfall was only about 3 feet wide, but in the darkness I could not see the other side of the chasm. I did not dare jump alone, so remounted my mule, held my breath, and gave him both spurs at once. His jump was successful.

The Indians called the Apurimac the 'Great Speaker' because of the noise it made. It was in spate over 100 feet deep, 300 feet wide and the water rose to within 25 feet of the narrow bridge that swayed in the wind on its six strands of telegraph wire.

To cross it seemed like tempting fate. So close to death did the narrow cat-walk of the bridge appear to be, and so high did the rapids throw the icy spray, that our Indian bearers crept across one at a time, on all fours and obviously wishing they had never been ordered by the Prefect to carry our luggage to Choqqequirau.

It was on this day that Bingham's exploration of 'Manco's hide-out' began:

Our guide pointed out that the ruins were more than a mile above us. It seemed a pretty serious undertaking to attempt to climb up a slippery little trail for 6,000 feet to an elevation twice as high as the top of Mount Washington ... At times the trail was so steep that it was easier to go on all fours than to attempt to walk erect.... As we mounted, the view of the valley became more and more magnificent. Nowhere had I ever witnessed such beauty and grandeur as was here displayed. The white torrent of the Apurimac raged through the canyon thousands of feet below us. Where its sides were not sheer precipices or scarred by recent avalanches, the steep slopes were covered with green foliage and luxuriant flowers. From the hilltops near us other slopes rose 6,000 feet above the glaciers and snow-capped summits ... About two o'clock, we

Above: *The Inca ruins at Choqqequirau.*

rounded a promontory and on the slopes of a bold mountain headland 6,000 feet above the river we caught our first glimpse of the ruins of Choqqequirau.

Bingham, having arrived, was at a loss what to do:

> Fortunately I had with me that extremely useful handbook *Hints to Travellers*, published by the Royal Geographical Society. In one of the chapters I found out what should be done when one is confronted by a prehistoric site – take careful measurements and plenty of photographs and describe as accurately as possible all finds. On account of the rain, our photographs were not very successful, but we took measurements of all the buildings and made a rough map.

The ruins were in several groups of terraces linked by stairs and pathways and naturally protected on three sides by precipices which dropped almost sheer to the river and made the site virtually inaccessible to enemies. The walls of the buildings, badly ruined and thickly overgrown, were made of stone, but compared with the best Inca masonry they were very roughly constructed. Of possible Inca artefacts, all Bingham found in the buildings was, resting on a stone niche, the stone weight from a spindle, exactly the same in shape and size as the wooden weights he had seen used by the 'campesinos' all over the Andes. It was a sudden reminder that the present-day Indians were direct descendants from the Inca past.

After four days' search, Bingham concluded that Choqqequirau was an Inca fortress that defended the approaches to Cuzco:

> The Prefect of Apurimac was much disappointed that I was unable to indicate to him the possible whereabouts of any buried treasure.... The chief satisfaction derived by the local gentry who had invested several thousand dollars in the unsuccessful enterprise was their claim that they had laid bare the capital of the last of the Incas. For this they took considerable credit.

Bingham, however, was equally certain that Choqqequirau was not Manco Inca's capital of Vilcabamba; but, if Choqqequirau was not to be identified with Vilcabamba, what was? And where was it? On the evidence of the Spanish Chronicles:

> ... probably over beyond the ranges in the region where I had seen snow-capped peaks.... Those snow-capped peaks in an unknown and unexplored part of Peru fascinated me greatly. They tempted me to go and see what lay beyond.

Bingham, determined to lead his own expedition to find Vilcabamba, prepared himself by studying the Spanish Chronicles and learning all that he could about the history and culture of the Incas. Some of that culture, despite looting and destruction by the Spaniards, still survived beneath the Spanish colonial buildings in Cuzco itself. The Spanish Chronicles gave a very good description of how the city had looked in 1553:

> Most of the city's buildings are of stone and the rest have half their façades of stone. There are also many adobe houses, very efficiently made, which are arranged along straight streets on a grid plan. The streets are all paved, with a stone-lined water channel running down the middle of each street. Their only fault is to be narrow: only one mounted man can ride on either side of the channel.

The city centre:

> ... is large and beautiful enough to be remarkable even in Spain. It is full of the palaces of nobles for no poor people live there. Each ruler builds himself a palace and so do all the chiefs ... The finest palace is that of the last Inca ... It has a gateway of red, white and multicoloured marble and has other flat floored structures that are almost as remarkable.

The palace was destroyed soon after the Conquest. Until that time, along with the other palaces of the dead Incas, it had been kept as a shrine, containing all the Inca's gold and silver belongings and fine textiles and the mummified body of the Inca himself which, on festival days, was paraded in a litter before the faithful in the main square. For the Incas worshipped their ancestors as they worshipped the stars, the moon and, in particular, the sun – for the sun was The Inca, and the sun was golden.

The most important building in Cuzco was the Coricancha, the 'Enclosure of Gold', also known as the Sun Temple, the cathedral of the Inca Empire. Here, beneath the walls of the church built by the Spanish Dominicans after the Conquest, Bingham found the remains of the smooth, ashlared walls of the temple itself; large blocks of stone laid in curving courses without mortar, 'so finely adjusted that it would be impossible to improve on them'.

The walls, until the Spanish came, had been covered in sheets of gold to reflect and imitate the sun and inside the temple was the image of the great sun rising, an enormous sunburst made of gold and studded with precious stones. It had been served by the high priest and the 'priestesses', the Women of the Sun:

... daughters of the nobility (who) claimed to be wives of the sun, pretending that the sun made love to them.

Bingham, as well as studying Cuzco's surviving Inca remains and learning local Indian traditions, consulted the Lima historian Carlos Romero. It was Romero who pointed out that, according to one of the contemporary Spanish Chronicles, Vilcabamba was located in an unexplored part of the High Andes:

... near a great white rock over a spring of water.

It wasn't much of a clue but it was to prove crucial.

In July 1911, the Yale Peruvian Expedition, led by Bingham, finally set out from Cuzco and headed in a quite different direction from Choqqequirau, down the Urubamba valley towards the Inca fortress temple of Ollantaytambo. Here, in May 1537, Manco Inca had regrouped with other Inca chiefs, after their last and failed attempt to remove the Spaniards from Cuzco. Although outnumbering the Spanish by ten to one, the Indians had been defeated by superior weapons, superior knowledge of siege tactics and the speed and manoeuvrability of an animal that they had not encountered before – the horse. Furthermore, in victory, the Spanish soldiers were totally ruthless. The Spanish priests were appalled:

... the injuries and injustices that have been done to the poor docile Indians cannot be counted. Everything from the very beginning is injury. Their liberty has been removed; their nobles have lost their nobility, authority and all forms of jurisdiction; and the Spaniards have stolen their pastures and many fine lands, and imposed intolerable tributes upon them.

Manco had no option but to retreat even further from the Spanish aggression, deep into the mountain and forest fastness of the Vilcabamba province, where his people could be safe. With his wives and sons, the mummies of his ancestors and some twenty thousand followers and their animals, Manco climbed 16,000 feet over the Panticalla Pass, descending into the Vilcabamba jungle.

For Bingham the journey was easier as, initially, he was able to keep to the recently opened trail along the river valley, although the region was still unmapped and largely unsettled. As well as a sizeable mule train, the expedition consisted of Bingham himself, an American doctor, a naturalist and a Peruvian army sergeant, Carrasco, who served as interpreter and liaison officer. Thirty miles downstream from Cuzco, the river entered a canyon:

In the variety of its charms and the power of its spell, I know of no place in the world which can compare with it. Not only has it great snow peaks looming above the clouds more than two miles overhead, gigantic precipices of many-coloured granite rising sheer for thousands of feet above the foaming, glistening, roaring rapids, it has also, in striking contrast, orchids and tree ferns, the delectable beauty of luxurious vegetation, and the mysterious witchery of the jungle. One is drawn irresistibly onward by ever-recurring surprises through a deep, winding gorge, turning and twisting past over-hanging cliffs of incredible height.

The party camped in a tiny clearing on the edge of the river, but their arrival aroused the suspicion of the local farmer, Melchor Arteaga, who lived in a nearby hut. Carrasco explained in Quechua that Bingham was looking for Inca ruins. Arteaga said that there were some good ruins on the opposite mountain called Huayna Picchu:

The morning of July 24th dawned in a cold drizzle. Arteaga shivered and seemed inclined to stay in his hut. I offered to pay him well if he would show me the ruins. He demurred and said it was too hard a climb for such a wet day. But when he found that we were willing to pay him a *sol* (a Peruvian silver dollar, fifty cents, gold), three or four times the ordinary daily wage in this vicinity, he finally agreed to guide us to the ruins. When asked just where the ruins were, he pointed straight up to the top of the mountain. No one supposed they would be particularly interesting. . . . Accompanied by Sergeant Carrasco I left camp at ten o'clock . . . After a walk of three quarters of an hour the guide left the main road and plunged down through the jungle to the bank of the river . . . Leaving the stream, we struggled up the bank through a dense jungle. For an hour and twenty minutes we had a hard climb. A good part of the distance we went on all fours, sometimes hanging on by the tips of our fingers. Here and there, a primitive ladder made from the roughly hewn trunk of a small tree was placed in such a way as to help one over what might otherwise have proved to be an impassable cliff. In another place the slope was covered with slippery grass where it was hard to find either handholds or footholds. The guide said that there were lots of snakes here.

Shortly after midday, 9000 feet above sea level and 2000 feet above the river, the three climbers reached, to their amazement, a little grass hut and a group of smiling Indians who welcomed them 'with dripping gourds of cool, delicious, water':

Through Sergeant Carrasco I learned that there were more ruins 'a little farther along'. In this country one never can tell whether such a report is worthy of credence ... Accordingly, I was not unduly excited, nor in a great hurry to move ... Furthermore, the view was simply enchanting. Tremendous green precipices fell away to the white rapids of the Urubamba below. Immediately in front, on the north side of the valley, was a great granite cliff rising 2000 feet sheer. To the left was the solitary peak of Huayna Picchu, surrounded by seemingly inaccessible precipices. On all sides were rocky cliffs. Beyond them cloud-capped mountains rose thousands of feet above us ...

Without the slightest expectation of finding anything more interesting than ... the ruins of two or three stone houses such as we had encountered at various places on the road from Ollantaytambo, I finally left the cool shade of the pleasant little hut and climbed further up the ridge and around a slight promontory.

Bingham was now accompanied only by a small boy supplied by the welcoming Indians as 'guide'.

Hardly had we left the hut and rounded the promontory than we were confronted with an unexpected sight, a great flight of beautifully constructed stone-faced terraces, perhaps a hundred of them, each hundreds of feet long and 10 feet high ... However, there was nothing to be excited about. Similar flights of well-made terraces are to be seen in the upper Urubamba Valley at Pisac and Ollantaytambo ...

So we patiently followed the little guide along one of the widest terraces, where there had once been a small conduit, and made our way into an untouched forest beyond. Suddenly I found myself confronted with the walls of ruined houses built of the finest quality Inca stonework. It was hard to see them for they were partly covered with trees and moss, the growth of centuries, but in the dense shadow, hiding in bamboo thickets and tangled vines, appeared here and there walls of white granite ashlars carefully cut and exquisitely fitted together. We scrambled along through the dense undergrowth, climbing over terrace walls and in bamboo thickets, where our guide found it easier going than I did. Suddenly, without any warning, under a huge overhanging ledge the boy showed me a cave beautifully lined with the finest cut stone. It had evidently been a royal mausoleum. On top of this particular ledge was a semi-circular building whose outer wall, gently sloping and slightly curved, bore a striking resemblance to the famous Temple of the Sun in Cuzco. This might also be a temple of the sun. It followed the natural curvature of the rock and was keyed to it by one of the finest examples of masonry I had ever seen ...

This structure surpassed in attractiveness the best Inca walls in Cuzco, which had caused visitors to marvel for four centuries. It seemed like an unbelievable dream. Dimly, I began to realize that this wall and its adjoining semi-circular temple over the cave were as fine as the finest stonework in the world.

It fairly took my breath away. What could this place be?

Bingham and the boy continued to climb up a steep hill and over what appeared to be a flight of steps. Surprise followed surprise in bewildering succession:

Suddenly we found ourselves standing in front of the ruins of two of the finest and most interesting structures in ancient America. Made of beautiful white granite, the walls contained blocks of Cyclopean size, higher than a man. The sight held me spellbound.

Each of the two buildings had only three walls so that they were open on one side. The walls of the principal temple were over twelve feet high and lined with the characteristically shaped Inca niches. Below them was a large block of stone which Bingham thought might be a sacrificial altar or, more likely, a throne on which could be set the mummies of dead Incas for worship. The building was roofless:

The top course of beautifully smooth ashlars was left uncovered so that the sun could be welcomed here by priests and mummies. I could scarcely believe my senses as I examined the larger blocks in the lower course and estimated that they must weigh from ten to fifteen tons each. Would anyone believe what I had found?

Opposite the principal temple, on the east side of a small plaza, was the other extraordinary building: a temple with three huge windows that looked out over the canyon towards the rising sun. It was, as far as Bingham knew, unique in its design and the beauty of its construction. This was clearly a ceremonial edifice of peculiar significance. Staggered by what he had found, Bingham asked himself the inevitable question:

Could this be 'the principal city' of Manco and his sons, that Vilcapampa where was the 'University of Idolatry' which Friar Marcos and Friar Diego had tried to reach? It behove us to find out as much about it as we could.

Friar Marcos and Friar Diego were two Spanish missionaries who, in the 1560s, penetrated surviving Inca territory to preach and to convert. It is the account of what they saw, written in the *Moralising Chronicle of the Activities of the Augustinian Order in Peru* by Father Calancha in 1639, that was to help Bingham identify the site that he had named 'Machu Picchu', after the mountain that stood over it.

Manco, in the safety of the Vilcabamba region, had settled first at a place called Vitcos and it was Vitcos that he used as a base from which to sally forth to attack the Spaniards. The attacks were rarely successful, and on one occasion, as Manco withdrew into the mountains, he was followed by Pizarro's brother. Manco realised that Vitcos was no longer secure and moved again, deeper and deeper into Vilcabamba territory to a place where he founded his newest-and-last capital, 'Vilcabamba City' or, as the friars were later to call it, the:

> ... largest city, in which was the 'University of Idolatry', where lived the teachers who were the wizards and masters of abomination.

Manco continued his guerilla war against the Spanish for six years until, giving sanctuary to five absconding Spanish soldiers, he was robbed by them and killed. His eventual successor was his son Titu Cusi and it was to Inca Titu that, according to Father Calancha, Friars Marcos and Diego bent their crusading steps.

From the mass of information in the Chronicle it gradually became clear that the friars were never allowed to see Vilcabamba, the 'University of Idolatry', itself but only Vitcos, which was described as being situated on a hill close to a village called Puquiura. As well as the name Puquiura, Bingham had already gleaned two other pieces of vital information. One was that Vitcos, as Romero had first told him, had been described by Father Calancha as being 'near a great white rock over a spring of water' and the second was that Vitcos was 'two long days' journey' from Vilcabamba. Bingham argued that, if he could find Vitcos and show that Vitcos was two days' journey from Machu Picchu then, *ipso facto*, Machu Picchu was Vilcabamba.

As soon as he had searched the ruins of Machu Picchu Bingham continued downstream looking for an Inca ruin that would match Father Calancha's 'white rock' description. It wasn't easy: there were no maps; Indian names were spelt by the Spanish phonetically and very inconsistently – 'Vitcos' was sometimes 'Uitcos' or 'Pitcos' – and names, after 350 years, could have changed altogether. No Indian and no Spaniard had heard of Vitcos and the expedition was frequently disappointed as one 'great ruin' after another turned out, once the jungle had been cleared, to be nothing but a solitary Inca dwelling.

After several days' tramp down the Vilcabamba river, offering money to the Indians if they could locate Inca ruins and doubling the price if the ruins were especially interesting, the expedition arrived at the modern village of Puquiura:

> We ... forded the Vilcamba River and soon had an uninterrupted view up the valley to a high, truncated hill, its top partly covered with a scrubby growth of trees and bushes, its sides steep and rocky. We were told that the name of the hill was 'Rosaspata', a word of modern hybrid origin – '*pata*' being Quechua for 'hill' while '*rosas*' is the Spanish word for 'roses'.

Could this be the hill close to the village of Puquiura?

> For it was to 'Puquiura' that Friar Marcos came in 1566 ... If this were the 'Puquiura' of Friar Marcos, then Vitcos must be near by, for he and Friar Diego walked with their famous procession of converts from 'Puquiura' to the House of the Sun and the 'white rock' which was 'close to Vitcos'.

They climbed the hill and found, on the summit:

> ... the ruins of a partly enclosed compound consisting of thirteen or fourteen houses arranged so as to form a rough square ... Due to the wanton destruction of many buildings by the natives in their efforts at treasure-hunting, the walls had been so pulled down that it is impossible to get the exact dimensions.

One building, however, remained almost intact. It was a great hall, 245 feet long by 43 feet wide, lit by thirty doorways, 'indeed a fit residence for a royal Inca, an exile from Cuzco'. So, Rosaspata might be Vitcos. For confirmation Bingham still needed to find the place that fitted Calancha's description that 'Close by Vitcos is a House of the Sun and near it a white rock over a spring of water.' The following day, the expedition followed a stream through thick woods:

Below: *The great 'white rock over a spring of water' at Vitcos.*

> We suddenly arrived at an open place called Nusta Isppana. Here before us was a great white rock over a spring. Our guides had not misled us. Beneath the trees were the ruins of an Inca temple, flanking and partly enclosing the gigantic granite boulder, one end of which overhung a small pool of running water ... It was late on the afternoon of August 9, 1911, when

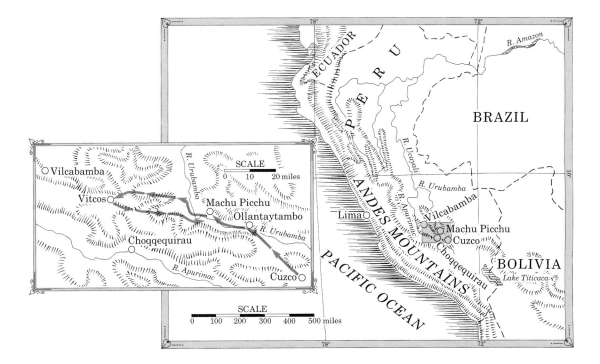

I first saw this remarkable shrine ... There was not a hut to be seen; scarcely a sound to be heard. It was an ideal place for practicing the mystic ceremonies of an ancient cult ... At last we had found the place where, in the days of Titu Cusi, the Inca priests faced the east, greeted the rising sun, 'extended their hands toward it', and 'threw kisses to it', 'a ceremony of the most profound resignation and reverence'.

All the pieces of the puzzle had fallen into place. The white rock had confirmed that Rosaspata, the hill near Puquiura, was Vitcos. And Rosaspata/Vitcos was, as the Chronicles had said, two long days' hard march from Machu Picchu. Machu Picchu and Vilcabamba certainly seemed to be one and the same place. Bingham concluded that he had found the last capital of the Incas.

In the summer of 1912, Bingham returned to Machu Picchu to clear and excavate the city and try to find confirmation of the city's identity.

Machu Picchu occupies the most spectacular archaeological site in the entire world. It lies on a narrow saddle of rock that links two precipitous peaks, the Machu and Huayna Picchu. On either side of the city the land falls away in man-made terraces before dropping sheer 2000 feet to the gorge of the Urubamba river which winds in a horse-shoe bend below. From the river, the city is completely invisible. The only access was at mountain level, from the Inca highway which entered through the city gate. This was the city's link with the Inca road network that covered the entire Inca Empire, which, at its height, stretched from Argentina to Ecuador, from the Pacific to the Amazon in the jungles of Brazil. The network was a system of paved road-ways and flights of steps which, as the Inca had no wheels but only pack animals, could follow the mountaintops.

The city was divided into two parts, an upper ward and a lower ward, separated by grass-covered plazas. Around the plazas were the temples, palaces, public buildings, artisan houses and agri-cultural terraces which, in their architectural form, their method of construction and their careful siting, reflected the rigid, hier-archical nature of the Inca social system. The agricultural ter-races in the lowest part of the city provided an abundant food supply. Despite Machu Picchu's elevation of 9000 feet above sea level, the climate is warm and the topsoil, carried up the mountains from the valley and laid on a base of river gravel, would have produced a good crop of tropical fruits and vegetables as well as maize and sweet potatoes.

The water supply was similarly well-organised. The Inca were expert hydraulic engineers. Crossing the ditch by the city gate was a stone aqueduct carrying a conduit which brought a plen-tiful supply of fresh water from mountain springs as well as rainwater collected in basins, used for both religious and dom-estic purposes as well as for irrigating the terraces. The water system, through a sophisticated use of storage basins, fountains and water channels, linked the houses on the edge of the city with those higher up and closer to the central plazas. The former have been identified as artisans' quarters: groups of two to eight single-roomed, steep-gabled thatched houses set around a court-yard which served as a compound in which all members of the extended family could cook, weave and do other domestic duties. The houses nearest the plazas belonged to the most prestigious members of the community. As with most cities throughout the world, the closer one was to the heart of town and the main religious buildings, the more important one was and at Machu Picchu more important also meant 'higher' geographically.

These houses included a set of buildings that Bingham dubbed 'the Ingenuity Group' because of the way the builders had skil-fully used the natural granite outcrop that projected through the floor. Instead of trying to remove this stone, the builders had

Right: *The forest being felled and burnt prior to excavation at Machu Picchu. The round building in the centre is the Royal Mausoleum.*
Below right: *The site after clearance, showing terraces of houses with thatched roofs and the Royal Mausoleum in the right foreground.*

converted it into a hollowed-out mortar that could be used for pounding maize and potatoes. This use of natural rock formations is a feature of Machu Picchu: staircases cut through the rock, buildings carefully keyed to the outcropping granite, and mountain slopes incorporated into the city wall. The Incas regarded architecture as a noble art to be practised only by the high-born. At Machu Picchu, as Bingham believed, the Inca masons produced 'art' the equal of anything in the world.

Bingham already knew and had charted the disposition of the main buildings. As well as 'the Ingenuity Group', there was a large collection of beautifully constructed buildings identified as royal residences and which he called the 'Kings Group' on the grounds that:

... no-one but a king could have insisted on having the lintels of his doorways made of great solid blocks of granite each weighing about three tons.

There was the Temple of the Sun with its elegantly curved wall and, beneath it, the 'Royal Mausoleum' for the deposit of the royal mummies; and there was the Principal Temple of the Sun, dedicated, Bingham thought, to Viracocha, supreme god of the Inca religion, source of divine power and the creator god. Most dramatically sited of all was the 'Hitching Post of the Sun', a six-foot finger of stone at the highest point of the city where Viracocha's main servant, Inti, the Sun (himself a divine ancestor of the royal Inca house) could, in the words of an American traveller who had seen similar stone fingers elsewhere in Peru:

> ... appear to be stopped or tied up for a moment in his course and on which, in his passage through the zenith, he might sit down in all his glory.

Bingham's first task was to excavate the principal structures to discover potsherds or other artefacts that might throw light on the former inhabitants:

> Our workmen, who fully believed in the 'buried treasure' theory, started with a will. Tests made with a crowbar in the Principal Temple enclosure resulted in such resounding hollow sounds as to give assurance that there were secret caves beneath the floor of the ancient temple. Amid the granite boulders under the carefully constructed floor our excavation was carried to a depth of eight or nine feet, but all the back-

breaking work ended only in disappointment. Although we penetrated many crevices and holes between boulders, there was nothing to be found; not even a bone or a potsherd.

The Temple of the Three Windows did supply, in the area beneath its windows, a quantity of potsherds, but no treasure, and Bingham's spirits began to flag:

> It began to look as though our efforts to learn any more of the life of the builders of Machu Picchu than could be gained by a study of their architecture and small fragments of earthenware would be a failure ... The next day all of our workmen were released from excavations ... in a feverish hunt for burial caves. At the end of the day the half-dozen worthies who had followed us from Cuzco came slowly in, one by one, sadder and no wiser, their hopes of the coveted bonus destroyed. They had been tattered and torn by the thickets and jungles and baffled by the precipitous cliffs of Machu Picchu. One of them had split his big toe with a machete.

Morale was low. The Indian workers had to be fed a morning diet of coca leaves and bribed 'with trinkets from Mr Woolworth's Emporium in New Haven, Connecticut', but perseverance paid off. In the ensuing weeks, dozens of burial caves were located with their skeletons and grave goods. Some were the bones of men but forty-six out of fifty individuals in 'Cemetery I' were young women:

> This was a very exciting and significant discovery. Apparently the last residents of Machu Picchu were Chosen Women, the 'Virgins of the Sun' associated with sanctuaries where the sun was worshipped.

Close by was the grave of the high priestess, the woman who looked after the virgins. She had been buried with her small personal belongings; bronze tweezers, shawl pins, some pieces of wool, the skeleton of her dog and a bronze mirror. It confirmed Bingham in his beliefs:

> Until we can find some other ruin within three days hard journey of Puquiura which answers the requirements of a 'University of Idolatry', an important religious centre, containing mostly remains of women and effeminate men, I am inclined to believe that we have at Machu Picchu the Vilcabamba-the-Old of Calancha's chronicle.

But that was not all. He postulated another theory even more surprising than the first. It concerned the Temple of the Three

Windows. According to Inca legend, the Inca tribe was founded by three brothers who travelled underground from Lake Titicaca in the south to emerge near Cuzco from the mouth of a cave called Tampu Tocco: the Tavern of Windows. The Spanish Chroniclers agreed that the location of the cave was at Paccaritambo, south of Cuzco, but there are no important buildings there and Bingham, having made the reasonable assumption that the three windows of the Machu Picchu temple represented the cave entrances of the legend, then went on to make one almighty leap of the imagination:

> Nowhere else in Peru, so far as I know, is there a similar structure conspicuous for being 'a masonry wall with three windows'. It will be remembered that Salcamayhua, the Peruvian who wrote an account of the antiquities of Peru in 1620, said that the first Inca, Manco the Great, ordered 'works to be executed at the place of his birth, consisting of a masonry wall with three windows'. Was that what I had found? If it was, then this was not the capital of the last Inca but the birthplace of the first ... He might have been buried in the stone-lined cave under the semi-circular temple.

Above left: *Indian workmen at Machu Picchu. Note the beautiful construction of the Inca wall, built without mortar.*
Above: *Jugs restored from sherds found by Bingham at Machu Picchu and described in painstaking detail in his report on the excavations.*

Hypothesis grew into conviction. Machu Picchu was both the

first *and* the last Inca settlement. It was Tampu Tocco, possibly for eight or ten centuries, until it was refounded after Cuzco's destruction as Vilcabamba:

> Undoubtedly in its last state the city was the carefully guarded treasure house where that precious worship of the sun, the moon, the thunder and the stars, so violently overthrown in Cuzco, was restored, where the last four Incas had their safest and most comfortable home and the Chosen Women whose lives had from early girlhood been devoted to the duties of the Sanctuary found a refuge from the animosity and lust of the conquistadores.

That Machu Picchu was Vilcabamba was a theory that, despite the lack of hard evidence in the form of precisely dateable objects, went almost unchallenged for half a century, until another American's expedition, that of Gene Savoy in 1964.

After Friars Marcos and Diego had attempted to exorcise the devil at the 'great white rock over the spring of water', the Incas, not happy at this abuse of hospitality, stoned Friar Marcos out of the province. Diego, however, was allowed to remain because of his medical knowledge, but when he tried to cure the Inca Titu Cusi of double pneumonia and failed, Father Diego was dubbed a murderer and killed.

The Spanish Viceroy of Peru, Don Francisco de Toledo, already irritated by the independent Inca enclave on the edge of his new territory, was furious at the murder of Friar Diego. He determined to destroy the Incas once and for all. In the spring of 1572, the Spanish marched against Vilcabamba and its new Inca, Tupac Amaru, Manco Inca's third son. The expedition's progress was recorded by a Spanish soldier:

> With arms and blankets and food for ten days, we set out. We went through mountains and ravines with very great difficulty

Top: *The Temple of the Three Windows at Machu Picchu.*
Above: *Carefully modelled handle for a ceremonial dish, probably representing a jaguar or other wild cat.*

for all. On the road we found sacrificed guinea-pigs in three or four places. It is common for the Indians to do this in times of war, famine or pestilence, to placate their deities and to divine what will happen.

The terrain, and the difficulties of crossing it, got even harder:

> The road, along which we had to march, ran around half a crescent, very narrow, with great rock outcrops and jungle and a deep turbulent river running beside the course of the road. It was all most dangerous and frightening to have to pass this and fight the enemy who would be in the heights which form a steep escarpment above this stretch. Some Indians came at us in ambushes but with artillery and arquebus we made them flee.

After crossing the high passes, the expedition began to descend into the jungle. Another Chronicle, unknown to Bingham, took up the story:

> At 10.00 in the morning on the 24th June 1572, which was the day of St John the Baptist, they entered the city of Vilcabamba all on foot since it is a very rough and rugged land and not at all suitable for horses. The whole town was found sacked. All the Indians had fled and hidden in the jungle, taking with them all that they could; they burned the rest of the maize and food that was in the storehouses, so that when the expedition arrived it was still smoking. The Temple of the Sun, where there was a principal idol, was burned.

Inca Tupac Amaru was chased into the jungle, caught and brought back to the capital, Cuzco, along with the mummies of his father Manco and his brother Titu Cusi. He was brought to the place of execution in the main square, made a speech denouncing his religion and his own sanctity, received Christian absolution and was immediately executed with a Spanish cutlass. After forty years, Inca resistance to Spain was at an end.

Gene Savoy was an amateur archaeologist like Bingham who also travelled widely in Peru and had read widely in the Chronicles. He came to the conclusion that Bingham's hypothesis that Machu Picchu was both the first and last Inca city was wrong – and wrong on both counts:

> Because Machu Picchu – and other ancient remains found in and around Cuzco – are the result of a classic period of Inca civilization, the stonework being most technical and the result of advanced skills, it had to be ruled out as both an early home and a refuge of the Incas.

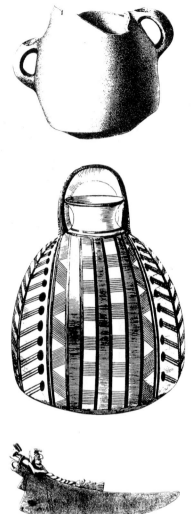

Above: *Jugs restored from fragments Bingham collected at Machu Picchu, and a bronze knife decorated with the life-like figure of an Inca boy hauling in a large fish. Bingham considered this knife the finest example of metal casting found at Machu Picchu.*

Above: *Bingham (top right) in the ruins at Espiritu Pampa, which he failed to recognise as Vilcabamba.*

The trapezoidal windows and niches that are a feature of the Temple of the Three Windows are an architectural conceit not found elsewhere in Inca buildings before about 1470. The artefacts and skeletons that Bingham found point to a similar date. Moreover, if it was true that Manco Inca escaped with upwards of 20,000 followers, there was no way that a small mountain citadel like Machu Picchu could have accommodated them.

For the real site of Vilcabamba, Gene Savoy looked beyond Machu Picchu, beyond Vitcos and the 'great white rock' to the steamy jungles by the headwaters of the Amazon. In the summer of 1964, Savoy's expedition arrived at a remote jungle habitat called Espiritu Pampa – the plain of the ghosts, where they discovered an old-fashioned Spanish-type horseshoe which suggested that at least one Spanish horse had reached the area. There were also signs of burnt timbers under the mat of the forest floor and, most significant of all, there were tiles:

> Many pieces are well preserved, colours still vivid. One piece is incised with serpentine lines, an Inca characteristic ... Who had used these tiles? Unknown in old Peru, roofing tile was introduced by the Spaniards shortly following the conquest. The Incas preferred ichu straw. Then I remembered that Manco had taken Spanish prisoners of war. These and the Augustinian friars under Titu Cusi may have passed on the use of this permanent roofing material.

Further clearance of the site revealed a city of at least 300 houses and several large buildings.

> For the first time I realise what we have found. We are in the heart of an ancient Inca city. Is this Manco's Vilcabamba – the lost city of the Incas? I am certain we are in parts of it.

Ironically, Hiram Bingham himself had come this way in 1911, shortly after his discovery of Machu Picchu and Vitcos. Guided by local Indians and in the heat and the rain:

> ... hidden behind a curtain of hanging vines and thickets so dense we could not see more than a few feet in any direction, the savages showed us the ruins of a group of Inca stone houses whose walls were still standing in fine condition ... Most of these buildings resemble those at Choqqequirau in being built of rough blocks of stone, not squared or otherwise fashioned except occasionally on the corners in the doorways. The stones were laid in mud.

In fact, it was exactly the kind of construction for a building that had been built in a hurry. The fragments of roof tile that

Bingham found were dismissed by him simply as evidence of later occupation, either 'made experimentally by recent Peruvians or possibly by Spanish missionaries'. And the few houses that he found were far too few to be evidence of 'the great city of Vilcabamba'. Thus, shortage of time and poor conditions denied Bingham his ultimate goal.

Final confirmation of Savoy's belief that Espiritu Pampa was Vilcabamba came from the British historian John Hemming. His careful reappraisal of the Spanish Chronicles and, in particular, the eyewitness description of Viceroy Toledo's expedition written by Martin de Murua, leaves no doubt. Murua describes Vilcabamba in a tropical location – a description of which both Bingham and Savoy were unaware:

> The climate is such that bees make honeycombs like those in Spain in the boards of the houses, and the maize is harvested three times a year. The crops are helped by the good disposition of the land and the waters with which they irrigate it. There are axials in the greatest abundance, coca, sweet canes to make sugar, cassava, sweet potatoes and cotton. The town has, or rather had, a location half a league wide, rather like the plain of Cuzco ... In it are raised parrots, hens, ducks, local rabbits, turkeys, pheasants, macaws and a thousand other species of birds of different vivid colours. There are a great many guavas, pecans, peanuts, papayas, pineapples, avocado pears and other fruit trees ... The Incas therefore enjoyed scarcely less of the luxuries, greatness and splendour of Cuzco in that distant or, rather, exiled land. For the Indians brought them whatever they could get from outside for their contentment and pleasure. And they enjoyed life there.

Reference by de Murua to roof tiles is conclusive:

> The Incas had a palace on different levels, covered in roof tiles, and with the entire palace painted with a great variety of paintings in their style – something well worth seeing.

Savoy had guessed right and Hemming had proved it: Bingham was wrong.

So, if Machu Picchu was not Vilcabamba, what was it? The cave beneath the Temple of the Sun might have been a royal mausoleum as Bingham suggested, and the Kings Group a royal palace. The Temple of the Three Windows probably did symbolise the three cave entrances from which the original mythical Incas emerged at Tampu Tocco and the predominance of female skeletons found at the site does indicate that there was a well-established cult of the sun god at the city. But convents for the

Chosen Women existed at many places besides Cuzco and there were many other 'temples of the sun'. Some archaeologists believe that Bingham's 'royal mausoleum' was perhaps the priest's lodging. In fact, it is almost easier to say what Machu Picchu was not than what it was. It was not the ancient Tampu Tocco and, in terms of Inca history, not an ancient site at all; it was not a mighty citadel (despite its mountain location) as the fortifications are militarily insignificant; it was not the refuge of the Virgins of the Sun escaping from Cuzco and, of course, it was not Vilcabamba – the lost city of the Incas.

All that can be said for certain about Machu Picchu is that it was an isolated holy place, late Inca, abandoned by its inhabitants before the Conquest and never found by the Spanish. But while it is not *the* lost city of the Incas, it has become the most dramatic and most evocative 'lost city' in the whole world.

Bingham, who died in 1956, had a distinguished career as a pilot in France during World War I, as Governor of the state of Connecticut, and as an academic, but nothing could rival the excitement of that first discovery on 24 July 1911:

> Above all there is the fascination of finding here and there under the swaying vines or perched on top of a beetling crag, the rugged masonry of a bygone race; and of trying to understand the bewildering romance of the ancient builders who, ages ago, sought refuge in a region which appears to have been expressly designed by nature as a sanctuary for the oppressed, a place where they might fearlessly, patiently give expression to their passion for walls of enduring beauty.

Chapter Nine

VALLEY OF THE KILNS
Reginald Le May in Thailand

It is not too much to hope that one day, as the years progress and people in Europe are able to look beyond the great barrier of India which screens the Far East from their eyes, the Indo-Chinese peninsula will come into its own and claim the attention that it deserves.*

By the end of the nineteenth century, most of the ancient civilisations of the world were known to archaeologists and their remains recorded. But there were still pockets to be discovered; even whole cities which were not, like Machu Picchu, up inaccessible mountains. One of those pockets was northern Thailand.

At the start of the twentieth century, Thailand, or Siam as it was then called, was virtually unknown to the West. It was not quite India, not quite China, and not colonised: a place that was a strange hybrid, exotic and mysterious like the king who ruled over it. King Chulalonghorn was the king of *The King and I*. He had ascended the throne in 1868 as Rama V, the first Siamese monarch to have been educated by a western governess, Anna Leonowens, and the first to be known world-wide through Anna Leonowen's book.

His capital was Bangkok, a city of temples – almost four hundred of them – and a city of canals: an eastern Venice, a city of low wooden houses and floating markets where the first road was not built till 1864. In the centre of the city was the Royal Palace, with its steep-gabled, multi-coloured roofs peering over

* R. Le May, *An Asian Arcady* (Cambridge: Heffer, 1926).

a high, white, fortified wall. It was a vast complex of buildings which, as well as the royal apartments, included the incredible Golden Pagoda, temples and audience halls glittering with tesserae of porcelain and mirror glass and, most sacred of all, the Wat Phra Keo or Temple of the Emerald Buddha, guarded by bronze lions and gilded mythical garuda birds. The Buddha himself, a small fourteenth-century figure of green jade, is still the talisman of the Siamese monarchy, venerated by all Buddhists.

Chulalonghorn, despite his traditionalism, his many wives and even more numerous progeny, was a reformer, struggling to modernise his state by curbing slavery, gambling and the dens of opium which flourished in his capital, and by opening the country to the trade and influence of the West.

It was into this strange but vital country that Reginald Le May arrived in 1907 as a student interpreter at the British Legation in Bangkok. He was to stay almost twenty-five years and, during that time, help balance the increasingly pervading western influence by helping to open the eyes of the West to the influence of the Far East – to the history, culture, art and artefacts of a country that the West had ignored for so long. In the process he travelled the length and breadth of Thailand and visited one of the most fascinating but, even today, least-known archaeological sites in the Far East, a ruined city in the jungle which dates from the golden age of Siam's past.

Like Alfred Maudslay, Le May was in many ways the archetype of the British consular official. He was born in 1885 in Wadhurst,

Sussex, and educated at Framlingham College in Suffolk, becoming senior prefect, captain of football and chairman of the Debating Society. When he left school he went to Zurich as confidential clerk to the British Consul-General and then, in 1907, at the age of twenty-two, came fourth in the country in the public exam for the Far Eastern Consular Service and was posted to Bangkok.

Unlike most British consular officials who turned wherever they were living into a little England, Le May took an increasing interest in his new surroundings. Scholarly, inexperienced, bureaucratic and reserved, there was in Le May a spirit of enquiry and adventure accompanied by a dry sense of humour.

From the outset, Le May kept a scrapbook:

> These are the four princesses practising golf in my garden – Poon, Pachung, Leur and Pilai.

But, in 1913, Le May travelled to the north of the country for the first time. It was to have a profound effect on him and was the start of his love affair with Siam. His destination was Chiang Mai, 450 miles north of Bangkok. His journey began at Bangkok railway station – a version of the train shed at Manchester Central or St Pancras, London:

Above: *Reginald Le May in consular uniform, 1916.*

> Leaving Bangkok early in the morning we presently passed the King's summer palace at Bang Pa In, on an island in the river, and soon after caught a glimpse of the ruins at Ayudhya, the old capital of Siam, which was finally sacked and destroyed by the Burmese in AD 1767.

It was this action by the Burmese which led to the foundation of Bangkok in 1782, further south and further away from the enemy:

> At the time I made my first journey north, the trains were not permitted to run at night, and the whole of the scorching day, from seven to seven, was spent in travelling through an extensive plain, with intervals of towns and villages, and here and there to the East a ridge of hills in the distance, standing out sharp and clear, and coming down to an abrupt end on the plain, like some forest-clad island in the sea. In fact, it did not need a great stretch of imagination to realise that this plain had once been covered by the sea, and that the sharply-outlined hills had actually been islands dotted about here and there. . . . Most of the land visible from the railway appeared to be under rice cultivation, but for the last hour or so of the journey to Pitsanulok, the end of the first day's travel, the cultivated area grew less and less, and we passed through wide stretches of swampy marshland, untilled and undrained.

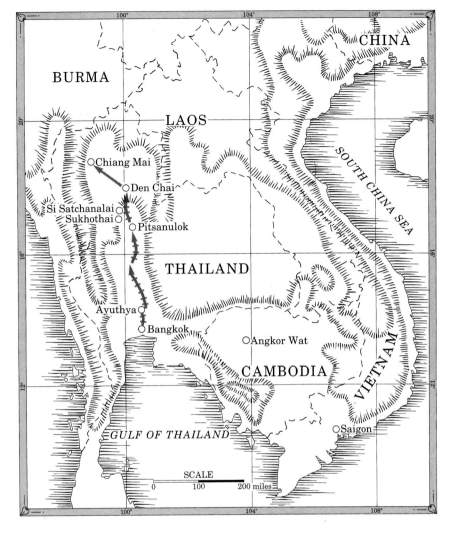

Right: *Le May's first journey, in 1913, by train to Den Chai and then on to Chiang Mai.*

The train stopped for the night at Pitsanulok and Le May took quarters in the station rest-house. During his early morning constitutional he found the town dreary and the markets squalid. Not until he was back on the train did his attitude change:

> The scenery from Pitsanulok to Den Chai was entirely different in character from that of the previous day, and was a source of unalloyed delight to one coming from the flat and uninteresting south ... The train goes up and up, winding slowly round the hillsides; on the one side are deep ravines, densely covered with jungle, and on the other, towering above in sharp contrast, a mass of sheer rock. All the while one is drinking a draught of the fresh mountain air, and breathing the scent of the jungle flowers. Innumerable butterflies of every hue and size swarm

on the permanent way, to an extent that, standing on the steps of the carriage, it is possible to catch them with one's hand; and the dense undergrowth of the jungle around conjures up visions of tiger, deer and elephant – visions, however, which do not materialise, as those animals have long since overcome their resentment to the railway and now maintain a dignified seclusion.

As the scenery changed, so did the people: no longer the Thai of southern Siam but the Lao from the north and, at every station at which the train stopped, a 'bevy of Lao beauties' selling fruits, pastries and sweet drinks swarmed around the 'wonderful train':

> I was filled with admiration ... They were dressed in the Lao 'Sin' or skirt (of red and black bands) with a close-fitting bodice above and had their hair dressed in layers, rather like the coils of a snake, with a red flower gracefully worn at the side. They laughed and chattered naturally and gaily, and seemed to possess a temperament different from that of the ordinary southern peasant, who is as a rule reserved and shy.

The railway ended at Den Chai. The rest of the railroad was still under construction and Le May had to continue his journey along roads that were often little more than grassy tracks, extremely bumpy in the dry season and, in the wet, a quagmire. The heat was stifling. When it was impossible to ride the push bike he had brought with him, Le May had to walk. Very occasionally he made use of a primitive local motor bus, but it had to be pushed up hills and dragged out of ditches and, in one instance, had to be abandoned by its passengers altogether when a wheel fell off in a swamp. Ponies or elephants carried his baggage. The journey covered a total of 450 miles – 330 by train – and took eleven days:

> I have described this journey from Bangkok ... at some length, since, as far as I am aware, it has never been described before; and also because, now that railway communication is through to Chiang Mai, these jungle tracks will probably gradually become overgrown and fall into disuse, and it is not likely that any European traveller will describe the overland journey again.

The account was published in his book *Asian Arcady* in 1926 and dedicated to HRH the Prince of Kambaeng Bejra. It proved an eye-opener, even for the new king himself, Rama VI, who told Le May that he'd read the book on the train going north and:

> As I knew nothing about that part of my country, I found it exceedingly helpful and I thank you.

Le May became British Vice-Consul at Chiang Mai in 1915. In 1916 he married, returned to Bangkok and was posted to Saigon in French Indo-China. But the memories of the evergreen jungle and the smiling Lao people of that first railway journey kept calling him back. He resigned his job as acting Consul-General in Saigon and became an economic advisor to the Siamese government in 1922. It was 1924 before he was able to return to the jungles of central Thailand and visit the ruined city of Si Satchanalai:

> It is now, alas, buried deep in the jungle and little remains of its former state ... I cannot find a single soul who knows any material facts about the history of this ancient city. I must wander alone among the pagodas and try to conjure up in my mind the kind of men who built them and why they fell into ruins.

The ruins of Satchanalai lie some 400 miles north of Bangkok on the River Yom. Here and there villagers have cleared spaces in the jungle for houses and small fields for farming but, for the most part, the city only makes its presence known through the occasional spire of a ruined pagoda rising above the jungle trees and through the sight of an occasional stretch of ruined wall in the undergrowth.

The city was originally called Chaliang after the first settlement there, and then, at the height of its prosperity in the fourteenth century AD, its name was changed to Si Satchanalai. Finally, during its period of decline when Ayuthya was capital of the Thai kingdom, it was called Sawankalok or 'Heaven on Earth' from the Sanskrit 'svanga loga'. As Si Satchanalai it was joint capital with Sukhothai of the first Thai kingdom, residence of the crown prince. Si Satchanalai retains much of its original atmosphere, but although the remains of Sukhothai, twenty miles south, have been excellently preserved, they have been so manicured that the city's identity has completely gone.

King Rama Gamhen ruled the first independent Thai kingdom from about AD 1279 to 1316. His story and that of his new kingdom he had inscribed in the new Thai language on a stela of black stone in 1292. It was discovered in the ruins of Sukhothai in 1833 by the future King Rama IV:

> In the Year of the Dragon, I Ramkamhaeng, sovereign of the Kingdom, ordered workmen to cut this stone slab. And I, as ruler of the cities of Si Satchanalai and Sukhothai, will preside over the assembly of noblemen and dignitaries and handle with them the affairs of the nation....

During the life of King Ramkamhaeng, the kingdom has become prosperous. In the water there are fish. In the paddies there is rice. The Lord of the Land does not raise taxes from his subjects who wander to and fro across his fields taking cattle to market or horses to be sold. Whoever desires to trade elephants does so.

The Thai were a Chinese people who moved south into southeast Asia and had, by the eleventh century, set up a series of small Thai principalities within the jurisdiction of the great Khmer Empire and were ruled from the Khmer capital of Angkor Wat, now in Cambodia. Shortly after King John in England had signed the Magna Carta, the Thai began to show signs of independence from their Khmer masters, but it was not until AD 1238 that there was a revolt and the kingdom of Sukhothai established. It was not until about 1280, under the warrior prince Rama Gamhen, Rama the Brave, that the independence was consolidated and the new kingdom flourished.

Below: *Le May's photograph of the Khmer-style stupa of Wat Maha Tat at Si Satchanalai, 1924. Le May was not a serious photographer.*

The old town of Satchanalai lies on the west or right bank of the river and can be reached by (motor bus) running along what passes for a road by a river bank ... To reach Wat Maha Tat, however, you must branch off to the right shortly before you come to the old town and the tall spire of the Pra Prang will soon be seen among the trees standing outside the walls on a peninsula caused by a bend in the river. The temple of Wat Maha Tat is, I think, of such interest that a discussion of its details may be carried on for many years yet before the history of its architectural beauties is finally determined. Also, although it has been described by HM the King and by M. de Lajonquière there is no account of it, that I am aware of, in English.

Wat Maha Tat, great temple of the Sacred Relic, is on the site of the original Chaliang settlement. It was from this temple that Rama Gamhen transferred the holy relics a mile downstream to a new temple in the new city of Si Satchanalai about AD 1285. What he left behind and what subsequent kings added produced, in the words of King Rama VI (1910–25):

One of the oldest and one of the very finest monuments in my entire kingdom.

Le May describes it in the prose and detail of the civil servant:

Going from west to east we have a Wihan, or assembly hall, completely ruined except for two Buddhas sitting on the main

Above: *Le May's photograph of the seven-headed cobra Buddha at Wat Maha Tat, Si Satchanalai, 1924.*

altar. Broken fragments of pillars lying on the floor show that they were formed of round blocks of laterite from six to eight inches thick, placed on top of one another and covered with cement.

Laterite is crumbly red clay which hardens when exposed to the air and looks like pumice stone or Gruyère cheese. Most of the buildings of the Khmer period are built of it; later buildings tend to be of brick covered with plaster:

> I was told by one of the local ancients that the cement in olden times was composed of pulverised stone mixed with sand together with molasses and the bark of a certain tree, the name of which was not remembered.

Through the gateway to the inner sanctuary with its principal Wihan stands the ruined Pra Prang, a large pagoda found only in royal monasteries and which contained the Sacred Relic. The image of the Buddha is throughout the monastery: the now headless 'girl' Buddha; the Buddha seated on the seven-headed cobra and protected by its spreading hood; the Buddha 'sitting in ever imperturbable contemplation':

> On a pillar close by the Standing Buddha, to the left, I was shown what appeared to be marks of fingers on the cement, said to be left by one of the masons. Such imaginative touches do but show how the people cling to the romance of life, and I would not disturb their beliefs for all the archaeological exactitude in the world, for whenever their hands touch this pillar, they are brought into affectionate contact with their forebears seven centuries ago.

That 'affectionate contact' was still evident in a tiny building that was still roofed, a small sanctuary called the Phra Ruang:

> There is only one entrance, to the east, with a high pointed arch and inside there is nothing now but the small altar heaped with remnants of bygone offerings and the usual miscellany of broken articles found in such ruins, although many of these being modern show that the chapel is still used on occasion.

Sixty years later, Le May's description remains accurate: flowers, ribbons, coloured candles and dolls with sacred yellow sashes to represent the King and Queen of Thailand are still brought:

> In Siam, how clearly one sees the result of Buddhist teaching – 'There is nothing abiding in man or on earth.' Historical tradition, the sense of continuity of policy or mind is entirely lacking in these people. Houses, temples, even cities fall to

ruin and decay. Not a hand is outstretched to save them. The weeds grow up and choke them, and they perish. There is no merit to be gained in 'repairing' a temple or a wall that someone else has built; so, as one temple falls, a new one is built, only to fall in its turn and time, a sign of the impermanency of all things and of how useless is the life of man.

Rama Gamhen's city of Si Satchanalai lies downstream from Wat Maha Tat, defended by the river and moats and a city wall which, in places, still stands several feet high. As the King declared:

And if any commoner in the land has a grievance which sickens his belly and grips his heart and he wants to make known to his ruler and lord, it is easy; he goes and strikes the bell which the king has hung at the city gate. Ramkamhaeng will hear the call, examine the case and decide it justly for him.

The best vantage point to see the layout of Rama Gamhen's city is the summit of the hill which lies at the city centre. Khao Pnom Ploeng, 'Mountain of Sacred Fire', is reached by a long staircase: at the top is a terrace with a temple that was probably the cremation place for the important people of the city. The city itself stretches out below, an oblong site surrounded by the still visible remains of its walls and ditches. There are tall grasses where the jungle has been cleared; tall trees where the jungle has encroached; signs of ancient roadways and paths; here and there what appear to be mounds of earth and stones, possibly the remains of buildings. The houses of the ordinary people built of wood and thatched with palm leaves like the village houses of today have all gone, but there stand the broken walls of royal buildings and temples, both important to Rama Gamhen:

The King, sovereign of the Kingdom, as well as princes and princesses, men as well as women, noblemen and dignitaries without exception, without distinction of hierarchy or sex, practise with devotion the Buddhist religion.

At the time of Rama Gamhen, three religions co-existed in Thailand, as, to some extent, they still do. There was animism: the worship of the spirits of the air, earth, forests and water, in which the country people believed and which explains the small models of animals that the country people today place on the altars in the ruins. There was also Brahminism, the religion of the people who built the Hindu temples of Ellora. This was the branch of the Hindu faith restricted to the upper castes who believed in a rigid caste system and who saw the king as a god on earth and which, during the Khmer Empire, was the religion of court

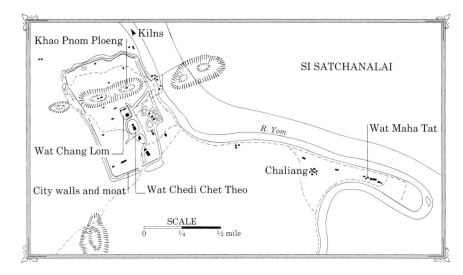

Wat Chang Lom · City walls and moat · Wat Chedi Chet Theo · Khao Pnom Ploeng · Kilns · SI SATCHANALAI · R. Yom · Wat Maha Tat · Chaliang

SCALE
0   ¼   ½ mile

Below: Wat Chang Lom (AD 1290) at Si Satchanalai, before restoration. The elephants on the lower terrace are almost covered with vegetation, and a tree sprouts from the upper terrace.

officials. And there was Buddhism: the belief in the Buddha as a prophet of the enlightenment, the One who will show the way, by doing good deeds in a miserable world, to Nirvana. Part of Rama Gamhen's revolution was to bring a 'pure' form of Buddhism from Ceylon to Siam, in which the king was no longer a god.

The most important temple in Si Satchanalai was Wat Chang Lom, built about AD 1290 probably by Rama Gamhen to house the Sacred Relic which he had taken from Wat Maha Tat at Chaliang. It is a symbol of the new Thai empire of Rama Gamhen, a symbol of change – religious, political and artistic – in its very structure a statement of national identity. The main stupa or pagoda at Wat Maha Tat is Khmer in style and fat, like an upturned marrow. The main stupa at Wat Chang Lom is deliberately different, a break from the architecture of the Khmer, and shaped like an upturned bell with the handle as the spire. It sits on two square terraces of laterite – the lower one buttressed by life-sized elephants, the celestial elephant carrying the world on its back; above it is the second terrace with arched niches and figures of the Buddha in each one. The Buddhist cave temples that Seely saw at Ellora in India were actual caves hollowed out from the mountain; here the caves are represented by the niches. The staircase which links the terraces is the sacred ladder linking the earth to the heavens above, the higher realms of enlightenment to which the Buddha, the great teacher, is showing the way through the finger of the temple's spire:

> I was fortunate enough to visit this temple shortly after the passage of royalty and so was able to obtain a photograph of it cleared of the jungle ... but I found it singularly uninteresting.

Today it is regarded as one of the most significant monuments in the whole of Thailand. Le May can be somewhat perverse:

> The Wat Chedi Chet Theo, on the other hand, entirely captured my imagination.

This complex, opposite the Wat Chang Lom, consists of a succession of small temples round an oblong courtyard. Each pagoda is different; each probably to house the ashes of a different member of the royal family. It was built by Rama Gamhen's grandson Lü Tai when he was crown prince. The plaster is falling away from the brickwork, which is white, pink, yellow and grey. Thick roots of bushes cling to the cement; the bricks are cracked, weeds sprout on the spires; but, in one of the niches there remains, in serene contemplation still, the Buddha:

> The aim of the eastern artist was to reach out after something unattainable, to try and define something beyond and above himself – a spirituality, whereas the western artist, with his intense individualism wishes the spectator to see form, or the scene exactly as he sees it, down to the very last detail. It is this spiritualism and economy of line combined with an intense feeling for form that, for me, are the reasons why the highest forms of eastern art are to me so immeasurably more satisfying than their compeers of the west.

Through the grasses ... and brambles is the Wat Nang Phaya:

> The Temple of Her Majesty the Queen now almost disappearing beneath the undergrowth but which still possesses some mural decoration in stucco in fine preservation.

The stucco, moulded to imitate wood, is almost the only indication of how rich the secular buildings of the city once were when the city was at its height. Finally, Le May came to a small shrine with a lotus bud carved on top, the Lak Muang:

> Which might be called the 'City's Luck' for no city of olden time was complete without it, and harrowing stories are told of the human sacrifices that were made at the time of its dedication in propitiation of the 'Phi' or spirit and to bring good fortune to the city and its people.

What human sacrifices he was referring to Le May doesn't say, but the 'Phi' smiled only briefly on this eastern Camelot. By AD 1365 it had become a vassal of the new Thai state founded at Ayuthya. Then, after constant incursions by the Burmese and the destruction of Ayuthya in the eighteenth century, the Si Satchanalai of Rama Gamhen was abandoned altogether:

> Coconuts, mangoes and tamarind abound in the kingdom:
> whoever sets up a plantation, the king will leave it to him.
> Those who want to play, play – those who want to laugh,
> laugh – those who want to sing, sing.

Whilst little of the glory of Si Satchanalai remains today above ground, 'treasure' lies beneath it:

> On issuing from the western gate you follow a narrow road for
> about four or five miles fairly close to the bank of the river
> going north-west, and presently come to a long row of kilns
> only distinguishable by the amount of debris and innumerable
> fragments of pottery and porcelain strewn about in every direc-
> tion. The place is so overgrown with jungle that, without a
> guide you might easily pass by without noticing it.

The 'treasure' of Si Satchanalai is to be found in its pottery kilns and it is this that makes the site and city of world-wide importance to archaeologists today. It is the beauty of the pottery itself, the method of its manufacture and the structure of a great medieval industry which even rivalled the Chinese, and whose product was traded throughout the East and Africa.

> As regards the kilns themselves, the more northerly series on
> both sides of the road is well-known and whether they were
> eventually abandoned suddenly by the potters fleeing before
> the attack of some northern horde who destroyed the kilns
> entirely, as Fournereau, de Lajonquière and others suppose,
> or whether they fell into peaceful, long drawn out decay,
> certain it is that the work of destruction has been carried out
> pretty thoroughly since, at the hands of generations of peaceful
> perpetrators with an eye to financial profit at the expense of a
> little manual toil.

It is a situation that still prevails. It is possible to buy green glaze celadon bowls of fourteenth century Sawankalok ware in the remoter corners of the Bangkok Sunday market. The trade is illegal, the purchase is illegal and the export is illegal, as the bowls come from protected sites. Illicit digging by villagers is prohibited, but despite the efforts of government officials and archaeologists the digging continues.

> Up to recent times, even in Siam, the pottery and porcellaneous
> stoneware made in the kilns of Sawankalok (Satchanalai) ...
> have always been shrouded in a certain veil of mystery, and
> nobody has ever made any serious attempt to study the subject
> from the student-collector's point of view.

Le May was to start to lift the veil:

> I may say that in August or September, after the heavy rains, it is almost impossible to find the kilns at all (but) I spent a very happy and profitable day and picked out a remarkable series of sherds and fragments illustrating the different kinds of ware produced at these kilns ... it can be easily imagined what a splendid collection systematic hunting and grouping would produce in the course of a year or two.

Weather always permitting, however:

> By 6.30 we began to hear distant rumblings in the sky and by 7.00 a torrential storm had broken over our heads. Within half an hour all the potholes were full, the river had risen and was overflowing its banks and there was at least six inches of water on the earth road. Soon we could not tell where the river began and the road ended. It grew pitch dark and all of a sudden the backwheels went bump! By the grace of God this was only in a pothole and not in the river and with the aid of our coolies we managed to lift the car out. For the next three or four hours we lived in a perfect nightmare.

Although fragments were easy to come by, Le May found it incredibly difficult to find or buy examples of pottery that were complete. Over a period of twenty years he was able to collect only fifty whole pieces. The one that he regarded as among the

Left: *Le May and guide on the site of the kilns in 1924, before the downpour.*

most significant in his whole collection was not even adjudged Sawankalok ware by 'ceramic authorities abroad':

> It came into my possession by chance, owing to the breakdown of the motor car near the old city. While waiting for repairs to be made, I was taken into the kind of general shop by the side of the road where a white-haired kindly old gentleman was induced to exchange this vase as well as other carefully guarded pieces of pottery from his store-cupboard, for certain magic and all powerful pieces of paper – but only after he had thoroughly satisfied himself that I was genuinely interested in the old ware and would not, like the last European to whom he had shown his treasures, dismiss them 'en masse' as *new*!

It is generally agreed that the 'factories' at Si Satchanalai were started some time between the eleventh and thirteenth centuries, contemporary with the Sung Dynasty in China which lasted from AD 960 to 1276, and that the original potters were Chinese brought from China at the invitation of the 'Thai' king himself. Le May accepted this:

> Even the most cursory glance will show the affinity between the Sung and Sawankalok wares and the influence of the former upon the latter.

But his studies began to enable him to refine his theories:

> My belief is as follows: The T'ai who came southwards from Chiengsen were accustomed to make pottery and they established kilns at Chaliang, which is the oldest name for Sawankalok, at an early date, perhaps even as far back as the tenth century.

The original influence was entirely Chinese but that influence gradually waned over the course of years until the transition was complete and, with an admixture of Indian influence, transformed the ware into something that was indigenously Thai.

> But the question that occupies students now is 'How long did these kilns remain in working order?'

His question was answered by a clever piece of academic sleuthing, when he was able to decipher a particular form of writing scrawled on a fragment of Sawankalok ware. Knowing when that kind of writing was first used in Thailand, he was able to date the ware to 1423:

> If the theory I am propounding, therefore, is correct, here we have a piece of porcelain on which the decoration is entirely

Thai in character, which shows (1) that the Sawankalok kilns were still working in 1423 (only 73 years after Ayudia was founded) and that (2) the Chinese influence had by that time entirely disappeared....

I do not pretend myself to have come yet to any definite decision on the question of the closing of the Sawankalok kilns (but there) is beginning to strengthen in my mind the conviction that the kilns must have been more or less moribund round about 1500.

And with the kilns moribund, so was the city of Si Satchanalai:

I myself saw two high mounds from which tall trees and great clumps of bamboos were growing, which my guide assured me were untouched kilns; and though the fact of their being untouched may not be literally true ... (investigation) under expert supervision as soon as conveniently possible, before the peaceful perpetrators get their fingers well into them, as they assuredly will before long, would be amply rewarded.

Most important archaeological sites were dug at the time of their discovery and many have been excavated again at least once, but an awareness of the kilns at Si Satchanalai and their significance is so comparatively recent that excavation is still in progress. Le May was unable to do any excavation himself and the 'peaceful perpetrators' were certainly able to get their fingers well in before an official programme of excavation, delayed by the Second World War, was set in motion. The responsibility for carrying out Le May's suggestion, with the help of the Thai government and Thai archaeologists, has fallen to the Australians. The 'Thai Ceramic Dating Project', a joint programme of the Thai Department of Fine Arts, the Art Gallery of South Australia and the University of Adelaide, has been excavating since 1980. Although the ceramics cannot always be dated too accurately and there are no contemporary Thai records of the industry and no potters' marks, it has now become possible to associate particular types of ware with particular types of kiln and the whole vast scope of the industry is now being recognised. It has also become possible to put Le May's ideas into context, to check his ideas and accuracy against those of modern scholars with up-to-date techniques: to take Le May not just at his own valuation but at the valuation of others. Don Hein is one of the leaders of the project:

In the beginning we did just what Le May did. We made observations, we did surface surveys. But then we had advantages that Le May didn't have with air photos and survey maps and, of course, we have the people with the techniques to make a closer study.

The principal technique for locating kilns is magnotometry. A kiln becomes magnetised through repeated firing, and the degree of magnetism can be registered by a magnotometer – a highly sophisticated electronic detector – which gives a clear indication of where the kiln is buried. Confirmation that the kiln is actually there is provided by drilling a core sample of soil down to a depth of five metres. Paleomagnetism, a technique which measures the age of magnetism by comparing in the laboratory the magnetism of samples of soil or kiln sherds with the movements of the magnetic pole, gives an idea of the age of the kiln and how long it was in use. According to Don Hein:

> The earliest dates go back to the tenth century so Le May was right about that. He said that he thought the industry might have begun about then, and it probably goes on well into the sixteenth century, which he also thought.

One of the largest kilns so far discovered is Kiln 61:

> We were excavating just nearby and there were signs in the stratigraphy (the soil changes in the walls of the pit) that suggested there was a kiln nearby. But the local people said 'No! There's no kiln.' But I was pretty determined to find something. We put a small pilot hole down, a test hole, and we struck the first jar standing upright. I thought then that we must have a kiln with jars and as we extended the excavation there it all was. We did have a very unusual find, basically a bank kiln made of slab clay; it would have contained hundreds of pots. Quite a number, perhaps twenty or so very large ones, up to a metre high and a metre wide and dozens of smaller jars. It gives a tremendous amount of information about how the potters worked; how many pots of what kind were in the kiln, and it gives dating information.

The kilns at Si Satchanalai were at first merely holes dug in the ground or in an earth bank, and operated by local farmers in the dry season as a part-time occupation. They produced simple pots for local domestic use. As better clays became available and techniques improved, demand grew. The kilns were brought out of the ground and placed on the surface; they were brick lined so that higher temperatures could be reached and higher quality wares produced; and eventually the part-time farmers became full-time potters.

Below: *Excavated kiln at Si Satchanalai, 1986.*

Whereas many kilns have been plundered or destroyed over the years as fresh kilns were built on top of older ones, Kiln 61, discovered in 1984, is of major importance as it remains virtually intact. Shaped like an elongated, upturned boat with a chimney projecting at one end and a fire hole at the other with the pots in between, the kiln, says Hein, would have been subject to considerable heat stress as the walls expanded and contracted during firing:

> The roof simply fell in on the pots and it did it by falling pretty much the fire-hole end and the chimney opening end and left most of the middle intact. The potters didn't know that. They could see the hole in the ground and they could hear noises and it seems they simply gave the whole lot up for lost – and preserved it for us today.

In addition to the kiln sites, the project is beginning to excavate burial sites too. The dead were cremated, probably in the nearby temples, and their ashes placed in large dark-grey burial jars. Some of the jars can be dated to the thirteenth century AD. They are everyday, utilitarian objects, but the range of wares produced at the height of the industry was enormous, and the best wares, mostly unknown to Le May, are amongst the very best in the world in design and quality. Among them are a fourteenth-century jug or 'kendi', in the form of a goose with a hole in the handle which, covered by the thumb, controls the flow of liquid from the bird's beak; the model of a sacred elephant with guards and the 'mahoot' or driver on its back in different coloured glazes; and a roof ornament for a temple in the form of a triple-headed mythical dragon.

Below: *Goose kendi jug, celadon Sawankalok ware c. AD 1400.*

Dick Richards, who is a member of the expedition, is curator and expert in Sawankalok ware at the Art Gallery of South Australia:

> It's difficult to describe the essential quality of this ware. On the one hand there are very simple, straightforward pots, on the other hand they have the most beautiful spare decoration and the most lovely subtle glazes, very beautiful greens and browns and blacks. And they have an extraordinary strength and liveliness. They seem to relate to the local architecture at Satchanalai; the temples also have this quality of simplicity and strength and, whereas the Chinese wares are often finer and more delicate, have more finesse, the wares that were made at Si Satchanalai have a tremendous earthy quality, have great beauty because of their simplicity, have a kind of flair, a life in the decoration, and more than hold their own.

Above: *Temple roof ornament of a mythical triple-headed dragon, Sawankalok ware c. AD 1300.*

It was this quality that so appealed to Le May:

> My inner eye sees beyond the form, as it is intended to do, and I experience something more than the sensation of enjoying the sight of mere physical beauty.

Where Richards differs from Le May is over the origin of the designs and, especially, the development of the methods of construction:

> Le May accepted the idea that King Ramkamhaeng brought several hundred potters from China to Si Satchanalai to set up the industry in the thirteenth century though, later, he believed it could have started earlier, in the tenth century. But our own research in the area would indicate that there is a very long pottery tradition on this site, probably from the first century even and that the Thais developed much of their own techniques of making ceramics. There may have been influence from northern Thailand or from China at various times but the dimensions of the site show that most of the techniques were invented right here.

When Le May first visited the site in 1924 he would have seen only some 40 or 50 kilns, mostly on mounds that were above the ground. Today, over 100 have been examined; more than 200 have been counted and it is estimated that, altogether, there must be 600 or 700. That makes it a very big industry; at its height, one of the biggest in Asia and, therefore, in the world.

How the site appeared at the peak of its output can be gauged both by the archaeological evidence and by the routine and methods still used in the small local village potteries that exist throughout Thailand today, as Don Hein explains:

> We should think of a large manufactory. Kilns surrounded by timber and bamboo buildings for making the ceramic wares – jars, bowls, architectural pieces, figurines – as well as for storage of clay, glazing materials, stacks of timber for fuel. There would be drying racks, stacks of fired and unfired pots; lots of people working and moving about, packing wares for transport in carts or on horses and perhaps even elephants. We know of five metal furnaces in the kiln site and these we think were used for iron smelting, so forges would have added their noise and fires to the scene. About ten religious buildings were also located on the site, so monks in their saffron robes would be officiating at weddings, cremations and other ceremonies. We would see roads and canals and farms and villages, and, I guess, the new Thai state in the making.

As the ceramic industry grew, the city grew with it. This expansion exercised great influence over production, improving efficiency and turning it into a professional industry. Why that industry ceased is still not known but the most likely explanation is simply that Si Satchanalai was no longer a viable centre politically, geographically and economically after the capital was moved south to Ayuthya. Ironically it is information coming from the south that will probably provide the final dates for Sawankalok ware production, as well as revealing some of its finest examples.

In the early days, Sawankalok ware was imported by road to the north over the mountains into China and Burma, but later (probably via Ayuthya) the wares went south by canal and river to the coast for export abroad by sea. Le May knew that examples of pottery had been found in Indonesia and the Philippines but, since then, examples have been found as far afield as the Middle East and North Africa. Some of the cargoes never reached their destinations but foundered at sea and were lost to the ocean floor. It is these vessels and cargoes (time capsules undisturbed, unlike land sites, by later buildings) that are being examined for the first time and the true extent of the world trade is being revealed.

In the Gulf of Thailand, Thai and Australian archaeologists, led by the Chief Marine Archaeologist for Western Australia, Jeremy Green, are excavating one particular vessel forty metres down. On board are three different kinds of 'porcellaneous' material: Sawankalok ware of Thai manufacture; Chinese blue and white material; and material of unknown origin. Part of the problem of identifying Si Satchanalai material is the fact that, towards the end of the fifteenth century, the Thai state acted the same way as Singapore or Hong Kong today – as a clearing house for a vast area, trading its own goods, re-exporting the goods of other nations and – additional complexity – making and exporting goods in the style of another nation to satisfy and capitalise on particular markets. But it is because of the very diversity of the cargo that accurate dating of Sawankalok ware might be possible.

Chinese blue and white material can be dated by its design and its potter's mark; so, if Chinese blue and white exists alongside a cargo of Sawankalok ware, the date of that Sawankalok ware and the blue and white will be approximately the same. And first indications from the wreck sites are that some of the Sawankalok ware dates from as late as the early seventeenth century, much later than Le May's 'moribund by 1500' would suggest. Le May,

Above: *Sawankalok bowl, collected by Le May and donated by him to the Victoria & Albert Museum in London.*

of course, was denied this source of information, as underwater archaeology only began in the late 1940s and, in the Thai gulf, only in the late 1970s. Although the work is still only in its very early stages, the evidence it has already produced and will continue to produce is crucial to a complete understanding of the history and aesthetics of a medieval industry and an art form of world significance that, until Le May, the world had forgotten. It will also help us to understand and appreciate that neglected and half-forgotten ruin in the jungle, the city of Si Satchanalai itself – that is, if the underwater 'peaceful perpetrators', the looters and plunderers, don't destroy all the evidence first.

Le May retired from Siam in 1932 and, at the age of forty-seven, returned to England. He took a Ph.D. at Pembroke College, Cambridge, and published his thesis 'Buddhist Art in Siam' in 1938. He brought home with him a caseload of fragments of Sawankalok ware, the best of which he presented to the British Museum, plus another fifty complete pieces, some of which were exhibited at the Victoria & Albert Museum. He continued to write books and lecture on his favourite subject, a subject on which he had become a world expert. He was praised by the King of Siam for having 'identified himself with the people of the Far East to a greater degree than most Europeans' and, although he

Left: *A roof tile of Sawankalok ware from the Le May collection in the V & A.*

was careful never to refer to himself as an archaeologist, he was praised by the great archaeologist Sir John Marshall for his pioneering work on Far Eastern art.

Recognition, however, did not bring financial reward. The longer he lived, the smaller his income became and the more embittered he felt. He had to sell his beloved collection. He retired to and became the archetype of 'Disgusted' of Tunbridge Wells, reduced to sitting in the corner of his favourite pub, talking to anyone who cared to listen and banging the table with his silver-topped cane to attract the attention of those who didn't.

To me the forest still calls, and memory brings back all the varying scenes of the jungle, plain, and mountain. Again I sit by the camp-fire at night by the bank of some forest stream. All the sounds of the jungle are still, but for the rippling of the water at my side and the fitful cry of some plaintive bird; and I gaze with growing awe at those skies of deep dark blue, which at night are set with myriads of gems, clustering around their central jewel.

Le May died in 1972 at the age of eighty-seven. He merited just two inches in the obituary columns of *The Times*. His books cannot be bought in London or New York but are readily on sale in Bangkok. However, compared with Hiram Bingham in the United States, Reginald Le May in Britain was and remains an unknown. As he once wrote:

How clearly one sees the result of Buddhist teaching – 'There is nothing abiding in man or on earth.'

It could serve as his own epitaph, as the epitaph of the city he discovered, and of the whole romantic period of archaeology.

BIBLIOGRAPHY

CHAPTER 1: STRONGMAN IN EGYPT
Giovanni Belzoni (1778–1823)

Belzoni, Giovanni, *Narrative of the Operations and Recent Discoveries within the Pyramids, Temples, Tombs, and Excavations, in Egypt and Nubia; and of a journey to the coast of the Red Sea, in search of the ancient Berenice; and another to the Oasis of Jupiter Ammon.* London: John Murray, 1820.
Burckhardt, John Lewis, *Travels in Nubia.* London: John Murray, 1819.
Hamilton, Sir William, *Remarks on Several Parts of Turkey.* Part I (Aegyptica), London, 1809.
Mayes, Stanley, *The Great Belzoni.* London, 1959.

CHAPTER 2: THE ROSE-RED CITY
Jean Louis Burckhardt (1784–1817)

Burckhardt, John Lewis, *Travels in Nubia.* London, 1819.
  Travels in Syria and the Holy Land. London, 1822.
Sim, Katherine, *Desert Traveller: The Life of Jean Louis Burckhardt.* London: Victor Gollancz, 1969.
Browning, Ian, *Petra.* London: Chatto & Windus, 1973.
Roberts, David, *The Holy Land.* London, 1842.
Rostovtzeff, M., *Caravan Cities.* Oxford, 1932.
Harding, G. Lankester, *Petra: Hashemite Kingdom of Jordan.* Department of Antiquities, Amman, 1938.

CHAPTER 3: THE WONDERS OF ELLORA
John B. Seely (1788–1824)

Seely, John B., *The Wonders of Elora; or, the Narrative of a Journey to the Temples and Dwellings excavated out of a mountain of granite, and extending upwards of a mile and a quarter, at Elora, in the East Indies, by the route of Poona, Ahmed-Nuggur, and Toka, returning by Dowlutabad and Aurungabad; with some general observations on the people and country.* London, 1824.
Anon., *Notes on the Rock-cut Temples and Rock-cut Palaces near Ellora, by a Recent Tourist.* Bombay, 1856.
Soar, Micaela, *The Tirtha at Ellora.* SOAS, University of London, 1986.

CHAPTER 4: THE MARBLE HUNTERS
Charles Fellows (1799–1860)

Fellows, Charles, *A Journal written during an excursion in Asia Minor by Charles Fellows 1838.* London: John Murray, 1839.
  An Account of Discoveries in Lycia, being a Journal kept during a second excursion in Asia Minor, by Charles Fellows 1840. London: John Murray, 1841.
  The Xanthian Marbles; their acquisition, and transmission to England. London: John Murray, 1843.
  Account of the Ionic Trophy Monument excavated at Xanthus. London: John Murray, 1848.
Beaufort, Francis, *Karamania, or a brief description of the South Coast of Asia-Minor and of the Remains of Antiquity; with Plans, Views, &c. collected during a survey of that coast, under the orders of the Lords Commissioners of the Admiralty, in the Years 1811 & 1812.* London: R. Hunter, 1817.
Spratt, Thomas Abel Bremage, and Forbes, Edward, *Travels in Lycia, Milyas, and the Cibyratis, in company with the late Rev. E. T. Daniell.* London, 1847.
Toksöz, Cemil, *Ancient Cities of Lycia.* Istanbul: Matbaacilik Ltd, 1986.

CHAPTER 5: THE TEMPLES OF KING SOLOMON
Karl Mauch (1837–1875)

Mauch, Karl, *The Journals of Carl Mauch: His travels in the Transvaal and Rhodesia 1869–1872.* E. E. Burke (ed.), F. O. Bernhard (trans.). Salisbury: National Archives of Rhodesia, 1969.
  African Explorer. F. O. Bernhard (ed. and trans.). Cape Town: Struik, 1971.

Bent, J. Theodore, *The Ruined Cities of Mashonaland: being a record of excavation and exploration in 1891.* London: Longmans, Green, 1892.

Hall, R. N. and Neal, W. G., *The Ancient Ruins of Rhodesia (Monomotapae Imperium).* London, 1902.

Hall, R. N., *Great Zimbabwe.* London: Methuen, 1905.

Prehistoric Rhodesia. London: T. Fisher Unwin, 1909.

Randall-MacIver, David, *Medieval Rhodesia.* London: Macmillan, 1906.

Posselt, Willi, in Southern Rhodesia Native Affairs Department *Annual Report.* Salisbury, 1924.

Caton-Thompson, G., *The Zimbabwe Culture: ruins and reactions.* Oxford: Clarendon Press, 1931.

Summers, Roger, *Zimbabwe: A Rhodesian mystery.* Johannesburg: T. Nelson, 1963.

Ellert, H., *The Material Culture of Zimbabwe.* Harare: Longman, 1984.

CHAPTER 6: PYRAMIDS IN THE JUNGLE
Alfred P. Maudslay (1850–1931)

Maudslay, Alfred P., *Biologia Centrali-Americana; or, Contributions to the Knowledge of the Fauna and Flora of Mexico and Central America,* vols. 55–9. London: R. H. Porter, 1889–1902.

Life in the Pacific Fifty Years Ago. London, 1930.

Maudslay, Anne C. and Alfred P., *A Glimpse at Guatemala, and some notes on the Ancient Monuments of Central America.* London: John Murray, 1899.

Maudslay, Alfred P., Unpublished notebooks, 1881, 1882. Royal Geographical Society, London.

'Explorations in Guatemala, Quirigua, Tikal and Usumacinta', in RGS Proceedings. London, 1883.

'Exploration of the Ruins and Site of Copan, Central America', in RGS Proceedings. London, 1886.

'Exploration in the Department of Petén', in *Nature,* London, 1911.

Adamson, David, *The Ruins of Time: Four and a half centuries of conquest and discovery among the Maya.* London: Allen & Unwin, 1975.

Tozzer, A. M., 'Alfred P. Maudslay', in *American Anthropologist,* 1931.

Coe, William, *Tikal.* Philadelphia: University of Pennsylvania Press, 1967.

Brunhouse, R. L., *Pursuit of the Ancient Maya.* Albuquerque: University of New Mexico Press, 1975.

Graham, Ian, *Art of Maya Hieroglyphic Writing.* Cambridge, Mass.: Harvard University Press.

Maudslay. London, 1977.

Willey, Gordon R., 'Towards an Holistic View of Ancient Mayan Civilisation', in *Man,* Royal Anthropological Institute, London, 1980.

CHAPTER 7: SPIRITS OF THE CANYON
Richard Wetherill (1858–1910)

Wetherill, Richard, Letters to Talbot Hyde, 1893–1902, in American Museum of Natural History, New York.

'The Cliff Dwellings of Mesa Verde', in *Mancos Times,* August 1895.

Field Notes, Grand Gulch, Utah, 1893–4, in American Museum of Natural History, New York.

Mason, Charlie, 'Account of the discovery of Mesa Verde', State Historical Society, Denver, Colorado, 1917.

Nordenskiold, Gustav, *The Cliff Dwellers of Mesa Verde.* New York, 1910.

McNitt, Frank, *Richard Wetherill, Anasazi.* Albuquerque: University of New Mexico Press, 1957.

Watson, Don, 'Indians of the Mesa Verde', Mesa Verde Museum Association, Colorado, 1953.

Fagan, Brian, *Elusive Treasure: Early Archaeologists in the Americas.* London, 1978.

Willey, Gordon R., *An Introduction to American Archaeology,* vol. I, 1966.

Gillmore, Frances and Wetherill, Louisa, *Traders to the Navajos: The story of the Wetherills of Kayenta.* Boston, 1934.

CHAPTER 8: LOST CITY OF THE INCAS
Hiram Bingham (1878–1956)

Bingham, Hiram, *Lost City of the Incas: The story of Machu Picchu and its builders.* New York: Duell, Sloan and Pearce, 1948.

Inca Land: Explorations in the Highlands of Peru. London: Constable, 1922.

Machu Picchu, a citadel of the Incas: Report of the Explorations and Excavations made in 1911, 1912 and 1915 under the auspices of Yale University and the National Geographic Society. New Haven: Yale University Press, 1930.

'The Ruins of Choqqequirau', in *American Anthropologist,* 1910.

'The Ruins of Espiritu Pampa, Peru', in *American Anthropologist,* April 1914.

'The Story of Machu Picchu', in *National Geographic,* February 1915.

Prescott, William H., *History of the Conquest of Peru* (rev. edn.), J. F. Kirk (ed.). London: Allen & Unwin, 1925.

Savoy, Gene, *Vilcabamba: Last City of the Incas.* London: Robert Hale, 1971.

Hemming, John, *The Conquest of the Incas.* London: Macmillan, 1970.

Machu Picchu: The Wonders of Man. New York, 1981.

CHAPTER 9: VALLEY OF THE KILNS
Reginald Le May (1885–1972)

Le May, Reginald, *An Asian Arcady: The land and peoples of northern Siam.* Cambridge: Heffer, 1926.

'A Visit to Sawankalok', in *Siam Society Journal,* XIX(2), 1925.

'The Ceramic Wares of North-Central Siam', in *Burlington Magazine,* October–November 1933.

A Concise History of Buddhist Art in Siam. Cambridge University Press, 1938.

'Sawankalok Wares from Siam', in *Antique Collector,* July/August 1948.

The Culture of South-East Asia, 1954.

Charoenwangsa, Pisit, *Archaeologia Mundi.* Bangkok, 1978.

Thai Ceramics Dating Project (D. Hein, P. Burns, R. Richards and S. Naenna), 'Sawankhalok Kilns: A Recent Discovery' (1980) and 'Further Discoveries', in Bulletin of Art Gallery of South Australia, Adelaide.

Stratton, Carol and Scott, Miriam McNair, *The Art of Sukhotai: Thailand's Golden Age.* Kuala Lumpur: Oxford University Press, 1981.

INDEX

PICTURE CREDITS

American Museum of Natural History, New York: pages 220–1 & 225; Ancient Art & Architecture Collection/Bruce Norman: pages 16 *inset*, 52, 62, 66–9 *all*, 70 *top* & *bottom left*, 71–2 *all*, 89, 93, 137, 138 *both bottom*, 139, 140 *centre* & *bottom*, 141 *both*, 143 *both insets*, 144, 183, 193, 209, 212 *top* & 213–4 *all*; Art Gallery of South Australia, Adelaide: pages 216 & 267–8; Aspect Picture Library/J. Alex Langley: page 65 *main picture*; BBC Enterprises Ltd/Derek Towers: page 210 *bottom*; BBC Enterprises Ltd/David Wallace: pages 140 *top*, 142–3 *main picture*, 157 & 165; BBC Hulton Picture Library: pages 10, 16 *main picture*, 24, 30, 37, 40, 43, 55, 73, 106, 127 & 252; Bibliothèque Nationale, Paris: page 25; British Museum: pages 11, 19 (photo: BPCC/Aldus Archive), 61, 116–20 *all*, 123 *right* & 129; J. Allan Cash Photolibrary: page 70 *bottom right*; Peter Clayton: page 34; David Drew: pages 38, 138 *top*, 210 *top,* 211, 215, 232, 239 & 266; Fotomas Index: page 103; Hauptstaatsarchiv, Stuttgart: pages 152 *all* & 155; India Office Library: pages 84, 86, 253, 257, 260 & 263; Mary Evans Picture Library: page 42; Maxwell Museum of Anthropology, Albuquerque, New Mexico/Werner Forman Archive: page 223; Mesa Verde National Park Museum, Colorado: pages 198, 200, 201 (photo: Werner Forman Archive) & 203; Museum of Mankind (British Museum): pages 168 *left*, 172, 184 & 187–8; National Archives of Zimbabwe, Harare: pages 133, 149, 158 *bottom*, 161 & 163; National Portrait Gallery: page 102; New Mexico State Records Center & Archives, Santa Fe (McNitt Collection): pages 196 & 205; Peabody Museum of Natural History, Yale University/National Geographic Society, Washington DC: pages 228, 230, 242–3 *all*, 245–8 *all* & 250; Royal Commonwealth Society: pages 158 *top* & 160; Royal Geographical Society: pages 168 *right* & 181–2; Royal Library, Copenhagen: page 229; Spectrum Colour Library: page 212 *bottom;* Victoria & Albert Museum: pages 53–4, 78, 91 & 270–1; Zefa Picture Library: page 65 *inset.*

Illustrations on the following pages are taken from the publications indicated:
Page 59: *Travels in Syria and the Holy Land* by J.L. Burckhardt; pages 92 *both*, 95 & 98–9: *The Wonders of Elora* by J.B. Seely; pages 104–5, 112–4 *all*, 122 *left* & 124: *A Journal written during an excursion in Asia Minor* by C. Fellows; page 159: *The Ruined Cities of Mashonaland* by J.T. Bent; pages 174 & 178–9: *A Glimpse at Guatemala* by A.C. and A.P. Maudslay; page 258: *A Concise History of Buddhist Art in Siam* by R. Le May.